C000262618
Adriatic Sea
65
ITALY
Portomaggiore
Molinella
Argenta
Valli di Comacchio
Comacchio
Conselice
Reno
Alfonsine
Castel San Pietro Terme
Lugo
Bagnacavallo
Marina di Ravenna
San Vitale e Sant' Apollinare Nuovo
Ravenna
Imola
Faenza
Cervia
Forlì
Forlimpopoli
Cesenatico
Brisighella
Bellaria-Igea Marina
Modigliana
Castrocaro Terme
Cesena
Rimini
Marradi
255
Santarcangelo di Romagna
Tempio Malatestiano
Riccione
Cattolica
P.N.Casentinesi-M.Falterona-Campigna
1654
M.Falterona
Mercato Saraceno
San Marino
SAN MARINO
Pesaro
San Leo
Fano
Bagno di Romagna
Poppi
Urbino
Marotta
Senigallia
Palazzo Ducale
Bibbiena
Pieve S.Stefano
Mondolfo
Urbania
Fossombrone
Metauro
Giovanni Valdarno
Montevarchi
Sansepolcro
Falconara Marittima
Cagli
Pergola
Chiaravalle
Cesano
Ancona
Arezzo
Città di Castello
259
Fonte Avellana
Sassoferrato
Grotte di Frasassi
Jesi
Esino
Osimo
Castelfidardo
Santuario della Santa Casa
Loreto
Porto Recanati
Marche
Mte.S.Savino
Castiglion Fiorentino
Gubbio
Fabriano
Cingoli
Recanati
Musone
Cortona
Macerata
Potenza Picena
Civitanova Marche
Umbertide
Matelica
Úmbria
Gualdo Tadino
Porto Sant'Elipido
Montepulciano
Magione
Perugia
S.Severino Marche
Tolentino
Corridonia
Porto San Giorgio
Castiglione sul Lago
Assisi
Camerino
Fermo
Quirico d'Orcia
Trasimeno
Bastia Umbra
Basilica di S.Francesco
Sarnano
Pedaso
Chiusi
Spello
P.N.dei Monti Sibillini
Grottammare
Città della Pieve
Amandola
San Benedetto del Tronto
Abbadia S.Salvatore
Marsciano
Foligno
Monti Sibillini
263
Montefalco
Trevi
2173
Ascoli Piceno
Piazza del Popolo
Martinsicuro
Piazza d.Popolo
M.Vettore 2476
Acquasanta Terme
Tronto
Todi
Spoleto
Norcia
Cascia
Arquata del Tronto
Civitella del Tronto
Giulianova
Orvieto
Duomo
Acquasparta
Teramo
Roseto degli Abruzzi
Pitigliano
Bolsena
Ferentillo
Amatrice
Monti della Laga
2458
Amelia
Terni
Atri
Pineto
Lago di Bolsena
Montefiascone
Leonessa
Silvi
Città Sant'Angelo
Montesilvano
Tuscania
Viterbo
Narni
P.N.del Gran Sasso e Monti della Laga
Corno Grande 2912
Pescara
Castro
Orte
Antrodoco
Pizzoli
Gran Sasso d'Italia
Penne
Necropoli etrusca
San Pellegrino
Rieti
Loreto Aprutino
Francavilla al Mare
Ortona
267
M.Nuria 1888
Basilica
L'Aquila
Chieti
Torre de'Passeri
Civita Castellana
Poggio Mirteto
Abruzzo
Fossacesia Marina
Tolfa
Borgorose
Lanciano
Lago di Bracciano
Bracciano
M.Velino 2487
Popoli
Guardiagrele
Necropoli etrusca
Monterotondo
Lázio
M.Amaro 2793
Casalbordino
Celano
Santa Marinella
Cerveteri
Mentana
Villa d'Este
Tagliacozzo
Sulmona
Casoli
Basilica di San Pietro
Tivoli
Avezzano
Piana del Fucino
P.N.d.Maiella
Atessa
Ladispoli
VATICAN CITY
Colosseo
Foro Romano
Villa Adriana
Monti Simbruini
Civitella Roveto
Pescina
Palena
Villa Sta.Maria
(ROME) ROMA
Subiaco
Trasacco
Scanno
Pescocostanzo
FCO
Frascati
Palestrina
P.N.d'Abruzzo
Pescasseroli
Fiumicino
San Paolo fuori le Mura
Fiuggi
M.Greco
Roccaraso
Agnone
Ostia Antica
Albano Laziale
Colleferro
Velletri
Anagni
Duomo
Alatri
Ferentino
Sora
2247 M.Petroso
2283
Castel di Sangro
Trivento
Colli Albani
Appennino Umbro-Marchegiano
Appennino Abruzzese
Tevere
Tiber
E45
E55
E35

Photo Guide

TUSCANY

Yes, the Leaning Tower of Pisa actually leans. Everyone knows that, and Tuscany's wealth of attractions draw visitors from across the world, but many of the assumptions made about this beautiful corner of Italy are as off-kilter as the tower itself.

Photo Guide

TUSCANY

Siena's architectural harmony can best be appreciated from the air. The "home of Gothic" is spread over three hills located in the heart of the Tuscan uplands. The city boasts fascinating red-brick villas and a quite unique atmosphere.

Note To telephone Tuscan numbers from abroad, dial the international prefix from your country + the code for Italy (39) and then the telephone number required. Also note that the first 0 of the number is not dropped; e.g. international prefix 39 055 12 345.

PROFILE

THE HIGHLIGHTS

CONTENTS

As lavishly illustrated as a coffee-table book and as informative as a travel guide, this *Photo Guide* is the perfect companion for your visit. Take an atmospheric journey of discovery through the greatest of Tuscany's tourist sites in the "Highlights" section, while in the practical "Explorer" chapter our experts have collated the most interesting sights and attractions, along with a selection of hotels and restaurants within easy reach at each location. There are also descriptions of the most beautiful cities and a selection of driving tours and excursions, followed by a comprehensive atlas section.

EXPLORER

ATLAS

TUSCANY PROFILE

Few other Italian regions can compare to Tuscany as far as variety is concerned. In the north the beautiful and dramatic Apuan Alps are also the source of Carrara marble, and in the west lie the islands of the Tuscan Archipelago, sandwiched between the Ligurian Sea and Tyrrhenian Sea, with their endless sandy beaches. In mainland Tuscany, the sparse, loamy soil of the central Crete region slowly merges into the rolling hills of the south, and the thick forests of the west were once a popular retreat for hermits. Among it all there are the cultural jewels: Tuscany's cities are unique, and the mighty churches and palaces with their overwhelmingly beautiful art collections attest to the great importance of the region's past.

PROFILE: QUINTESSENTIA

Gently rolling hills, pine groves, avenues of cypresses, priceless art treasures, delicious food – Tuscany is a place for art lovers and gourmets alike. Its historic cities and unmistakable scenery make it a universal work of art that is uniquely European – it is little wonder that Pope Boniface VIII described it as the heart of the world, the *quintessentia.*

Typically Tuscan: Macchia

Macchia, which means "thicket" or "undergrowth", is a type of vegetation found all over Tuscany, especially in the south. Consisting of low trees, ground cover plants, thorny bushes, and brambles, it is nowadays principally used as grazing land for sheep and goats or for the cultivation of oils, spices, and aromatics (sage, bay trees, juniper, myrtle). The heath plants of the *macchia*, known to botanists as sclerophyll vegetation, do however represent a potential danger that annually threatens even entire cities in Tuscany; the leaves and grasses can dry out in the summer, leading to extensive forest fires which affect the whole region.

Between March and May, when the *macchia* is in bloom, the evergreen undergrowth exudes an aromatic scent.

On the shin of the Italian boot

Tuscany lies in the northwest of the Italian peninsula, bordering the Ligurian and Tyrrhenian Seas to the west. Liguria and Emilia-Romagna lie to the north, Umbria and Le Marche to the east, and Latium to the south. Rome, the heart of Italy, is less than 150 km (93 miles) away.
Tuscany's longest north-south axis measures 215 km (113 miles), while the greatest distance from west to east is 235 km (146 miles). It has a total surface area of approximately 23,000 sq km (8,880 sq miles), making it Italy's fifth-largest region.

Mild temperatures

The climate is mild and temperate here: average temperatures rarely drop below freezing and in July and August can climb to over 30°C (86°F) in the shade. Such figures only tell part of the story, however, because of the region's diverse landscape. There is a continental climate in the Apuan Alps in the north, for example, which makes it much cooler than Tuscany as a whole, with higher average rainfall. The coast and indeed much of the interior has a maritime climate, with warm summers and great heat, especially in the valleys.

Pick your time

The ideal time to visit the region is in spring. May, when everything is in bloom and has not yet been dried out by the sun, is especially good for exploring the Tuscan countryside, and a trip to one of the spa towns with their restorative volcanic springs is recommended. Many tourists also visit Tuscany in the winter; the cities are less crowded and the day-time temperatures still rather pleasant, compared to more northerly latitudes. Those determined to sunbathe, however, would do best to go in July, the hottest month on average.

provide a habitat both for highly endangered species and for those driven from their natural home by the presence of man. Bears, lynxes, and wild goats have just recently taken up residence here, and there are plenty of different birds to admire, in particular the mighty golden eagle, which now nests here regularly.
The habitats of all these animals have long been threatened by the intensive quarrying carried out in the Apuan Alps, the source of the world-famous and much-coveted Carrara marble. Although this valuable stone is quarried at more than 150 locations in the area, the recent growth of tourism in Tuscany's mountainous regions, such as Garfagnana, has generated an awareness that a balance needs to be struck between exploiting the local resources and putting into effect the appropriate legislation to preserve the natural landscape.

Always popular: the thermal spa resort of Saturnia in the province of Grosseto.

Marble and mountains

Northern Tuscany has many steep Alpine rock features and large tracts of the Apuan Alps (Alpi Apuane), with Monte Pisanino (1,945 m/ 6,380 feet) at their highest point, have been placed under protection since 1985. Attempts are being made in the national park – Parco Naturale delle Alpi Apuane – not only to conserve the rare mountain plants as well as other vegetation, but also to

SCENERY AND THE NATURAL WORLD

Sea and islands

The Arno, the longest river in Tuscany and its main artery, flows into the sea among long bathing beaches on the Tuscan coast south of Pisa. Two rivieras, the Riviere della Versilia and degli Etruschi, run from the foothills of the Apennines in the north to the flatlands of the Maremma in the south.

The islands of Elba (the largest island of the Tuscan Archipelago and Napoleon's first place of exile), Giglio, Capraia, Giannutri, Pianosa, Montecristo (which gained notoriety in the mid-19th century thanks to Alexandre Dumas' fictional Count), and the prison island Gorgona all lie just off the coast and belong to the region. The islands are said to have fallen from the diadem of the Venus of Tyrrhenia as she rose from the sea by the Tuscan coast.

In 1990 the Parco Nazionale Arcipelago Toscano, which also includes part of the mainland, was established to protect these "jewels in the crown". The park concerns itself particularly with the marine world, which attracts thousands of snorkelers every year.

The bird life in the park – Europe's largest marine park – is unique: the southern part in particular attracts large breeding colonies of endangered shearwaters as well as seagulls, including rare Audouin's gulls.

The Maremma

The Maremma, a region of sparsely populated flatlands covered in pine groves and *macchia* (see sidebar, opposite), lies in south-western Tuscany. This region, which covers an area of approximately 100 sq km (40 sq mi), has been protected as a nature park since 1975. The Ombrone river, the second most important waterway in Tuscany, flows into the sea here, and its delta has preserved much of the marshland that, until drainage was carried out during the 20th century, was typical of the whole Maremma area. Conservation lobbies have prevented the remaining area from being reclaimed and this has ensured the survival of many species of wading bird and reptiles.

Crete – a manmade desert

Taking its name from its clay hills (*crete* means clay), the strange landscape of the Crete, near Siena, is typical of central Tuscany. This sparse region is characterized by low, flat hills upon which very little grows, with just a few cypress trees dotted about in clusters between the hills.

The scant level of rainfall in the area – some parts even qualify as deserts according to current criteria – has dried out the land with the result that the layer of topsoil has been lost right back to the hard clays, which have now become visible. This eroding action has been further accelerated by the merciless felling of the vast oak forests that once covered the whole region of Tuscany; traces of their eastern extremities are still to be found in Mugello and Casentino.

The mountains of the north: the Apuan Alps at Carrara.

A national park in the south: sunflowers in the Maremma.

Idyllic Tuscany: a cypress grove at San Quirico d'Orcia.

A number of structures can be distinguished in Etruscan necropolises (right, Sovana in Grosseto): grave chambers carved from soft volcanic rock, topped with tufa or earth mounds called tumuli; trench graves, simple underground tombs, and rock burials. Common to all is that they were furnished as dwelling-places: the masons carved pillars, tables, beds, and benches from the tufa.

Mezzadria

Until a few decades ago, the great majority of the inhabitants of Tuscany made a living from agriculture organized according to a system called *mezzadria* (sharecropping). This system provided that the landowner would meet half the production costs – tools and seeds, for example – and would receive half the profits from the tenants. The system, which barely guaranteed the farmers a subsistence income, came to an end only when cooperative farms and larger farms appeared in the 20th century, and the result was that many small tenants simply lost their livelihoods. The problem is now rather in abeyance: only about three percent of the population still works in agriculture, with more than 65 percent employed in the service industries.

Rural life in Tuscany is becoming more and more threatened.

Home of the Etruscans

Quite who the Etruscans were is still disputed among historians to this day. It is likely that Greeks emigrated to Italy, intermarrying with local tribes, and the civilization that resulted formed the basis for Etruscan culture, of which there is evidence in Tuscany from about 1000 BC. Although the Etruscans thought of themselves as a discrete people, instead of coalescing into a coherent nation their society formed a loose alliance of 12 independent states. For this reason it would be wrong to think in terms of the Etruscan empire being "conquered" by the Romans in the 3rd century BC – a better image is that of a gradual agglomeration. Some Etruscan cities were defeated militarily, but many adopted Roman culture willingly.

Tuscia is Christianized

Civilization in Tuscia flourished under Roman rule: theaters and great thermal baths were constructed, and reliable water supplies were installed. At the same time the region shrank as a commercial center – grain imported from the Asian provinces of the empire was cheaper than local produce and the topsoil was already being lost as a result of the logging demanded by the ore-smelting trade. Tuscany was a poor area, long past its cultural heyday, by the time Rome fell in the dark days of tribal migration. For around two centuries after this it was part of the kingdom of the Lombards and towards the end of the 8th century it came under Charlemagne's Frankish control.
By this time, the Christianization of Tuscany, which had begun with the martyrdom of St Minias of Florence in AD 250, had been completed.

The "Manhattan of the Middle Ages": San Gimignano's dynastic towers attest to the town's wealth.

The rise of the cities

Independent city states began to develop during the Middle Ages. These soon gained in importance as a result of their localized self-government, which proved to be more effective than receiving orders from a distant emperor or pope, and also because of the rise in sea trade, which brought prosperity to the area.
Another important contemporary component of this rise was the development of the modern banking system, which began in Tuscany – Pisa, Siena, and Florence in particular benefited, and there was much jostling for position between these regional bases. However, by the 15th century Florence

had firmly established itself as the dominant power and brought large portions of Tuscany under its rule.

The Medici

Control of the cities passed initially to an oligarchy of elite mercantile families. The regime was republican in the sense that each city leader – known in Florence as the *Gonfaloniere*, from the word meaning "flag" or "banner" – was elected into office by the families.

The Florentine Medici family soon came to prominence, gradually curbing the political influence of the other families before seizing overall power in 1434, the year that Cosimo de' Medici (1389–1464) was named *Gran Maestro* by the pope. This sealed the fate of the republic and marked the beginning of three hundred years of supremacy for the Medici family; the head of the dynasty was to adopt the title of Grand Duke of Tuscany in 1569 and the clan was extinguished on the sword side only when Gian Gastone (1671–1737) died without male issue.

From the Habsburgs to Napoleon and back again

After Medici supremacy came to an end, the Grand Duchy of Tuscany became part of the Habsburg Empire, which imposed a new constitution in the spirit of the Enlightenment: torture and capital punishment were abolished, the Inquisition banned, and the equality of citizens enshrined in law. This regime was interrupted by Napoleon's first Italian campaign in 1796. The kingdom of Etruria was established, but this proved to be only a short intermezzo, and Napoleon's empire crumbled upon his defeat at the Battle of Waterloo in 1815.

Habsburg rule was restored by the Congress of Vienna, signed just a few days before Waterloo, but this was also relatively short-lived and *Risorgimento*, Italy's independence movement, successfully crowned Victor Emanuel II as the first king of a united Italy in 1859. He chose Florence as his capital from 1865 to 1871 and Tuscany became a region of the newly independent state.

The arrival of modernity

The 20th century brought Tuscany, and especially the area around Livorno, into the industrial present. The country suffered greatly during both world wars, but the economic booms of the 1950s and the 1980s encouraged expansion in heavy industry and mining, bringing a renewed prosperity.

At the same time, more and more cultural tourists and nature enthusiasts were being drawn to the region, and this in turn helped promote the conservation of tourist attractions, as more and more of the economy was turned over to the services sector.

Tuscany's capital investments for the 21st century reside in its unique natural and cultural landscape, now recognized as UNESCO World Heritage Sites.

Cosimo de' Medici – captured here in oils by Jacopo da Pontormo (1494–1557) – became *Gran Maestro* of Florence.

Many of the masterpieces created in Florence set standards that were to last for centuries; Andrea del Castagno's *Last Supper* fresco in Sant'Apollonia in Florence, which depicted Judas as the only apostle to sit on the other side of the table, established a compositional practice for all later depictions of this biblical scene that was to last throughout the Renaissance until the time of Leonardo da Vinci.

Macchiaioli: the Tuscan impressionists

Many art enthusiasts are principally drawn to Tuscany by masterpieces from the Roman era to the baroque, but they often overlook a remarkable school of Italian impressionist painting: a group of artists, slighted as *i Macchiaioli*, literally "the daubers", who turned away from the "official" formal language of the Accademia in Florence. Their works, which can be seen in the Palazzo Pitti, generally choose rural motifs, fleeting impressions captured out of doors. Artists such as Telemaco Signorini, Giovanni Fattori, and Giuseppe Abbati, who considered their work to be contributions in developing an independent concept of Italian culture, were somewhat sidelined after Italy's political independence in 1861.

The Galleria d'Arte Moderna in Florence also possesses works by the most prominent Macchiaioli: Telemaco Signorini (above) and Giovanni Fattori.

Rich pickings

Tuscany has a rich store of art treasures from virtually every era of human civilization. The oldest surviving works and masonry fragments date back to the beginning of the 1st century BC. Archeological excavation of Etruscan "necropolises", the cities of the dead, have yielded rich finds; valuable grave goods, ornate urns and wall art, jewellery, and weapons have come to light in the areas around Volterra, Grosseto, and Pitigliano in particular.

The remains of settlements, viewable today at open-air museums, and comprehensive archeological exhibitions attest to the region's first cultural expansion, and these Etruscan monuments far outshine what remains of the Roman period. The ruins of ancient theaters, such as at Volterra, and the fragments of historic roads and aqueducts attest to the cultural achievements of these centuries, but the absence of any greater works of art is also indicative of the decline of Tuscany in the dark ages at the beginning of the Christian era.

Through every epoch

Enthusiasts of Tuscan art from the Middle Ages to the modern period soon realize that every movement arising in central Europe is represented somewhere here, from Romanesque and Gothic to Renaissance and the baroque, which found its apotheosis in the mannered style of rococo. It is nonetheless striking how the time frames of these periods are out of kilter with those in northern Europe. Tuscan Romanesque lasts from the 10th century into the 13th century – a time when the monastery of Saint-Denis north of Paris was already completed and the Gothic cathedral at Cologne was under construction. It is also worth noting that the late Romanesque period, which eventually gave way to Gothic, has been described as a "proto-Renaissance" because of the regionally specific formal language that was adopted.

The Renaissance as a period in art history was already under way here by the 15th century, a good hundred years earlier than in France, Germany, or England, and Italy was the base from which it began its triumphal procession through the Western world. With influences already discernible in the late 16th century, the baroque in northern Italy began contemporaneously with Spain, but considerably earlier than in England or the Netherlands, for example; in Florence especially, however, the *barocco* would never aspire to the lavish excesses that were to characterize it further north.

The Libreria Piccolomini, a library created in 1445 in the cathedral at Siena for Pope Pius II, is decorated with a cycle of frescoes by Pinturicchio depicting events from the life of the pope, who started life as Enea Silvio Piccolomini.

The cradle of modern art theory

Art flourished in Tuscany particularly in times of commercial prosperity; the Piazza dei Miracoli in Pisa, financed with war booty, and the proto-Renaissance church of San Miniato in Florence are early proof of this. The buildings of Giovanni and Andrea Pisano and the paintings of Cimabue are impressive examples of Gothic art. Masterpieces in their own right, a modern view might also perceive in them the starting point of a still more impressive and almost more perfect style – that of the Renaissance.

Giotto di Bondone, a pupil of Cimabue's, architects such as Filippo Brunelleschi, sculptors such as Donatello and Michelangelo, and painters such as Piero della Francesca and Leonardo da Vinci conspired to develop a completely new concept of art underpinned with an equally new understanding of the world, and Man's place in it. What are seen as the commonplaces of our modern world – viewing Man as an individual, for example, or the use of perspective – were born during this period and found lasting expression in Michelangelo's figure of *David* and Botticelli's *Birth of Venus*. Even modern art theory and historiography can be traced back to Tuscany: Giorgio Vasari was the first to produce comprehensive biographies and prototypical *catalogues raisonnés* of Italian artists.

The conversion of the Florentine Palazzo degli Uffizi from administrative buildings to an important art gallery that could be used for the purposes of academic study was the first step in the journey

The pulpit in the cathedral at Pisa was created by Giovanni Pisano, the son of Nicola Pisano. The so-called Pisani pulpits were famed for their exceptionally three-dimensional figures, which broke new ground for sculpture.

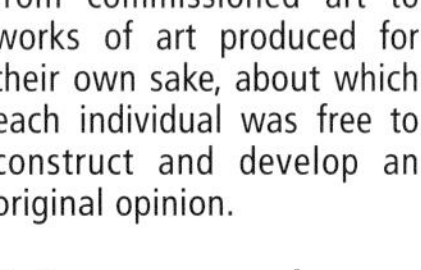

from commissioned art to works of art produced for their own sake, about which each individual was free to construct and develop an original opinion.

Arte nuova and foreign artists

Tuscan art experienced a second heyday at the beginning of the 20th century. The cities in the north and west were particularly influenced by the architecture of the *arte nuova*, the Italian take on art nouveau; the most striking example of this is the seaside promenade at Viareggio.

There was little more in the way of avant garde work in Tuscany after World War I; artists who were born here, such as Amadeo Modigliani from Livorno, were to seek their fortune in larger European cities such as Paris. After World War II, however, the region began to attract foreign artists, who appreciated the easy lifestyle and good climate and who created works of international stature. An excellent example are the female figures sculpted from the 1970s onward in the Giardino dei Tarocchi at Capalbio by the Franco-American Niki de Saint Phalle and her Swiss husband Jean Tinguely. The garden is now an open-air museum, as is the garden created in 1990 by the Swiss artist Daniel Spoerri, which exhibits sculptures in a landscaped garden of his own creation. Spoerri's garden in Seggiano houses more than 50 installations by artists such as Nam Jun Paik and Meret Oppenheim.

Florence, city of art

Florence is a city of culture par excellence: no less than four universities, 12 theaters, any number of academies and cultural institutes, and more than 50 famous museums and permanent exhibitions – not to mention the historic architecture – provide a background for a wide-ranging cultural life which still has time for smaller events. Florence is also a city of private galleries such as the Il Bisonte è Aperto, exhibiting original prints by important Tuscan artists, or the Galleria Poggiali e Forconi with its modern international painting. These are worth a visit simply for the tension they generate between old and new, as exhibitions of contemporary art are often held in rooms in old *palazzi*.

Santa Croce beside its eponymous square (top) and the Fountain of Neptune on the Piazza della Signoria (bottom).

PROFILE: QUINTESSENTIA

A pizzeria in Pisa: what could be better than spending the evening over a typical local pizza after a long day of sightseeing among the amazing art and cultural treasures of Tuscany? The *dolce vita,* literally "sweet life", is a given in Tuscany, and locals are prepared to pay more for it than perhaps many central and northern Europeans.

The finer things in life

Hardly any visitor to Tuscany leaves without having succumbed to the shopping bug, so it is little wonder that the alabaster and pottery industry is just as geared to the souvenir trade as the paper-making business, which produces handmade and marbled paper of exquisite quality. Designer fans are also well looked after in Tuscany: the twin stirrups of

Souvenirs and knick-knacks: the range in the many souvenir shops varies from the sublime to the ridiculous.

Gucci and the top fashion label Emilio Pucci are both based in Florence. Here you can buy the original versions of the leather goods, sunglasses, and clothing you find illegal traders offering for sale as low-rent knock-offs on the corner of every big city.

City and country

Until the 20th century, there was a great divide in Tuscan society between the city-dwellers on one side and the peasants and fishermen on the other. More recently, however, the ever-increasing levels of tourism and the corresponding growth of competiton in the service sector have blurred this division; the tourists are no longer just visiting the big cities to educate themselves about art. With the rise of down-sizers looking for a quiet holiday home and a growth in low-impact "agritourism", which focuses on experiencing the countryside in a hands-on way, rural communities have increasingly set aside old rivalries and the area has reinvented itself as a region of nature and culture combined – "Tuscany" proper. Italy's capital is still Rome, but Tuscan patriotism is a growing force.

Poetry and language

One reason for this patriotism is the fact that three Italian national poets – Dante, Petrarch, and Giovanni Boccaccio – were either born in Tuscany or wrote their greatest works here. Of these, Dante Alighieri (1265–1321) is the most important; his *Divina Commedia*, the *Divine Comedy*, has not only come to be regarded as the apotheosis of Italian poetry, it also uses Tuscan dialect throughout, cementing the idiom as the language of poetry, alongside Latin, and establishing nothing less than the fundamentals of modern Italian. Tuscan patriots maintain that they don't speak Italian in Tuscany, but the rest of Italy has learnt to speak Tuscan.
The area also became important for Italian children's literature in the late 19th century when Carlo Lorenzini, known by the pen name Carlo Collodi, wrote the world-famous story of the wooden puppet with a heart, *The Adventures of Pinocchio.* Collodi is the name of the Tuscan village where the author's mother was born and where he spent part of his childhood.

***Fatto in casa* – homemade – are the magic words for most Italians when it comes to food, and *la mamma* makes it better than anyone.**

Feasts and festivals

People here are justifiably very proud of their local traditions, which most often come to the fore on feast days; there is hardly a town in Tuscany that does not celebrate at least one elaborate festival a year.
In Siena, for example, the Palio, a traditional horse race preceded by a pageant in the Piazza del Campo, has since 1644 been held twice annually, on 2 July and 16 August. In Florence, the Calcio Storico is held every June, when different districts compete in a ball game that is a cross between soccer and rugby, dating back at least to the 16th century. The same month sees Pisan rowers in four boats, each representing one of the four ancient town districts, racing on the Arno in the Regata di San Ranieri. The Festival Puccini, held in July/August in Torre del Lago, celebrates the great composer Giacomo Puccini (1858–1924), who was born in Lucca and lived for many years in nearby Torre del Lago.
All these festivals, which are invariably accompanied by an elaborate procession with the participants dressed in contemporary costumes, give the towns an atmosphere of the Middle Ages intended to remind visitors of Tuscany's heyday. And quite right too.

Dolce Vita

Italian rents are lower, and the size of the apartments smaller, than in many other countries. The Italians choose to spend their money on the pleasures of everyday life instead. Produce such as vegetables, fish, and cheese are purchased fresh at the local market, which is to be found even in the smallest of villages. Bread and meat are bought daily at the baker's and butcher's around the corner, rather than at a supermarket, although these are slowly and inevitably starting to creep in.

Keeping up traditions, holding up flags: the Palio in Siena.

The other essentials for a good life here – olive oil, without which hardly a dish is prepared, and wine, without which hardly a meal is consumed – are also sourced directly from the producer, who will invariably be from the same region.

Honey, balsamic vinegar, preserved antipasti, and of course fine grappa, the popular pomace brandy, are also all produced locally.

Dinner is served

It is worth mentioning that people here regularly eat in public, often outdoors. This is of course partly a result of the relatively mild weather, which means you can comfortably stay out until quite late in the evening, but it's also because eating in Tuscany has always been something of a sociable event – although it is something of a debatable point as to whether people meet up over food for conversation, or just meet and then happen to have something to eat at the same time.

Breakfast is generally restricted to a cup of strong coffee with pastries or a filled bread roll (*panino*). It is often taken at one of many standing cafés, an opportunity to read the paper while you eat. Large lunches are less popular, especially during the hot summer months. Instead, people prefer to have a little something in a bar near work or home – *tramezzini* perhaps, which are a bit like sandwiches with regional fillings, all washed down with a glass of wine and a chat.

The main meal in Tuscany is supper, which is not usually served until after eight o'clock in the evening. As everywhere else in Italy, supper comprises a starter (*antipasti*); a first course (*primo piatto*), usually either pasta or pizza; a second course (*secondo piatto*), which is a meat or fish dish; and finally the essential *dolci*, a sweet dessert. At the end of the meal there is a cup of espresso – or perhaps a glass of grappa.

Properly butchered meat – another Tuscan strong point.

THE HIGHLIGHTS

LUCCA AND THE NORTH

A land of dreams: northern Tuscany, with the foothills of the Apennines and the Apuan Alps to the north, and the Riviera della Versilia to the west, is one of the most geographically varied areas in the whole region. It boasts the highest point in Tuscany, Monte Prado, 2,053 m (6,740 feet) above sea level, and the sandy beaches of the Riviera are among the longest in Italy. The Parco Naturale delle Alpi Apuane has been protected as a national park since 1985 and is an area of outstanding natural beauty, offering great walks for hikers. The area around Carrara is where the world-famous marble of the same name is quarried.

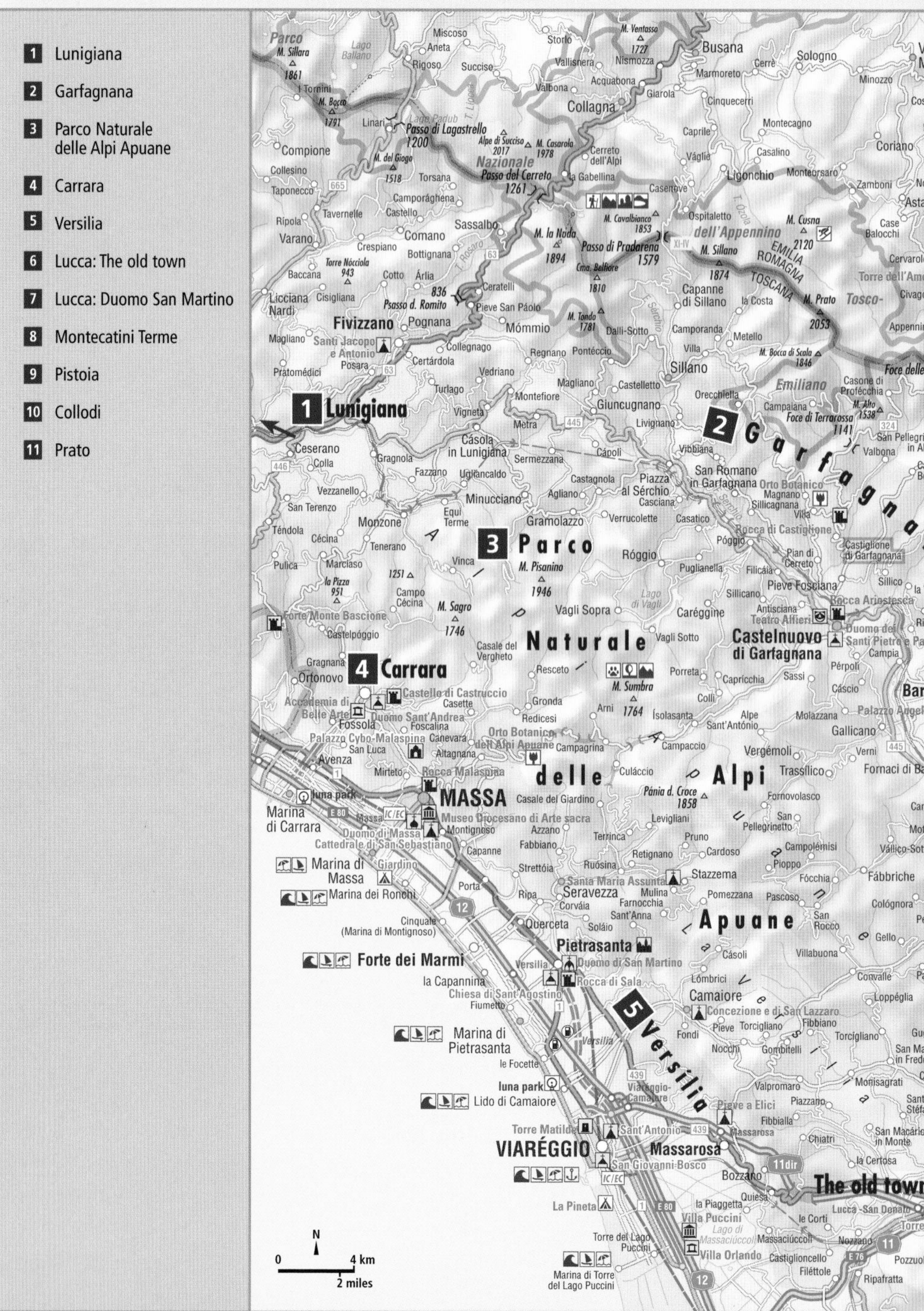

1 Lunigiana
2 Garfagnana
3 Parco Naturale delle Alpi Apuane
4 Carrara
5 Versilia
6 Lucca: The old town
7 Lucca: Duomo San Martino
8 Montecatini Terme
9 Pistoia
10 Collodi
11 Prato
1 Lunigiana
2 Garfagnana
3 Parco Naturale delle Alpi Apuane
4 Carrara
5 Versilia
The old town
Parco Nazionale dell'Appennino Tosco-Emiliano
Passo di Lagastrello 1200
Passo del Cerreto 1261
Passo di Pradarena 1579
M. Pisanino 1946
M. Sagro 1746
M. Sumbra 1764
Pània d. Croce 1858
M. Prato 2053
M. Cusna 2120
Fivizzano
Castelnuovo di Garfagnana
Sillano
Collagna
Busana
Ligonchio
MASSA
Marina di Carrara
Marina di Massa
Marina dei Ronchi
Forte dei Marmi
Marina di Pietrasanta
Lido di Camaiore
Pietrasanta
Seravezza
Camaiore
VIARÉGGIO
Massarosa
Torre del Lago Puccini
Marina di Torre del Lago Puccini
Castello di Castruccio
Duomo Sant'Andrea
Accademia di Belle Arte
Palazzo Cybo-Malaspina
Orto Botanico dell'Alpi Apuane
Rocca Malaspina
Museo Diocesano di Arte sacra
Duomo di Massa
Cattedrale di San Sebastiano
Forte Monte Bascione
Santa Maria Assunta
Duomo di San Martino
Rocca di Sala
Chiesa di Sant'Agostino
Concezione e di San Lazzaro
Pieve a Elici
Torre Matilde
Sant'Antonio
San Giovanni Bosco
Villa Puccini
Villa Orlando
Lago di Massaciúccoli
Rocca di Castiglione
Castiglione di Garfagnana
Rocca Ariostesca
Teatro Alfieri
Duomo dei Santi Pietro e Paolo
Santi Jacopo e Antonio
Orto Botanico
San Romano in Garfagnana
Piazza al Sérchio
Vagli Sopra
Lago di Vagli
Gallicano
Barga
N
0 4 km
2 miles

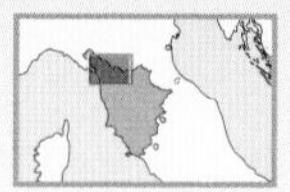

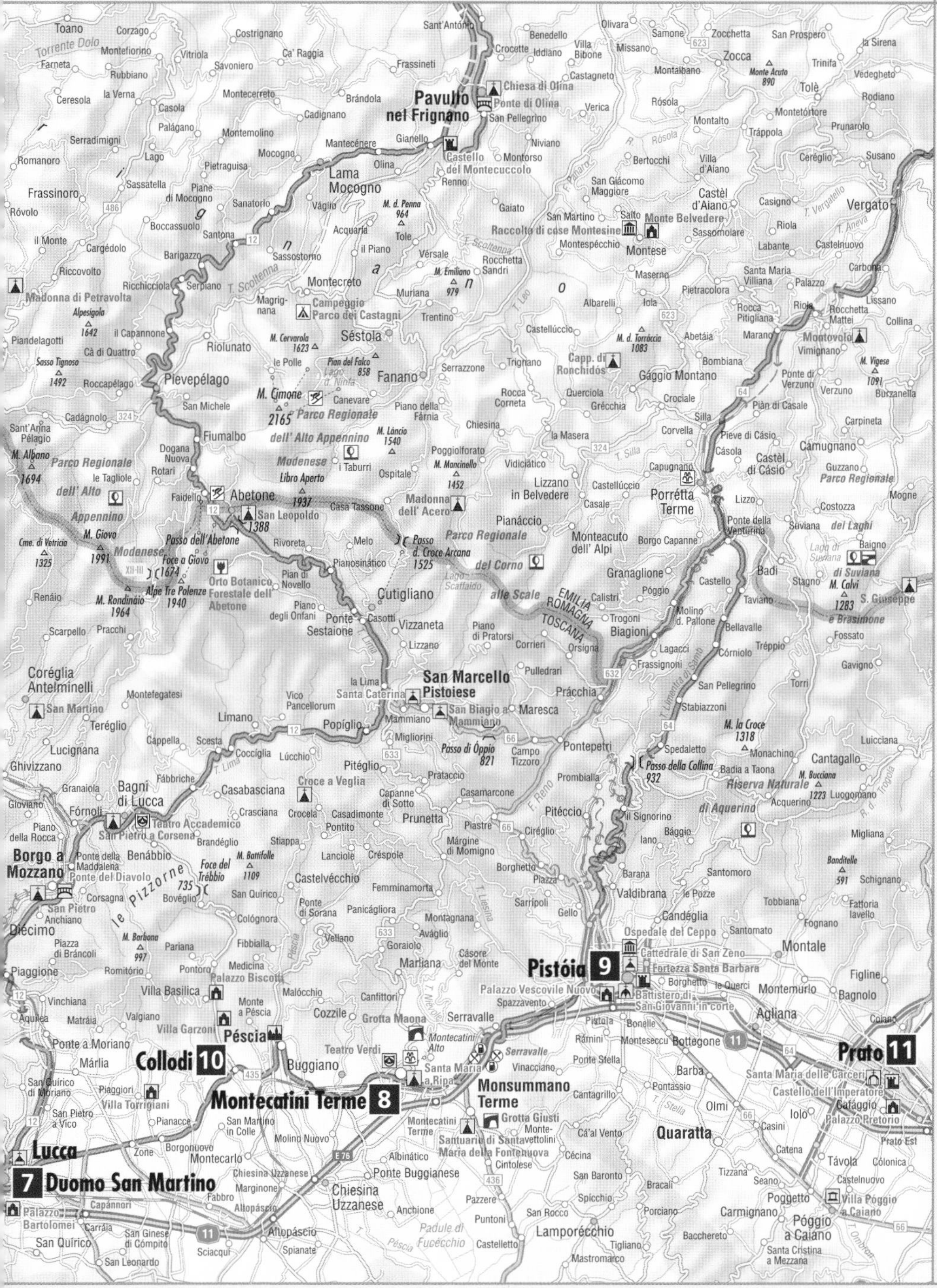

Toano
Corzago
Costrignano
Sant'Antonio
Benedello
Olivara
Samone
Zocchetta
San Prospero
Torrente Dolo
Montefiorino
Vitriola
Ca' Raggia
Crocette
Iddiano
Villa Bibone
Missano
Zocca
Monte Acuto 890
Trinità
la Sirena
Farneta
Rubbiano
Savoniero
Frassineti
Castagneto
Montalbano
Vedegheto
Ceresola
la Verna
Montecerreto
Brándola
Pavullo nel Frignano
Chiesa di Olina
Ponte di Olina
Tolè
Casola
Cadignano
San Pellegrino
Verica
Rósola
Rodiano
Palágano
Montemolino
Montalto
Montetortore
Trappola
Prunarolo
Serradimigni
Mantecénere
Gianello
Niviano
Romanoro
Lago
Mocogno
Castello del Montecuccolo
Montorso
Bertocchi
Villa d'Aiano
Ceréglio
Susano
Pietraguisa
Olina
Lama Mocogno
Renno
San Giácomo Maggiore
Frassinoro
Sassatella
Piane di Mocogno
Castèl d'Aiano
Casigno
Vergato
Róvolo
Sanatorio
Vaglio
M. d. Penna 964
Gaiato
San Martino
Salto
Monte Belvedere
Boccassuolo
Acquaria
Tole
Raccolta di cose Montesine
Sassomolare
Riola
il Monte
Cargédolo
Santona
Sassostorno
il Piano
Montespécchio
Montese
Labante
Castelnuovo
Barigazzo
Vérsale
Rocchetta Sandri
Riccovolto
M. Emiliano 979
Maserno
Santa Maria Villiana
Palazzo
Carbona
Ricchicciola
Serpiano
Montecreto
Muriana
Pietracolora
Madonna di Petravolta
Magrignana
Campeggio Parco dei Castagni
Albarelli
Iola
Rocca Pitigliana
Riola
Rocchetta Mattei
Lissano
Alpesigola 1642
Trentino
Collina
Piandelagotti
il Capannone
M. Cervarola 1623
Sèstola
Castellúccio
M. d. Torráccia 1083
Abetáia
Marano
Montovolo
Cà di Quattro
Riolunato
Pian del Falco 858
Bombiana
Vimignano
Sasso Tignoso 1492
le Polle
Lago d. Ninfa
Fanano
Serrazzone
Trignano
Capp. di Ronchidós
Gággio Montano
M. Vigese 1091
Roccapélago
Pievepélago
M. Cimone 2165
Canevare
Rocca Corneta
Querciola
Crociale
Ponte di Verzuno
Verzuno
Burzanella
San Michele
Parco Regionale
Piano della Fárnia
Grécchia
Pian di Casale
Cadágnolo
Silla
Carpineta
Sant'Anna Pélago
Fiumalbo
dell' Alto Appennino
M. Láncio 1540
Chiesina
la Masera
Corvella
Pieve di Càsio
Camugnano
M. Albano 1694
Parco Regionale dell' Alto Appennino Modenese
Dogana Nuova
Poggiolforato
Cásola
Castèl di Càsio
Rotari
Modenese
i Taburri
M. Mancinello 1452
Vidiciático
Capugnano
Guzzano
le Tagliole
Libro Aperto 1937
Ospitale
Lizzano in Belvedere
Castellúccio
Porrétta Terme
Parco Regionale
Faidello
Abetone
Madonna dell' Acero
Casale
Lizzo
Costozza
Mogne
San Leopoldo 1388
Casa Tassone
Pianáccio
Ponte della Venturina
Suviana
dei Laghi
Cme. di Vetricia 1325
M. Giovo 1991
Passo dell'Abetone
Rivoreta
Melo
Passo d. Croce Arcana 1525
Parco Regionale del Corno
Monteacuto dell' Alpi
Borgo Capanne
Lago di Suviana
Baigno
Foce a Giovo 1674
Pianosinático
Granaglione
Badi
di Suviana
Alpe Tre Potenze 1940
Orto Botanico Forestale dell' Abetone
Pian di Novello
Lago Scaffaido
Castello
Stagno
M. Calvi 1283
S. Giuseppe
Renáio
M. Rondináio 1964
Cutigliano
alle Scale
EMILIA ROMAGNA
TOSCANA
Calistri
Póggio
Taviano
e Brasimone
Piano degli Onfani
Ponte Sestaione
Casotti
Vizzaneta
Piano di Pratorsi
Molino d. Pallone
Trogoni
Biagioni
Bellavalle
Scarpello
Pracchi
Lizzano
Corrieri
Orsigna
Lagacci
Trèppio
Fossato
Frassignoni
Córniolo
Gavigno
Coréglia Antelminelli
la Lima
Santa Caterina
San Marcello Pistoiese
Pulledrari
San Pellegrino
Torri
Montefegatesi
Vico Pancellorum
Prácchia
Stabiazzoni
San Martino
Mammiano
San Biagio a Mammiano
Maresca
T. Limentra di Sambuca
Teréglio
Limano
Popíglio
Migliorini
M. la Croce 1318
Luicciana
Cappella
Scesta
Passo di Óppio 821
Campo Tizzoro
Pontepetri
Spedaletto
Monachino
Cantagallo
Lucignana
Cocciglia
Lúcchio
Badia a Taona
M. Bucciana 1223
Ghivizzano
Fábbriche
Pitéglio
Passo della Collina 932
Prombialla
Riserva Naturale
Luogomano
Granaiola
Bagni di Lucca
Casabasciana
Croce a Veglia
Pratáccio
Acquerino
Gioviano
Capanne di Sotto
Casamarcone
Pitéccio
di Aquerino
Fórnoli
Crasciana
Crocela
Casadimonte
Prunetta
Piastre
il Signorino
Piano della Rocca
Teatro Accademico
San Pietro a Corsena
Brandéglio
Stiappa
Pontito
Margine di Momigno
Cirèglio
Bággio
Migliana
Borgo a Mozzano
Ponte della Maddalena
Benábbio
M. Battifolle 1109
Foce del Trébbio 735
Lanciole
Créspole
Iano
Banditelle 591
Ponte del Diavolo
Castelvécchio
Borghetto
Santomoro
Schignano
Corsagna
le Pizzorne
San Quirico
Bovéglio
Femminamorta
Piazza
Barana
Valdibrana
le Pozze
Tobbiana
Fattoria Iavello
San Pietro
Anchiano
Cológnora
Ponte di Sorana
Panicágliora
Sarrípoli
Gello
Candéglia
Fognano
Diécimo
Montagnana
Ospedale del Ceppo
Santomato
M. Barbona 997
Pariana
Fibbialla
Vellano
Aváglio
Piazza di Bráncoli
Goraiolo
Cásore del Monte
Montale
Cattedrale di San Zeno
Piaggione
Romitório
Pontoro
Medicina
Palazzo Biscotti
Marliana
Pistóia 9
Fortezza Santa Barbara
Borghetto
Figline
Vinchiana
Villa Basilica
Malócchio
Canfittori
Palazzo Vescovile Nuovo
le Querci
Montemurlo
Bagnolo
Matráia
Valgiano
Monte a Péscia
Cozzile
Spazzavento
Battistero di San Giovanni in corte
Aquilea
Grotta Maona
Serravalle
Pistoia
Bonelle
Agliana
Villa Garzoni
Péscia
Ponte a Moriano
Teatro Verdi
Montecatini Alto
Serravalle
Ramini
Montesecco
Bottegone
Prato 11
Colle
Collodi 10
Buggiano
Vinacciano
Ponte Stella
Márlia
Santa Maria a Ripa
Barba
Santa Maria delle Carceri
San Quirico di Moriano
Piaggiori
Monsummano Terme
Pontassio
Castello dell'Imperatore
Villa Torrigiani
Montecatini Terme 8
Cantagrillo
Olmi
Cafággio
San Pietro a Vico
Pianacce
San Martino in Colle
Montecatini Terme
Grotta Giusti
Iolo
Palazzo Pretorio
Molino Nuovo
Santuario di Santa Maria della Fontenuova
Montevettolini
Cá'al Vento
Quaratta
Casini
Prato Est
Lucca
Zone
Borgonuovo
Montecarlo
Albinático
Cécina
Catena
Távola
Cólonica
Cintolese
7 Duomo San Martino
Chiesina Uzzanese
Ponte Buggianese
San Baronto
Tizzana
Castelnuovo
Marginone
Seano
Fabbro
Bracali
Poggetto
Villa Póggio a Caiano
Palazzo Bartolomei
Capánnori
Altopáscio
Pazzere
Spicchio
Carmignano
Póggio a Caiano
Carráia
San Ginese di Cómpito
Anchione
San Rocco
Porciano
Puntoni
Padule di Fucécchio
Lamporécchio
Baccherreto
San Quírico
Altopáscio
Castelletto
Tigliano
Santa Cristina a Mezzana
Sciacqui
Spianate
San Leonardo
Mastromarco

THE HIGHLIGHTS: LUCCA AND THE NORTH

Rising up like an island in a green sea (below): Montereggio, near Pontremoli. The Museo delle Statue-Stele Lunigianesi in the castle at Piagnaro in Pontremoli has an exhibition of prehistoric sandstone figures (below, inset). There is a view of all Lunigiana from the vantage point of Mulazzo (right).

TIP Wine festival

Mulazzo is the wine-making center of Lunigiana. There is a top-quality wine fair here every year in July, where you can sample the local produce.

Bancarel'Vino, Via della Liberazione 10, 54026 Mulazzo; Tel (01 87) 43 90 05. www.bancarelvino.it

LUNIGIANA 1

Lunigiana is an area of interlocking valleys surrounding the Magra river in the far north-west of Tuscany between the Tyrrhenian Sea and the foothills of the Apennine mountain range. This is a region of fortresses and castles, some well preserved but most now in ruins, which were predominantly built for the family of the Margrave of Malaspina, one of the leading dynasties during the Middle Ages. Lunigiana means "land of the moon" and was named after the Roman settlement of Luni, a port whose exported marble was held to have the hue of pale moonlight. At the heart of Lunigiana lies the little town of Pontremoli, and the Castello Piagnaro here houses the Muso delle Statue-Stele Lunigianesi, a sculpture museum displaying sandstone figures dating from the first two millennia BC. These were created by the original inhabitants of the valley to venerate their gods.

THE HIGHLIGHTS: LUCCA AND THE NORTH

The 11th-century Ponte della Maddalena (below), also known as "the devil's bridge", leads to Borgo a Mozzano on the opposite bank of the Serchio river. Little-known plants such as pastinaca and elegant Madonna lilies grow in the Apuan Alps (below, inset, from left).

TIP Gourmet festivals

Many local festivals, especially in the summer, celebrate regional produce. Food is served up with great ceremony and you can try local specialties for very little money – such as Serchio trout at the Sagra della Trota in the Villa Collemandina (12–15 August). *www.garfagnanaturistica.info*

GARFAGNANA 2
PARCO NATURALE DELLE ALPI APUANE 3

Nestling between the peaks of the Apennines and the Apuan Alps, Garfagnana is a paradise for hikers and has been protected as a national park, the Parco Naturale delle Alpi Apuane, since 1985. The mountain valley north-west of the little town of Castelnuovo di Garfagnana is filled with deciduous forests through which wild mountain streams flow into the Lago di Vagli, the largest reservoir in Tuscany, built between 1947 and 1953. When water is let out of the reservoir, the ruins of the flooded village of Fabbrica di Caréggine reappear above the surface of the lake, a peculiar sight. The Grotta del Vento, a limestone cave more than 3 km (2 miles) long, is also worth visiting, and a trip in the direction of Lucca will take you past the Bagni di Lucca thermal baths (see p. 209).

THE HIGHLIGHTS: LUCCA AND THE NORTH

Open-cast mining has changed the face of the mountains around the city of Carrara (right); cables are used for cutting work in the quarry (below, inset). The mighty blocks of valuable marble are cut out of the living rock with heavy equipment (below).

INFO Marble quarries

The marble quarries at Cave Fantiscritti, 4 km (2.5 miles) from Carrara, are open to the public. There is a museum at the Galleria Ravaccione quarry where you can buy marble artifacts.

Tourist information: Viale XX Settembre, 54036 Carrara; Tel (05 85) 84 41 36.

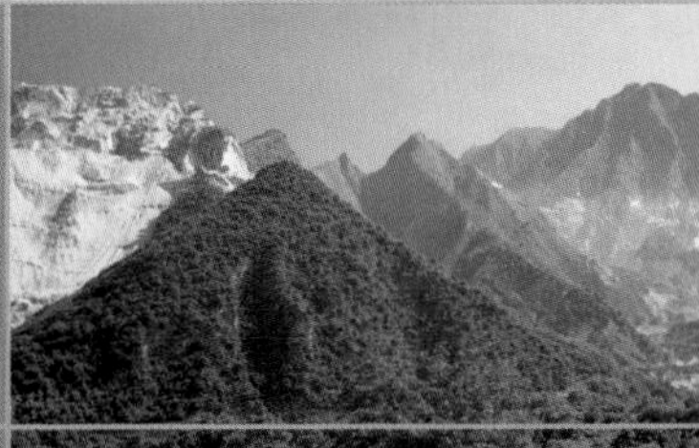

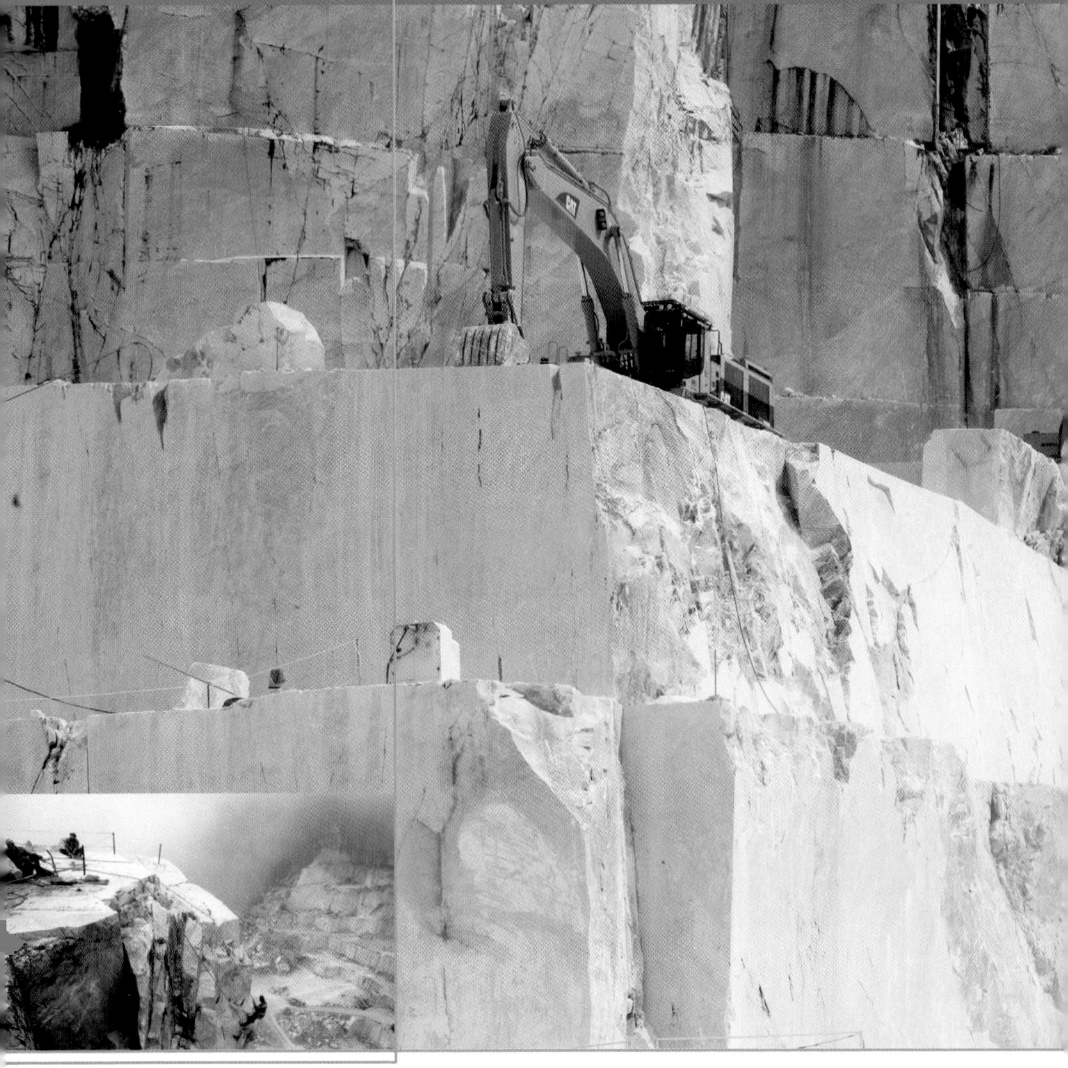

The name "Carrara" has Celtic roots and means "a quarry" – and to this day, quarries are the symbol as well as the main source of income of the whole region, which bears the same name. The prosperity brought to the area by Carrara marble is manifest in the city of Carrara – in the marble-clad building, originally a princes' residence dating back to the late 12th century, that since the early 1800s has housed the Carrara Academy of Fine Arts; in the beautiful fountain that stands before it; and in the *trompe l'oeil* Romanesque colonnade of the 11th–14th-century three-nave cathedral of Sant'Andrea. A house that stands next to the cathedral is decorated with reproductions of the tools of the artist who breathed life into marble like no other: Michelangelo lived here whenever he was in Carrara, searching for the finest material for his great sculptures (see p. 208).

From classical beauty to kitsch – the marble workshops around Carrara (below) have always known the value of this precious material. Right: The statue of Ludovica Albertoni, canonized only three years previously, is a mature late work by the great baroque sculptor Gian Lorenzo Bernini (1598–1680). The piece is located in the church of San Francesco a Ripa in Rome.

MARBLE: THE SCULPTOR'S WHITE GOLD

The word "marble", derived from the Greek word *mármaros* ("shining stone"), describes a medium- to coarse-grained metamorphic (i.e. changed through heat and pressure) crystalline limestone – any so-called "marble" that has not undergone this process is not the real thing. Often used as a building material, the stone has found its best use in art, especially in the Renaissance and baroque periods. Two of Italy's greatest Renaissance artists used marble from the province of Massa-Carrara: Michelangelo, in his famous figure of *David*, now on display in the Accademia Gallery in Florence, and Donatello, in his *John the Baptist*. Also known as *Bardiglio*, Carrara marble varies in tone from brilliant white and light gray to various shades of red, and was formed within the earth under high pressure, coming to the surface as the Apuan Alps were created out of folds in the ground. It is quarried at more than 150 locations in the province, and its uses are not confined to artistic endeavors: *lardo di Colonnata*, a north Tuscan culinary specialty made in Colonnata and elsewhere, involves large pieces of pork belly – the pigs have to have been slaughtered in the fall – which are packed in salt and a herb mixture called *conca* and then pressed into a sort of marble sarcophagus to pickle for six to eight months. During this time, apparently, the meat takes on the taste of the stone.

THE HIGHLIGHTS: LUCCA AND THE NORTH

A tourist destination with tradition: the beaches at Viareggio, with the Gran Caffè Margherita on the beach promenade (below) and the resort of Forte dei Marmi (right), can look back on a long history of European seaside holidays extending into the first half of the 19th century.

TIP Gran Caffè Margherita

Viareggio's famous art nouveau café burnt down completely in 1917. In 1928, it was rebuilt in its full pomp, and the oriental-looking cupolas once again draw admiring glances.

Viale Margherita 30, 55049 Viareggio; Tel (05 84) 96 25 53; 9.00–24.00 daily.

Versilia, a coastal area nestling in the shelter of the Apuan Alps, is sometimes called the "Tuscan Riviera" because of the many seaside resorts on this 30-km (19-mile) stretch of shoreline between Marina di Carrara and Marina di Torre del Lago Puccini. Towns situated a little way back from the coast, such as Massa, Pietrasanta, and Camaiore, were establishing ports and lidos on the stretches of coast under their control as far back as the 18th century, and in the 19th century artists, writers, and other characters were attracted to what had become the most fashionable bathing region in Tuscany. The elegant resort of Forte dei Marmi, with its fine sandy beaches, has played host to the great mime Eleonora Duse, and the writers Thomas Mann and Aldous Huxley. The town has always retained a discreet charm; Viareggio, perhaps more worldly, has beautiful art nouveau architecture.

THE HIGHLIGHTS: LUCCA AND THE NORTH

The Piazza del Mercato (below) in the heart of Lucca is turned into one big open-air café and restaurant in summer. The foundations of the Roman amphitheater that stood here in the 2nd century BC have been used for the surrounding houses.

INFO Villa Oliva

Another Renaissance jewel is to be found about 6 km (4 miles) outside Lucca: the Villa Oliva is an impressive 15th-century country house, and its parks and water features are open to the public.

San Pancrazio; Tel (05 83) 40 64 62; 15 Mar–5 Nov 9.30–12.30, 14.00–18.00 daily.

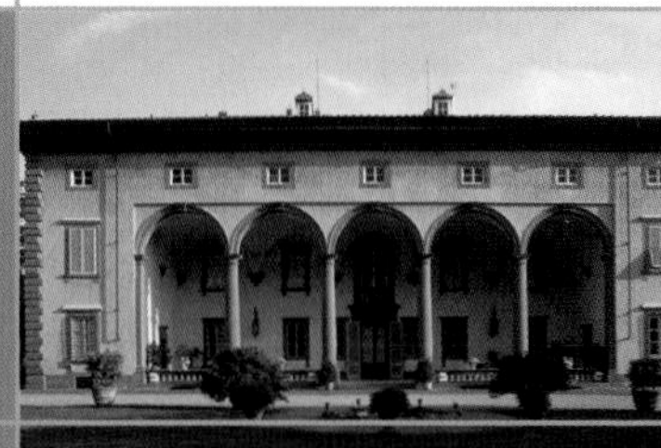

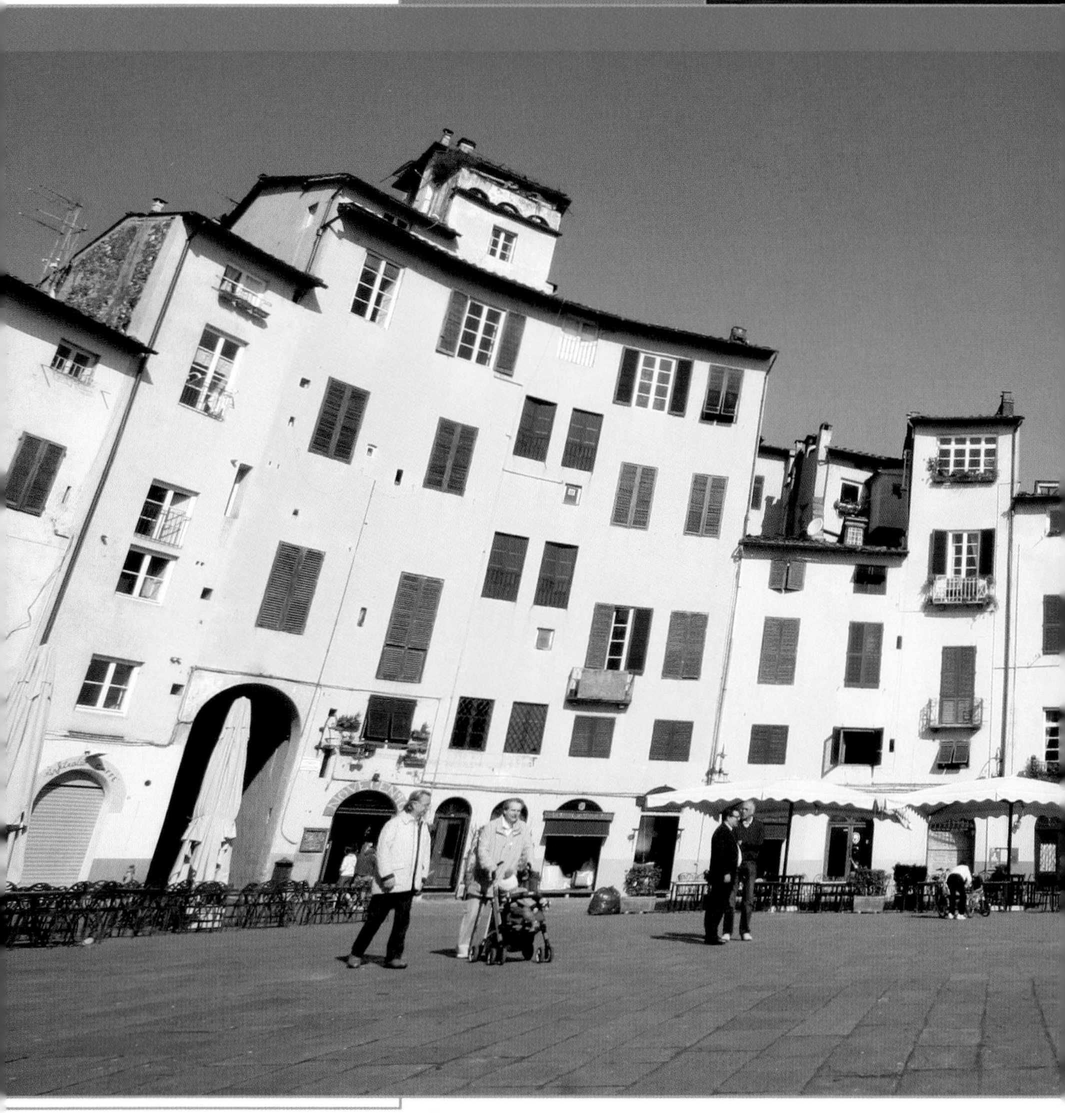

Anyone who wishes to know what a town looked like from the air in Renaissance times need only visit the city of Lucca. One of its symbols is open to the public: the Torre dei Guinigi, a tower erected by an aristocratic dynasty in the Middle Ages as a fortified home. There are large oak trees growing at the top of its 44-m (145-foot) turret. There are also good views from the city wall, which is 12 m (40 feet) high and some 4 km (2.5 miles) long. The Via Fillungo has exquisite art nouveau architecture and some excellent cafés. Two locations in Lucca betray its ancient past: the Piazza San Michele and the church of San Michele in Foro were built on the site of the old Roman forum, and the oval shape of the Piazza dell'Anfiteatro is easily explained; the houses were simply built around an old amphitheater (which no longer exists; see p. 209).

Among the finest works of art in the cathedral is the tomb of Ilaria del Caretto, who died in childbirth at the age of 19; it was wrought from the finest Carrara marble by Jacopo della Quercia in 1408 (below). Below, inset: The cathedral exterior.

INFO Cathedral museum

The displays in San Martino's museum illustrate the artistic activity of the period. It is worth taking time to view the large collection of precious silks, richly embroidered in the Luccan tradition.

Piazza San Martino; Tel (05 83) 49 05 30; 10 Mar–2 Nov 10.00–18.00 daily, 3 Nov–9 Mar Mon–Fri 10.00–14.00.

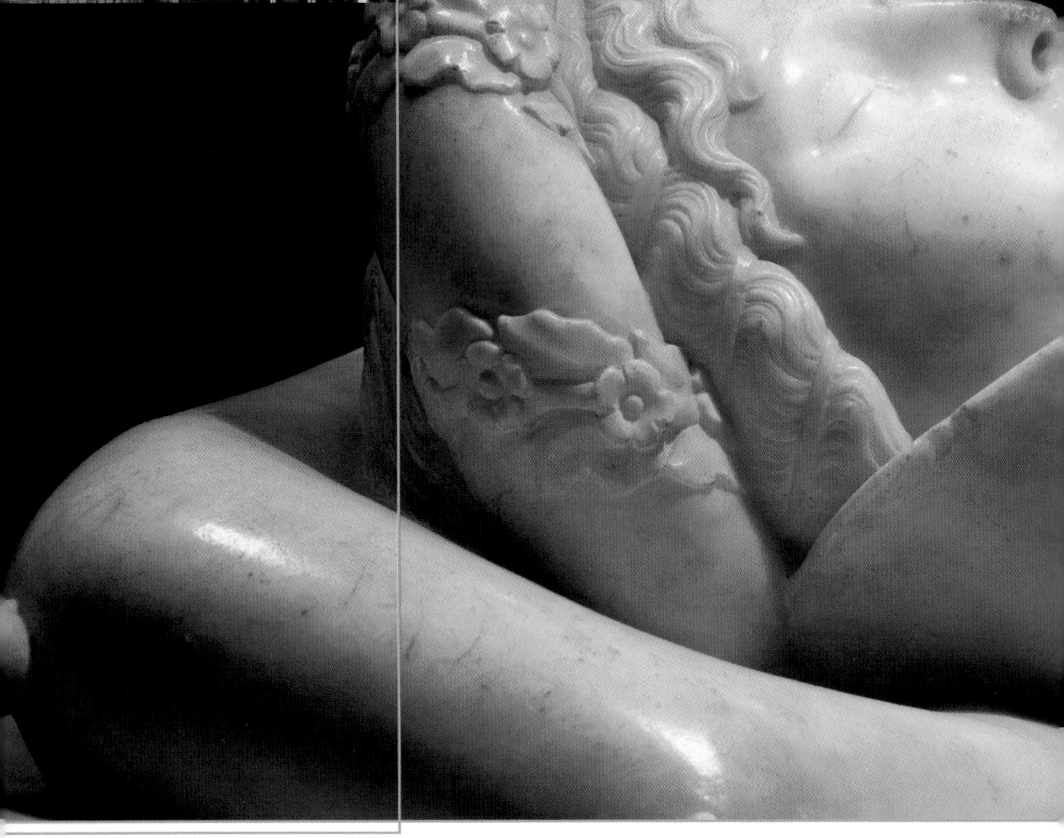

Lucca's cathedral is a three-nave construction with a two-nave transept. The church was probably designed by the Lombard architect Guidetto da Como. The portico arches, to the right of which there stands a mounted statue of St Martin, are topped with three ranges of open galleries, each with a different style of column. The 69-m (235-foot) *campanile* (bell tower) is situated to the right of the façade. The exterior of the transept is decorated with moulded arches topped with floral capitals. San Martino's most precious object is a crucifix for which Matteo Civitalis created a marble chapel within the cathedral in 1484. According to legend, the cross was carved by St Nicodemus himself and miraculously conveyed to Lucca in 782. The cathedral is also home to Federico Zuccari's *Adoration of the Magi* (1595) and Tintoretto's *Last Supper* (see p. 209).

A monument in front of the house of his birth commemorates a maestro beloved of opera fans the world over (below). Examples of his work are displayed throughout the Villa Puccini in Torre del Lago (below, right); during his lifetime, the great composer will no doubt have often enjoyed the idyllic view across the Lago di Massaciuccoli (right).

HIGH EMOTION AND WONDERFUL MUSIC: PUCCINI

One of the greatest opera composers of all time displayed life-long loyalty to his Tuscan homeland: Giacomo Puccini was born on 22 December 1858 in Lucca, where his father was leader of the municipal orchestra and organist at the cathedral. Puccini's very first opera, *Le Villi* (1884), which he wrote soon after graduating from the conservatory at Milan, became a hit. Further triumphs soon followed, with *Manon Lescaut* in 1893 and *La Bohème* in 1896, whose premiere in Turin was conducted by no less a figure than Arturo Toscanini. *Tosca*, probably Puccini's best-known work, was first performed at the Teatro Constanzi in Rome. A drama of love and jealousy which ends in murder and suicide, the beauty of its arias leaves no opera lover unmoved; set in Japan, *Madame Butterfly* (1904) has also entered opera history.

Suffering from throat cancer, Giacomo Puccini moved to Torre del Lago near Viareggio in 1921, to work on Turandot, his unfinished last opera (which was completed by Franco Alfano in 1926). He died on 29 November 1924 after an operation in Brussels, and his tomb can be seen in the chapel of his art nouveau villa in Torre del Lago. Lucca celebrates its greatest son every summer in the "Festival Puccini", which moved to the open-air theater in 2008.

THE HIGHLIGHTS: LUCCA AND THE NORTH

The Tettuccio baths in Montecatini Terme feature a charming mixture of neo-baroque designs and art nouveau decor. Take a glass of the healing waters after your treatment (right) among the Tiffany windows and decorated tiles (below, inset, from left).

TIP Montecatini Alto

A Roman castle stood on the hill above the springs in Montecatini long before the spas were founded. Its ruins are now surrounded by a cheerful collection of restaurants and bars, accessible by car or, best of all, by funicular railway.

MONTECATINI TERME 8

Most of the facilities here in the most famous hot spas in Tuscany date back to the 1920s and 1930s, although the baths were first promoted in the 18th century by Grand Duke Peter Leopold, the later Habsburg emperor Leopold II; the Terme Leopoldine, built in the style of an ancient temple, are named after him. The Romans were well aware of the healing power of spa treatments and were the first to exploit the volcanic hot springs in Tuscany. Under Medici rule – the family owned Montecatini from 1583 – people drank the water; bathing cures were not to become fashionable for another two centuries, when the town and its extensive spa complex became the playground of the fashionable and wealthy in the 19th and 20th centuries. The *funiva*, one of the oldest funicular railways in the world, will take you up to the picturesque mountain village of Montecatini Alto (see p. 210).

THE HIGHLIGHTS: LUCCA AND THE NORTH

Evening lends a mysterious air to the Piazza del Duomo and the cathedral (below and right). The cathedral's interior features Verrocchio's *Madonna* (below, inset left) and majolica work (below, inset right). The pulpit of the church of Sant'Andrea (below, right) is a masterpiece by Giovanni Pisano.

TIP Market

Early on Wednesday and Saturday mornings the cathedral of San Zeno becomes an impressive backdrop for a large market selling all kinds of items: a real find for souvenir hunters. The best bars in Pistoia are to be found nearby.

Piazza del Duomo

The city of Pistorium gained a worthy place in history in the 1st century BC, under Roman rule; the armies of the conspirator Catalina were comprehensively defeated and their leaders executed here in 62 BC. The centuries that followed were equally scarred with warmongering; rivalry between this small commercial town and the nearby towns of Pisa, Bologna, and Florence ended in the 13th century with Pistoia bowing to Florentine rule. Even today, the town is somewhat overshadowed by its bigger neighbors, although its many medieval churches and the neat houses on the Piazza della Sala have a charm of their own. The bell tower of the Romanesque cathedral (Duomo San Zeno) has become Pistoia's iconic symbol, and the dome of the church of the Madonna dell'Umità, commissioned by Cosimo I de' Medici, is one of the largest in Italy (see p. 210).

THE HIGHLIGHTS: LUCCA AND THE NORTH

The grounds of the Villa Garzoni in Collodi (right) with its butterfly house (below, to left of the image) and the magnificent steps (below, inset left), a jewel of baroque garden design. The Parco di Pinocchio recreates scenes from Carlo Collodi's famous fairy tale (below, inset right).

INFO Exhibition

At the end of the tour of the Parco di Pinocchio there is the Laboratorio delle Parole e delle Figure, an exhibition illustrating the life and works of Pinocchio's creator, Carlo Collodi.

Via S. Gennaro 3, 51014 Collodi; Tel (05 72) 42 93 42; Mar–Nov 8.30 until dusk, winter from 9.00 daily.

Many a tourist has been surprised to stumble upon one of the most important baroque gardens in Tuscany in the sleepy mountain village of Collodi. Synthesizing elements of French and English garden design, it lies within the grounds of the 17th-century Villa Garzoni, one of the largest villas in the province of Lucca. An artful double flight of steps forms the centerpiece of the garden, which boasts water features and a fascinating butterfly house. Collodi has also become famous for its connection with the writer Carlo Lorenzini, whose mother was born here. Under the *nom de plume* of Carlo Collodi he wrote the tale of *Pinocchio* between 1881 and 1883, creating one of the most successful figures in world children's literature. Scenes from the life of the wooden boy, whose nose grew whenever he told a lie, are artfully recreated in the Parco di Pinocchio theme park (see p. 211).

THE HIGHLIGHTS: LUCCA AND THE NORTH

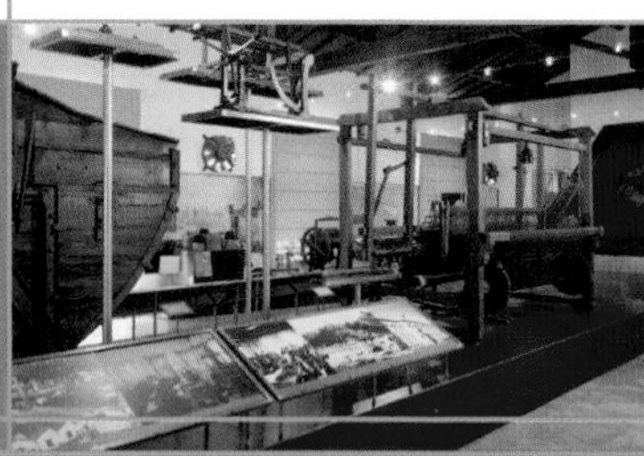

The green and white marble façade of the cathedral of Santo Stefano dominates the square (below). The unusual external pulpit (below, left) is to the left of the main entrance. Filippo Lippi's fresco *Salome and Herod* (below, inset right).

INFO Textile museum

Textiles put Prato on the map, and the Museo del Tessuto illustrates the development of the trade. The exhibits include costumes from various international film productions.

Via Santa Chiara 24, 59100 Prato; Tel (05 74) 61 15 03; Mon–Fri 10.00–18.00, Sat 10.00–14.00, Sun 16.00–19.00.

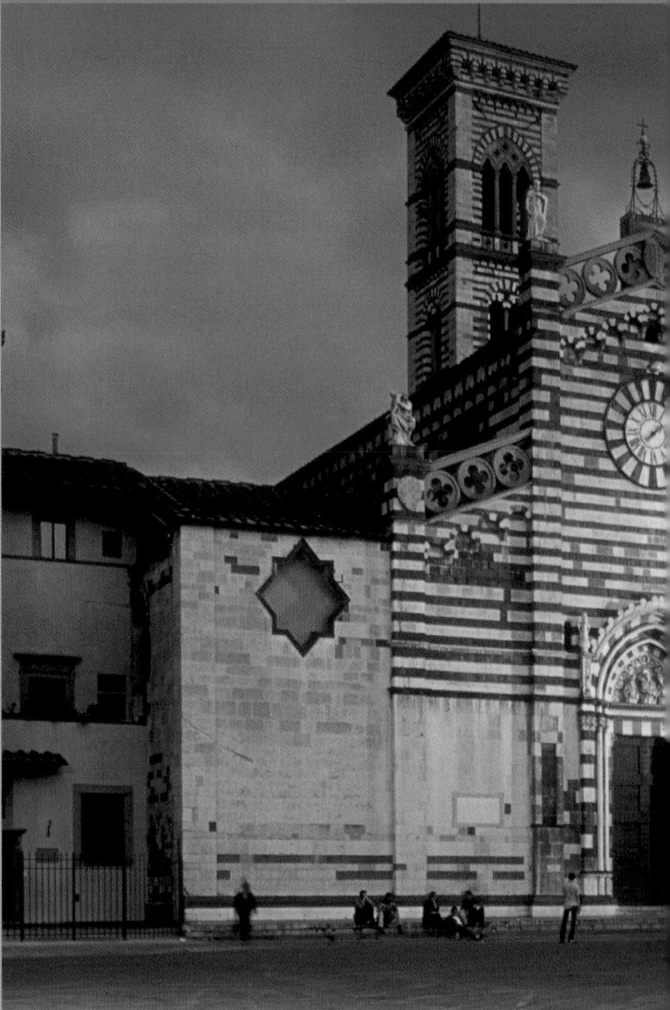

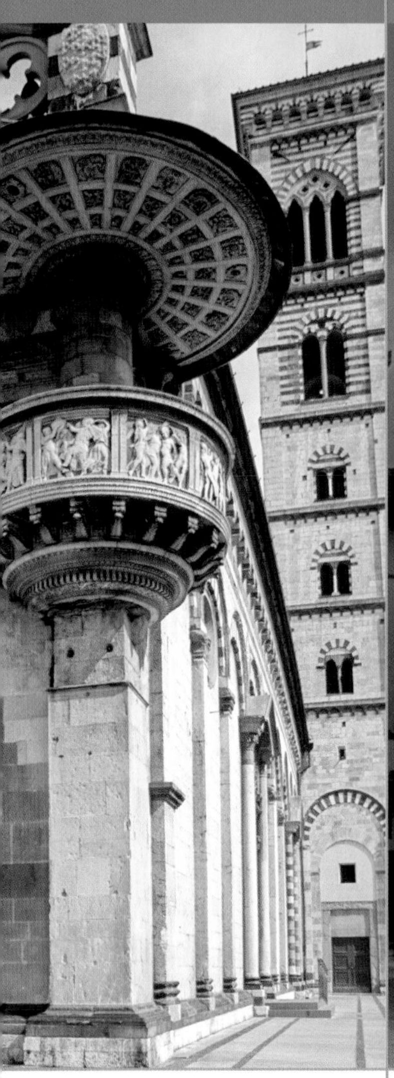

The Castello dell'Imperatore was built as the last bulwark of Prato's hexagonal medieval fortifications (parts of which are still clearly visible today) by the Staufer emperor Frederick II in the 13th century. The ornate cathedral is evidence of the early prosperity of the city, which soon became a leading textile center. The cathedral's present form dates back to 1400; it was later given an exterior pulpit designed by Donatello and Michelozzo, which was intended to allow the faithful to view a Marian relic. An impressive cycle of frescoes depicting the lives of St Stephen and John the Baptist was begun in the cathedral's main choir chapel by Fra Filippo Lippi in 1456. Located a short way outside Prato, the Villa Medicea, a house maintained in the style of an ancient palace or temple, was used as a residence by both the Medici pope Leo X and the 19th-century king of Italy, Victor Emanuel II (see p. 211).

THE HIGHLIGHTS

FLORENCE AND SURROUNDINGS

Lying on the River Arno, Florence, the region's most populous city, is not just the political capital of Tuscany. Its Old Town, unique in the history of art, became a UNESCO World Heritage Site in 1982. Both the formal language of the Renaissance, rooted in the ancient world, and classically influenced humanist philosophy started in Firenze before spreading throughout the world. With the exception of Rome, no other Italian town has produced a comparable number of creative artists and poets, or as many important thinkers, statesmen, and popes. Florence was ruled for a time by the highly influential Medici family, who founded the Medici Bank and were bankers to the pope.

Florence:

- **12** Duomo Santa Maria del Fiore
- **13** Battistero San Giovanni
- **14** Piazza della Signoria
- **15** Palazzo Vecchio
- **16** Ponte Vecchio
- **17** Palazzo Pitti
- **18** Santa Maria del Carmine
- **19** Galleria dell'Accademia
- **20** Santa Maria Novella
- **21** San Lorenzo
- **22** Cappelle Medicee
- **23** Santa Croce
- **24** San Miniato al Monte

- **25** Fiesole
- **26** Vinci
- **27** Empoli
- **28** San Miniato
- **29** Colle di Val d'Elsa
- **30** Chianti

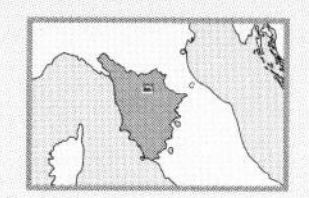

Pratolino
Parco Demidoff
Olmo
65
Uccellatojo
Cercina
Via Bolognese
Rosigbano
la Querciola
Montorsoli
S. Miniato Pagnolle
Céllole
Montereggi
Le Molina
PIÀN DI BARTOLO
302
Villa Corsini
Torrente Mugnone
Via Faentina
Caldina
Saletta
QUINTO
Villa di Castello
Villa Petráia
TRESPIANO
CASTELLO
Piàn di Mugnone
S. Michele a Muscoli
Valle
CAREGGI
Via Bolognese
Fiesole
LE PANCHE
25 Fiesole
Via Reginaldo Giuliani
RIFREDI
Ontignano
SAN DOMÉNICO
Museo Stibbert
20 Santa Maria Novella
Vincigliata
IL ROMITO
21 San Lorenzo
MAIANO
Paiatici
PONTE DI MEZZO
Montebeni
IL PELLEGRINO
Éllera
Ex Fortezza da Basso
Stazione Leopolda
19 Galleria dell' Accademia
SETTIGNANO
Compiobbi
12 Duomo Santa Maria del Fiore
Via F. Rosselli
Coverciano
Stadio Artemio Franchi
Terenzano
22 Cappelle Medicee
Staz. Centrale
alazzo Vecchio 15
13 Battistero San Giovanni
Anchetta
67
14 Piazza della Signoria
Rignalla
Ponte Vecchio 16
VARLUNGO
Casavecchia
Giardino di Bóboli
17 Palazzo Pitti
23 Santa Croce
Candeli
2
Viale Giannott
Via Marco Polo
Vicchio Di Rimaggio
SAN GÁGGIO
San Miniato al Monte 24
Bagno a Rípoli
Via Senese
BANDINO
Via Roma
BADIA A RÍPOLI
ARCETRI
Via del Poggio Imperiale
CASCINE DEL RICCIO
BARONCELLI
Paterna
GALLUZZO
SAN PIERO A EMA
Quattro Vie
E 35
30 Chianti
Firenze Sud
1
RUBALLA
Osteria Nuova

THE HIGHLIGHTS: FLORENCE AND SURROUNDINGS

The harmoniously integrated marble façades of the cathedral and the baptistry to the west (below); the separate *campanile*, designed by Giotto di Bondone, (below, right) is considerably shorter than the high dome of the cathedral (right).

INFO Cathedral music

From 1997, between April and September, the gloom of the basilica has been lit up with *Musica – O flos colende*, traditional concerts of sacred music. There is usually one evening concert a month, and admission is free.
Piazza del Duomo;
Tel (055) 230 28 85.

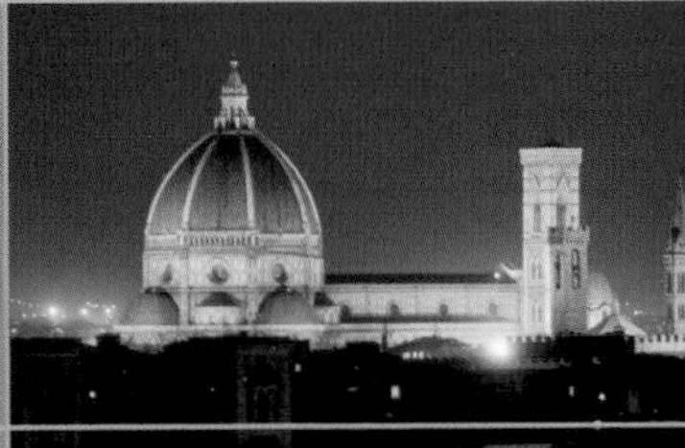

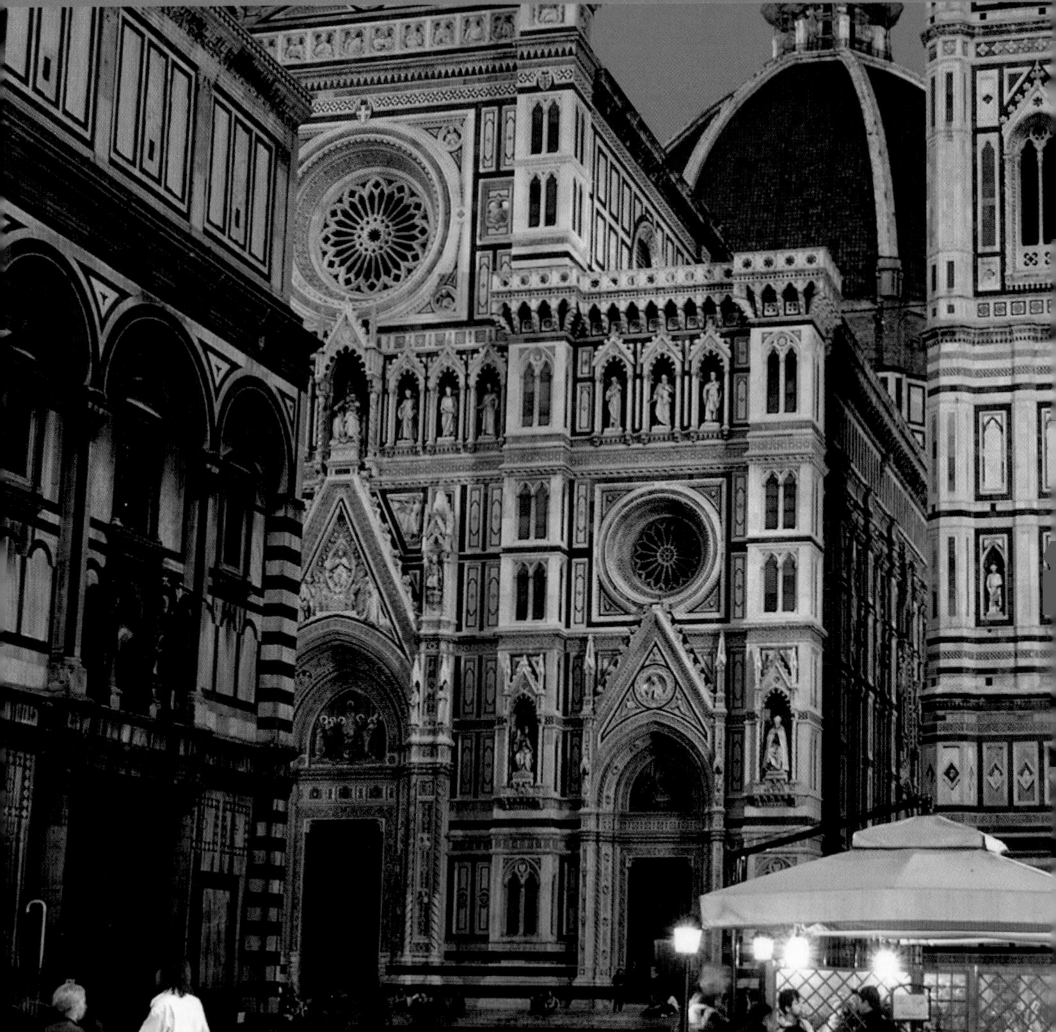

FLORENCE: DUOMO SANTA MARIA DEL FIORE

One of the largest churches in the world, the cathedral in Florence is 153 m (502 feet) long, 38 m (125 feet) wide, and the dome has an external height of 114 m (374 feet). It was consecrated in 1436, while still unfinished; its 19th-century neo-Gothic façade reflects the style of the *campanile* designed by the great 14th-century Renaissance artist Giotto, for which Andrea Pisano created terracotta reliefs. The cathedral's crowning glory is the dome, built between 1418 and 1436 by Filippo Brunelleschi; its 46-m (151-foot) diameter made it the largest in the world at the time. The interior reveals a series of frescoes, begun by Giorgio Vasari and completed by Federico Zuccari in 1579, which depict the Last Judgement. The climb to the top of the dome is worthwhile – you are rewarded inside with a good view of the ornate marble floor of the cathedral and outside with a panorama of the rooftops of the city (see p. 212).

Giotto di Bondone played a crucial role in decorating the Franciscan Santa Croce church in Florence. The artistic genius created frescoes depicting the *Death of St Francis* (below) and his subsequent appearance at Arles (below, inset) for the Cappella Bardi. Right: *Joachim and Anna Meeting at the Golden Gate.*

GIOTTO: FORERUNNER OF THE RENAISSANCE

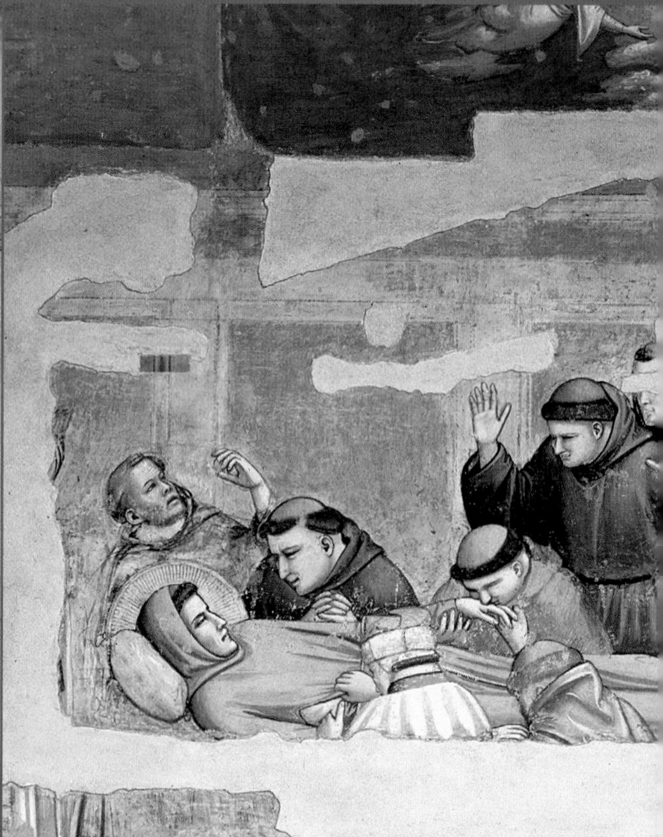

The Florentine painter and architect Giotto di Bondone (*c.* 1267–1337) began a completely new movement in the history of European art. Constantly switching between different genres in the creative arts, he paved the way for the Renaissance, freeing painting from convention and rigid Greek and Byzantine influences. Previously, church wall art had been confined to mosaics or panels completed in a stiff, two-dimensional style inherited from iconic painting. By contrast, Giotto painted people made of flesh and blood, with natural gestures and authentic facial expressions, and he placed them in space using perspective. His picture cycles tell complete stories, with religious themes, of course – art was to depart from restrictions to sacred content only a century and a half after Giotto's death. This new naturalness and vivacity was enabled by a new technique: Giotto was the first great master of medieval fresco painting. Painting onto wet plaster replaced mosaic as the decoration of choice for large areas of wall, not least for the rather worldly reason that it was much cheaper and thus more congruent with contemporary notions of the ideals of poverty. Giotto himself was not poor, and his art brought him considerable position and wealth during his lifetime.

Filippo Brunelleschi's magnificent dome graces the cathedral at Florence (below), whose interior was decorated with frescoes by Giorgio Vasari and Federico Zuccari in the 16th century (below, right). Right: The painter Masaccio depicted both himself (second from left) and his artistic colleagues in the Cappella Brancacci in Santa Maria del Carmine.

FILIPPO BRUNELLESCHI: INNOVATOR AND ARCHITECT

Born the son of a Florence notary, Filippo Brunelleschi (1377–1446) completed an apprenticeship as a goldsmith at the Arte della Seta, at the same time teaching himself the necessary sculptural and architectural skills to enable him to follow his vocation. Research trips to Rome and intensive study of buildings from the ancient and Byzantine world were necessary to develop his own style, which was characterized by strong geometric forms and an almost total lack of ornate decoration. Other elements essential to Brunelleschi's success included his use of mathematical calculations to determine the perspective and the invention of tools that made possible this new "humanist" building style. In 1418, Brunelleschi and Lorenzo Ghiberti competed for the commission to build the dome for the cathedral in Florence. Brunelleschi won, and the dome was completed in 1436. For this construction Brunelleschi used the so-called "fishbone" technique first developed in the ancient world, an approach that hitherto had only been adopted in buildings with a circular floor plan. He succeeded in adapting this technique to the octagonal floor plan of the sanctuary, creating not only the largest but also the first double-skinned church cupola in the world, with self-supporting ribs.

Lorenzo Ghiberti created the doors – described by Michelangelo as the "Gates of Paradise" – for the east portal of the baptistry (below, left); detail showing the giving of the Ten Commandments (below). The interior is decorated with marble panels (right), and ornate frescoes adorn the cupola.

INFO Museo del Bargello

The greatest artists of the period competed to design the north portal of San Giovanni. The bronze reliefs designed by the runners-up to Ghiberti can be seen in the Museo del Bargello.

Via del Proconsolo 4; Tel (055) 238 86 06, 8.15–14.00 daily, in summer 18.00.

FLORENCE: BATTISTERO SAN GIOVANNI 13

The origins of the octagonal San Giovanni baptistry are assumed to date back to the 4th century. Constructed in the so-called "proto-Renaissance" style around 1100, the building became an inspiration for later Renaissance architecture. The interior of the dome is completely covered with 13th-century tesserae, a masterpiece of Western mosaic art, centered on an 8-m (27-foot) figure of Christ enthroned as the judge of the world. The baptistry doors are also of great art historical importance. The design of the north doors echoes Andrea Pisano's doors on the south side – a division into 28 quatrefoil panels, of which 20 depict scenes from the Old Testament. The doors were designed by Lorenzo Ghiberti, who also created the gilded bronze eastern doors, known as the "Gates of Paradise", a masterpiece of the sculptor's art consisting of ten exquisite bas-relief panels (see p. 212).

Few buildings are more beautiful than the Palazzo Medici-Riccardi, one of the first non-sacred buildings of the Florentine Renaissance. Benozzo Gozzoli created the fresco *The Journey of St Balthasar* for the east wall of the chapel in 1460, Giorgio Vasari produced a portrait of Lorenzo "il Magnifico", and Agnolo Bronzino painted Archduke Cosimo I (1519–1574).

THE MIGHT OF THE MEDICI

In 13th-century Italy, the resolution of the feud between two great political entities – on one side the Ghibellines, loyal to the emperor, and on the other the Guelphs, loyal to the pope – resulted in the founding of the independent city state of Florence. The influence of the aristocracy had been checked and the rights of citizens were now enshrined in a constitution. The so-called *Signoria* took on the role of government, led by an elected *Gonfaloniere.* The Florentine republic soon gained in commercial power, becoming the dominant force in Tuscany, and individual aristocratic dynasties such as the Albizzi, the Rucellai, and the Strozzi held sway over politics in the Arno region. The beginning of the end of this new state form was signaled by the appointment of Cosimo de' Medici, a protégé of the pope, to the office of *Gran Maestro* in 1434. His incumbency ushered in a period of dominance for his family which lasted into the 18th century, with a high point during the reign of Lorenzo the Magnificent (1449–1492). The Medici rulers had adopted the title of Grand Duke of Tuscany in 1569, and the family went on to produce cardinals and even popes. To display their enormous wealth and power, the Medici took to building imposing palaces and patronizing the arts. After the male line of the Medici died out, the Grand Duchy of Tuscany fell to the house of Habsburg-Lothringen.

THE HIGHLIGHTS: FLORENCE AND SURROUNDINGS

The Piazza della Signoria with the Palazzo Vecchio and the Loggia dei Lanzi (below and right) is the place to rub shoulders with Giovanni Bandini's *Hercules* or Michelangelo's *David*. Below, left: Bartolomeo Ammanati's *Fountain of Neptune*.

TIP Rivoire

Enrico Rivoire, chocolatier to the royal House of Savoy, founded his workshop, devoted to the finest chocolate, in 1872. People still meet here to enjoy the chocolate treats, which, as always, are handmade.

Piazza della Signoria, corner of Via Vacchereccia; Tel (055) 21 44 12; Tues–Sun 8.00–24.00.

The Loggia dei Lanzi is testament to the importance of the Piazza della Signoria in the political life of the republic. Constructed between 1376 and 1382, the building and its arcade received its current name under the rule of Duke Cosimo I, who had stationed German lancers (*Lanzichenecchi*) here. Giambologna's group sculpture *The Rape of the Sabine Women* (1583) and Benvenuto Cellini's bronze of *Perseus* (1554) are both to be found here. The equestrian statue of Cosimo I (1595), also by Giambologna, and Bartolomeo Ammanati's *Fonte del Nettuno* fountain (1575), intended to commemorate various successful sea battles, are expressions of the city's political self-confidence. Girolamo Savonarola, the revolutionary friar who had briefly wrested power from the hands of the Medici at the head of a band of religious fanatics, was burnt at the stake on the Piazza in 1498 (see p. 212).

THE HIGHLIGHTS: FLORENCE AND SURROUNDINGS

The "Hall of the Five Hundred", meeting-place of the political elite, is the heart of the Palazzo Vecchio (right and below). The hall ceiling (below, inset left) is the creation of Giorgio Vasari and other painters of his school. The Sala dei Gigli was used for formal occasions (below, inset right).

INFO Palazzo Vecchio

Visitors wishing to learn more about the treasures in the Palazzo Vecchio can book a guided tour with the official city guides:

Florapromotuscany; Tel (055) 21 03 01; Palazzo Vecchio, Piazza della Signoria; Tel (055) 276 83 25; 9.00–19.00 daily, Thurs 9.00–14.00.

The "Old Palace", built in 1300 by Arnolfo di Cambio, used to be Florence's town hall. Cosimo I also lived here, before moving to the Palazzo Pitti. As the focus of the city's power, the Palazzo Vecchio was appropriately decorated: the first courtyard, designed in 1470 by Michelozzo, an associate of both Lorenzo Ghiberti's and Donatello's, has impressive frescoes, a *putto* fountain, and magnificent columns. Panels in the coffered ceiling above the "Hall of the Five Hundred", where Michelangelo's *Genius of Victory* is displayed, celebrate the city's history. The next floor reveals the private chamber of Eleonora of Toledo, Cosimo's wife and thus Duchess of Florence, for whose chapel Agnolo Bronzino created a series of frescoes. The Hall of Lilies has entrancing wall frescoes by Ghirlandaio. The Collezione Loeser has an exhibition of works by the Tuscan school from the 14th to the 16th centuries (see p. 212).

The Galleria degli Uffizi (right) is one of the world's greatest art collections. Bernardo Buontalenti created the luxurious golds and reds of the octagonal *Tribuna* (below) for Francesco I de' Medici. The greatest treasures in the Uffizi were once kept in a shrine here.

THE MEDICI AND ART

In 1560, Cosimo I ordered the construction of a building to accommodate the *uffici delle magistrature*, the municipal administration offices. Architects such as Giorgio Vasari, Bernardo Buontalenti, and Alfonso Parigi the Younger collaborated to produce plans for a horseshoe-shaped building behind the Palazzo Vecchio and the Loggia dei Lanzi, with an extended eastern and western gallery connected by the classical façade of the southern gallery. The development of the Palazzo degli Uffizi into one of the most important art galleries in the world began under Francesco I, Cosimo de' Medici's successor, who began an art collection here on the upper floor; this was augmented by subsequent rulers before falling into the possession of the city in 1743. The collection enjoyed such respect that the term "gallery" to describe the parts of the palace where the art was kept became synonymous with "art collection". The Uffizi has magnificent works in many styles, from the Early Modern to the Renaissance in particular. Sandro Botticelli's *Birth of Venus* and his mythically inspired *Allegory of Spring* always draw crowds, as do Titian's *Venus of Urbino*, Caravaggio's *Medusa*, Michelangelo's *The Holy Family*, and *Leda and the Swan* by Leonardo da Vinci.

This humanizing spirit is unmistakable even where the Renaissance addressed more spiritual themes or chose highly Christian motifs, although it is most apparent in images of classical mythology. Sandro Botticelli created a symbol of love in his *Birth of Venus* (1486, below, left), and his *Spring* is a charming allegory of our feelings at the birth of the year (below). Titian, too, gave love a body and a face in his *Venus and Cupid* (*c.* 1550, right).

OUT OF DARKNESS, INTO THE LIGHT: RENAISSANCE CULTURE

The French term Renaissance (Italian: *Rinascimento*) literally means "rebirth", and with this is meant a spiritual return to the ancient world. This was chosen as an alternative to the "darkness" of the Middle Ages, which had lasted for many centuries. In this sense, the Renaissance, which began in Italy, can be understood as the beginning of the modern period. One of the spiritual hubs of Renaissance philosophy, so-called "humanism", was the Platonic Academy in Florence, where renowned 15th-century philosophers such as Marsilio Ficino and Giovanni Pico della Mirandola rediscovered the works of Plato, Aristotle, and other geniuses of pre-Christian antiquity. Italian Renaissance poetry, whose famous exponents include Dante Aligheri, Francesco Petrarca (Petrarch), and Giovanni Boccaccio, was also to have lasting influence. However, the Renaissance was to leave its greatest mark on the creative arts. Reminiscent of ancient temples, the columns and geometric forms of buildings such as those at Pienza were the signal to abandon the Gothic style; the central perspective typical of a Renaissance painting provided a new feeling of space; and sculptures such as Michelangelo's *David* revealed a new, more "natural" notion of Man.

The so-called "Vasari Corridor" runs along the first level of the bridge (below), a secret passage connecting the Palazzo Vecchio and the Palazzo Pitti. Below, inset left: A goldsmith's shop on the Ponte Vecchio. Bernardo Bellotto (Canaletto) painted this view of the Arno in 1742 (right).

INFO Historic river trips

The boats are called *renaioli* and were once used to transport sand for building purposes in Florence. The I Renaioli cultural association has had several painstakingly restored and now organizes atmospheric cruises beneath the bridges of the Arno between June and September.
Mobile: 34 77 98 23 56.

FLORENCE: PONTE VECCHIO 16

The Arno was of the greatest importance for Florence as a natural line of defense as well as a thoroughfare and a water supply. It was probably first bridged at its narrowest point in the Etruscan period, centuries before the Christian era; it is more certain that the Via Cassia, a Roman consular road, crossed the river here via a wooden bridge. The Ponte Vecchio was built on the same spot in the 14th century. The "Old Bridge", the oldest in the city, is lined with little stores and workshops that jut out over the water; butchers, tanners, and smiths once worked here, but as the distinctive noise and smell of their trades became increasingly intrusive, they were banished by Grand Duke Ferdinando I in a decree of 1593 which is still in force. The decree "for the benefit of strangers" established that only goldsmiths should be allowed to ply their trade on the bridge (see p. 212).

THE HIGHLIGHTS: FLORENCE AND SURROUNDINGS

The monumental façade of the Palazzo Pitti (below) is impressive from the outside; inside, the exquisite treasures of the throne room and the Galleria Palatina, including Fra Bartolomeo's *Deposition* (*c.* 1514, bottom left), will quicken the pulse of any art enthusiast.

INFO The Boboli Gardens

In the 16th century the Medici had a garden laid out behind the palace, which was later landscaped; it now features elements from several periods of garden design.

Recommended entrances: Forte Belvedere or Via Romana; 8.15–19.30 daily, Apr, May, Sept, Oct until 18.30.

The 200-m (660-foot) rusticated façade and high window embrasures of the Palazzo Pitti have an almost monumental feel. The palace was designed by Brunelleschi and begun in 1457 for the banker Luca Pitti, whose family was subsequently ruined by the building costs; it was sold by his heirs to the Medici in 1550. King Victor Emanuel II of Italy was in residence here in the 19th century (until 1871, at least) and the royal apartments have been preserved. The core of the Galleria Palatina in the palace, which is open to the public, is a collection of paintings begun in 1620 by the Medici with works by artistic greats such as Raphael, Titian, Tintoretto, Rubens, van Dyck, Murillo, and Velázquez. The palace also holds works from the 19th and 20th centuries in the Galleria d'Arte Moderna, concentrating especially on the Tuscan Macchiaioli school – the "daubers" (see p. 212).

THE HIGHLIGHTS: FLORENCE AND SURROUNDINGS

In 1424 Francesco Brancacci, a silk merchant, commissioned the decoration of a chapel in Santa Maria del Carmine. Below: The frescoes created by the Renaissance painters Masolino, Masaccio, and (below, inset) Filippino Lippi, depict biblical scenes. Right: The central nave.

TIP Antico Setificio Fiorentino

All the intricacies of Florentine silk-weaving are revealed behind an inconspicuous door in the district of San Frediano. Silk has been woven on hand looms here for more than 200 years. The show-room has a display of hundreds of different fabrics.
Via Bartolini 4; Tel (055) 21 38 61.

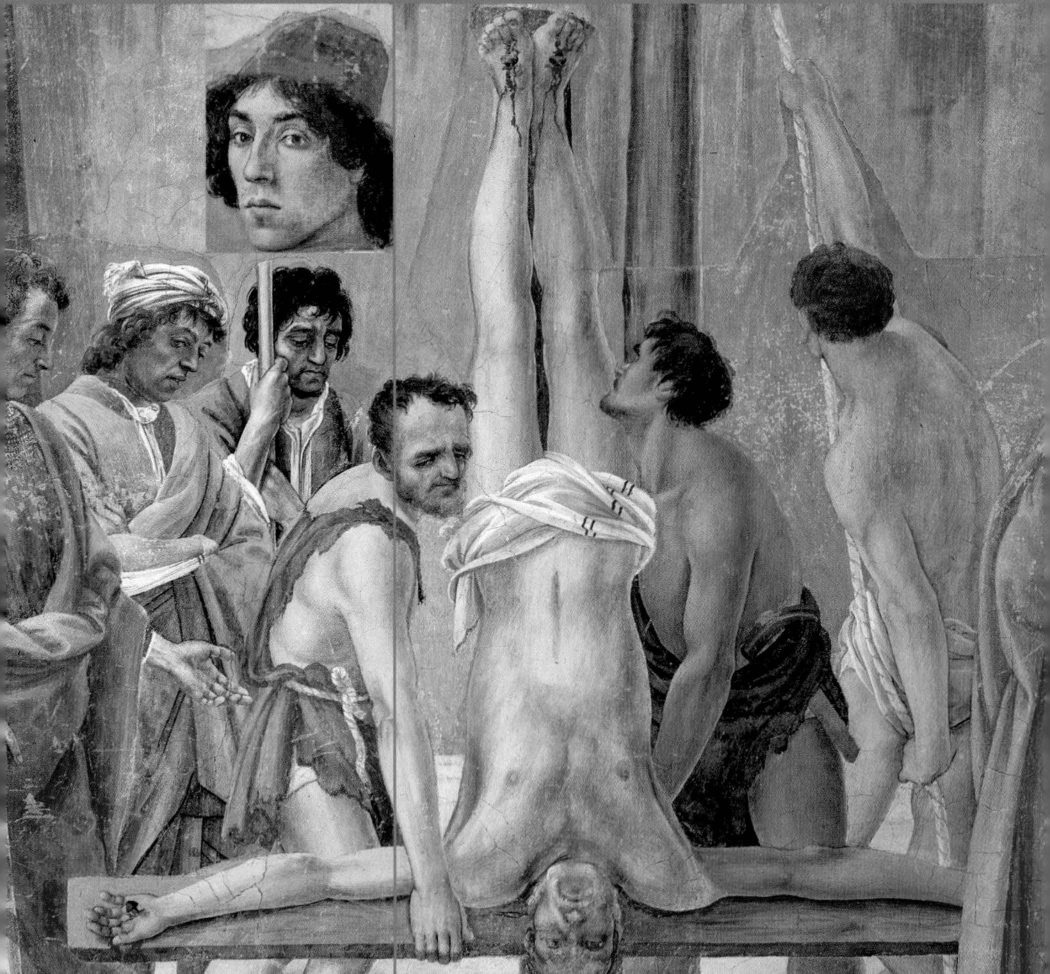

Looking at the unfinished façade of the church of Santa Maria del Carmine, south of the Arno, you would hardly guess the remarkable treasure that is to be found in its interior: the Cappella Brancacci conceals precious early Renaissance frescoes that were begun in 1425 by Masolino, continued by his pupil Masaccio, and finally completed by Filippino Lippi. The original form of the images, the most famous of which is Masaccio's *Expulsion from the Garden of Eden*, was re-established during restoration work in the 1990s. The works are a milestone in the journey from the medieval, Gothic style of fresco painting to the Renaissance, pointing the way for many later artists. A further reason to visit Santa Maria del Carmine is the baroque Cappella Corsini, added in 1675, with its 1682 cupola frescoes by Luca Giordano depicting the *Glory of St Andrew Corsini* (see p. 212).

THE HIGHLIGHTS: FLORENCE AND SURROUNDINGS

Below: The original *David* is the central exhibit in the Galleria dell'Accademia, but other great works of art are also to be found here, such as Lorenzo Monaco's *Man of Sorrows* (right), Botticelli's *Madonna of the Sea*, and Masaccio's *St Peter Baptizing the Neophytes* (below, inset, from left).

INFO One-hour tour

If the number of people queuing in front of the Accademia is just too intimidating, try the one-hour guided tour of the highlights offered daily by "Ciao Florence". Afterwards, you can stay and look round the museum a little longer.
Bookings: Via Benedetto Marcello 1; Tel (055) 35 40 44.

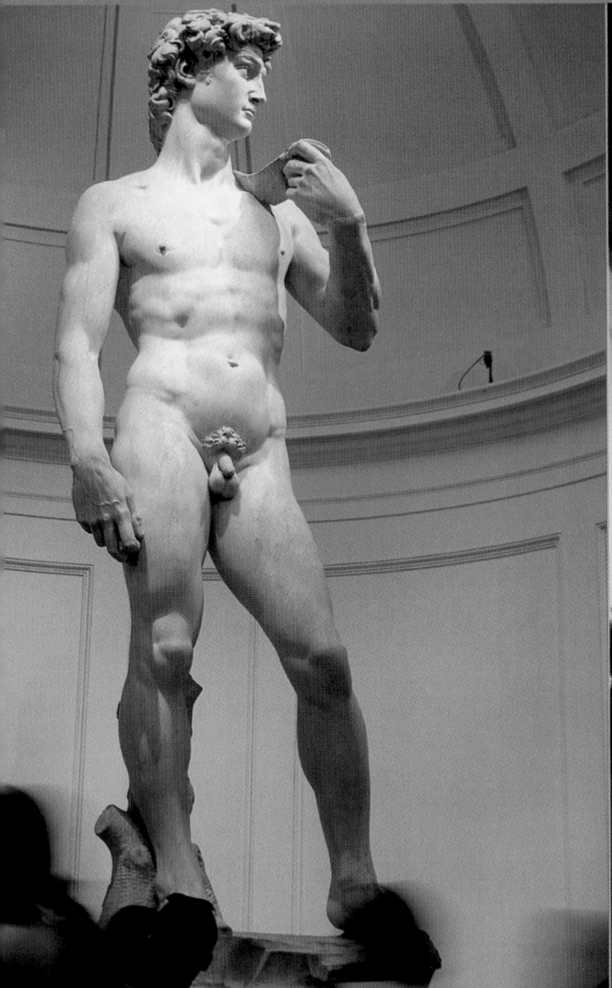

Retreating from the public gaze: in 1873, Michelangelo's 4-m (13-foot) statue of *David*, completed in 1504, which had always stood on the terrace of the Palazzo Vecchio, was replaced with a copy. The original, a world-famous icon of Renaissance genius, has since formed the core of the Galleria dell'Accademia collection, housed in the Ospedale di San Matteo, a former hospital. Grand Duke Pietro Leopoldo, later to become the emperor Leopold II, established the Galleria in 1784 as a collection of exceptional works for the education of young artists, and it soon became an art museum of the first water, acquiring masterpieces by Michelangelo such as the sculpture of *St Matthew* and the four *Prigioni*. There are also several painted masterpieces by Giovanni da Milano and Lorenzo Monaco; the *Madonna of the Sea* is ascribed to Botticelli (see p. 212).

Michelangelo's 1510 portrait by his pupil, Giuliano Bugiardini, depicts him as a contemporary Turk (below, left). The master was 35 years old at the time. *David's* mighty head can be seen on the right. Michelangelo's last resting place is in the right-hand nave of the Basilica of Santa Croce. His tomb, with allegorical depictions of Sculpture, Painting, and Architecture (right), was designed by Giorgio Vasari.

MAN AT THE CENTER: MICHELANGELO BUONARROTI

Michelangelo's *David* is a milestone in the history of art, embodying all kinds of new ideas: departing from traditional iconography, which emphasized the military nature of the victory over Goliath and represented David's heroism as the triumph of religion, Michelangelo approached the biblical figure from a more "human" standpoint. He was more concerned with representing youth, wisdom, and martial prowess – all virtues that were politically very much in vogue in contemporary Florence.

Michelangelo Buonarroti was born in 1475 in a little mountain village called Caprese (now known as Caprese Michelangelo), just south of La Verna. He trained in the workshop of Domenico Ghirlandaio in Florence, subsequently working there, at Carrara, and then in Rome from 1496. He was active in Rome from 1534 until his death in 1564. His multifaceted work as a painter, sculptor, and architect has made Michelangelo the epitome of the High Renaissance artist. His ceiling in the Sistine Chapel, completed in 1512, and the construction of St Peter's in Rome, on which he collaborated from 1546, are among the greatest works of art on earth. If the central feature of "modern" thinking is taken to be the notion of the individuality of each and every person, Michelangelo's portraits and sculptures are the works that usher in this modernity.

THE HIGHLIGHTS: FLORENCE AND SURROUNDINGS

Santa Maria Novella: the magnificent Renaissance façade (below, left) is most famous for its numerous frescoes and paintings (right). Below, right, from top: The main choir chapel, dedicated to the Virgin and John the Baptist; a view of the central nave; and the verdant cloisters.

TIP Monastery apothecary

The monks of Santa Maria Novella were specializing in the production of aromatic essences as early as 1200. The apothecary was officially founded in 1612 and is now a museum of historic scents.

Via della Scala 16; Tel (055) 21 62 76; Mon–Sat 9.30–19.30, Sun 10.30–18.30.

The splendid Gothic Santa Maria Novella began life as the church of a Dominican monastery, built between the mid-13th and mid-14th centuries. Completed in 1479, its Renaissance façade in green and white marble was designed by Leon Battista Alberti. Inside are many notable works of art, including frescoes by Filippo Lippis (painted 1497–1502) and *The Holy Trinity* by Massacio, one of the first Renaissance works to show a grasp of the rules of perspective. The tomb designed by Benedetto da Maiano for statesman Filippo Strozzi lies behind the altar. Domenico Ghirlandaio's fresco cycle in the choir depicts the life of John the Baptist and the Virgin Mary, portraying them in 15th century Florence, with the faces of some of the figures thought to represent notable Florentines of the time. Commissioned as a funerary chapel and later assigned to Elenora of Toledo, wife of Cosimo I, the Spanish chapel contains a wealth of art and frescoes.

THE HIGHLIGHTS: FLORENCE AND SURROUNDINGS

Below: Brick-built San Lorenzo houses art treasures of inestimable value. Below, inset, from left: Brunelleschi's Old Sacristy; the cupola, completed to his designs by Antonio Manetti; Agnolo Bronzino's fresco *The Martyrdom of St Lawrence*, completed in 1569.

TIP Mercato Centrale

Gourmets will be in heaven on the two floors of the Mercato Centrale di San Lorenzo, where they have everything that eating and drinking in Tuscany has to offer: market stalls, stores, and excellent little bars serving local specialties.
Piazza San Lorenzo; Mon–Sat 7.00–14.00.

The Basilica di San Lorenzo is one of the oldest and largest churches in Florence. Its origins date back to the 4th century and it served for many years as the cathedral. Construction of its current incarnation, with a façade that was to remain incomplete, was begun in the 15th century to a design by Filippo Brunelleschi. The later builder of the cathedral dome in Florence first realized here his ideas of central perspective and a linear arrangement of space, a concept whose impact is only reinforced by an impressive coffered ceiling. Next to the transept he also created the Old Sacristy, now filled with striking works by Donatello. Built to a design by Michelangelo, the Laurentian Library is to be found above the first level of the cloisters attached to the church. It contains more than 11,000 valuable manuscripts, some 2,500 incunabula, and 150,000 often highly valuable books (see p. 212).

THE HIGHLIGHTS: FLORENCE AND SURROUNDINGS

The Sagrestia Nuova is considered Michelangelo's first architectural work. The versatile artist went on to complete at least two tombs for the Medici. Lorenzo the Magnificent's last resting place is adorned with allegories (below). Right: The marble cladding in the crypt, designed in 1604 by Matteo Nigetti.

INFO Museum marketing

The Florentine Museum Group (Firenze Musei) maintains a series of official stores where comprehensive brochures, art guides, and well-made replicas of various works of art are sold.

Medici Chapel shop: Piazza Madonna degli Aldobrandini; Tel (055) 28 29 84; 8.15–17.00 daily.

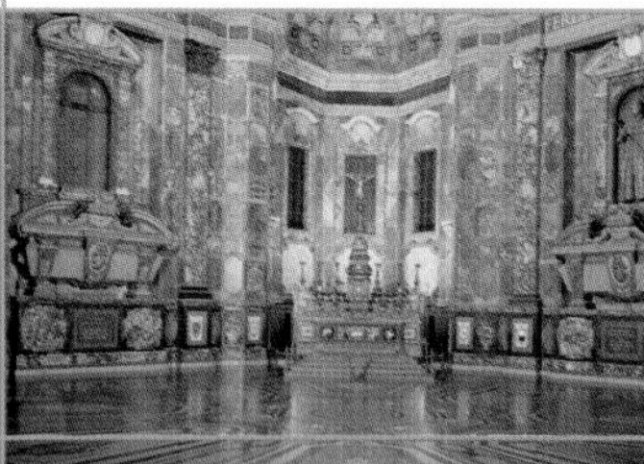

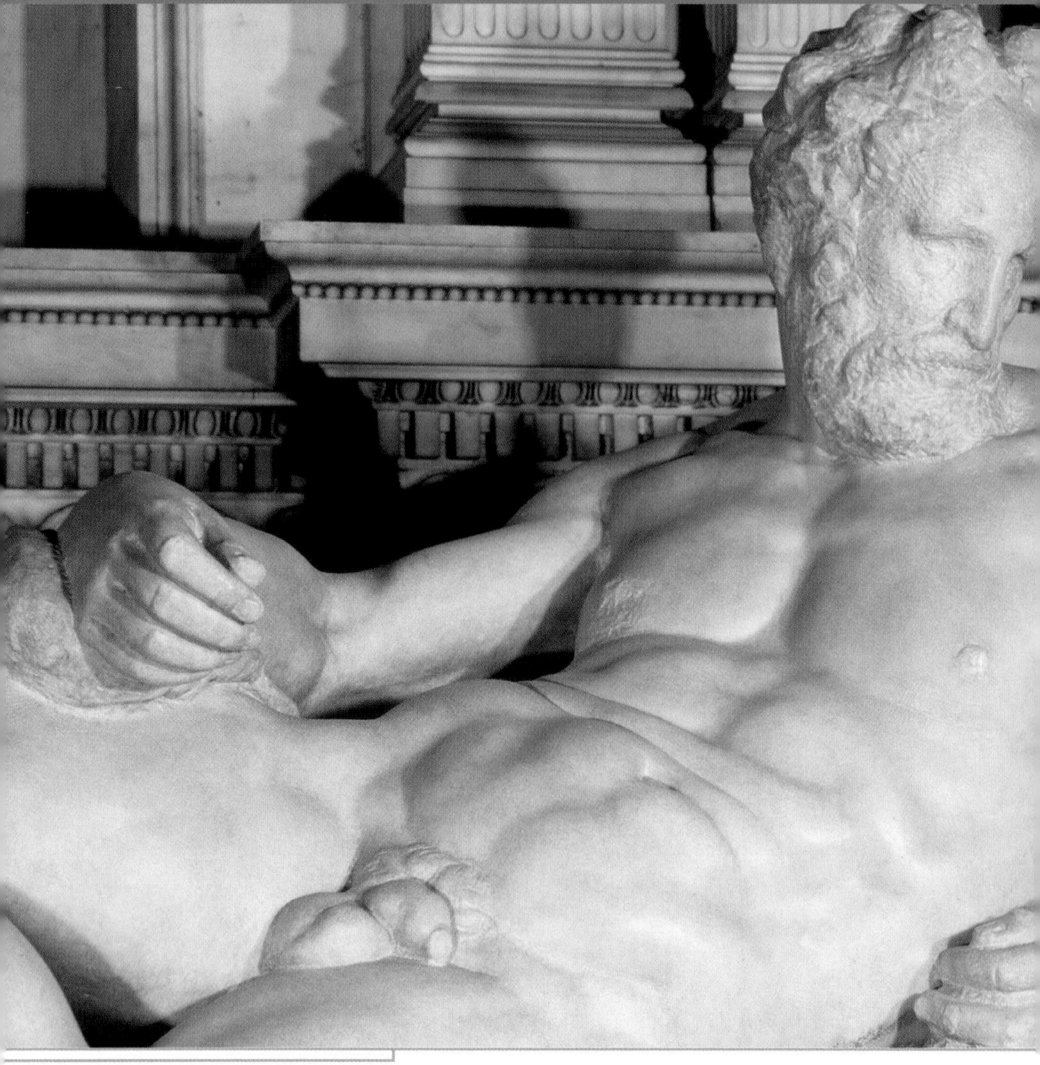

FLORENCE: CAPPELLE MEDICEE 22

In 1520, Michelangelo Buonarroti was commissioned to build the New Sacristy, the Sagrestia Nuova, as a sort of counterpart to Filippo Brunelleschi's Old Sacristy (Sagrestia Vecchia) in San Lorenzo. The Cappelle Medicee is part of a complex of Medici chapels accommodated in a spacious, apse-like extension to the Basilica di San Lorenzo; it is only accessible from the outside and was long used as the dynastic crypt. More than 50 members of the family were buried in the undercroft beneath the chapels, designed by Bernardo Buontalenti, and a further six important Medici princes were laid to rest in the Cappella dei Principi above, which was begun at the beginning of the 17th century. The octagonal building is decorated with the coats of arms of the Tuscan cities and with ceiling frescoes extolling the virtues and achievements of the Medici (see p. 212).

THE HIGHLIGHTS: FLORENCE AND SURROUNDINGS

The three-naved basilica, whose façade dates back only to the 19th century (below, inset), nonetheless contains several important 14th-century picture cycles. Taddeo Gaddi, a colleague of Giotto's, worked on frescoes depicting scenes from the life of the Madonna in the Baroncelli chapel from 1332 to 1338 (below).

INFO Casa Buonarroti

Michelangelo's earthly surroundings can be visited in his house just a few steps from his tomb in Santa Croce. Some of the master's juvenilia are exhibited in the extravagantly decorated rooms.

Via Ghibellina 70; Tel (055) 24 17 52; Wed–Mon 9.30–14.00.

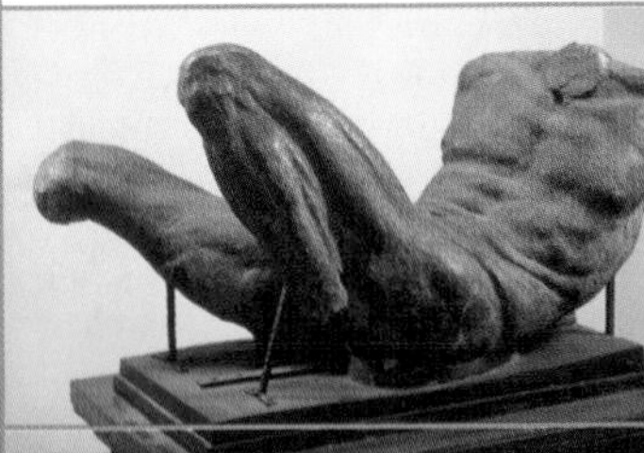

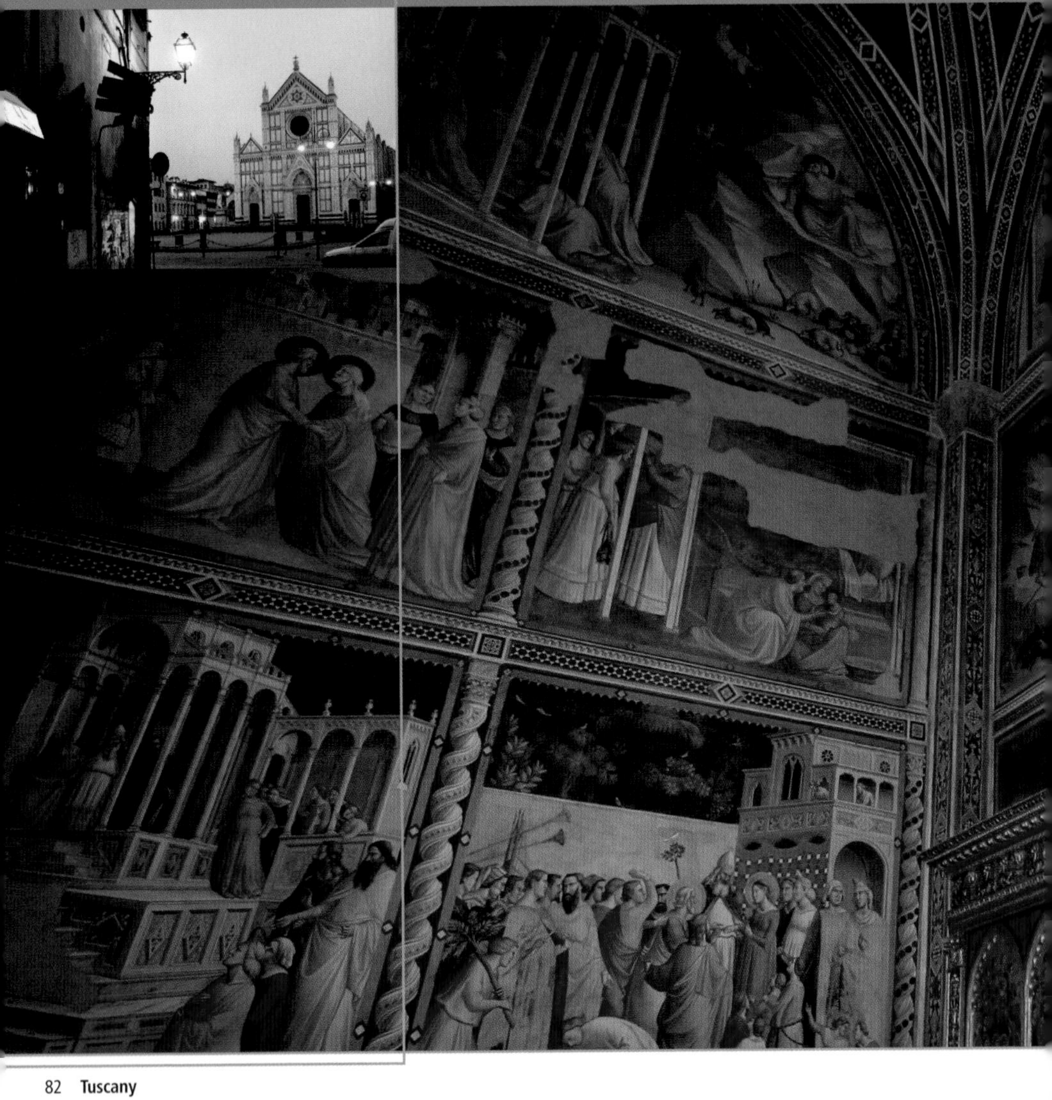

It took over 500 years to build the Gothic church of Santa Croce, from around 1300 to the completion of the façade in 1863. The presence of works by great master painters have made this large Franciscan basilica a jewel in the history of art, and many famous personalities have been laid to rest here: Michelangelo's tomb was designed by Giorgio Vasari in 1570, the tomb of the great humanist Leonardo Bruni was created by Bernardo Rossellino in 1447, and in the 18th century the great scholar Galileo Galilei was recognized with a memorial by Giulio Foggini. Niccolò Machiavelli, the political philosopher, is buried here, as is the master sculptor Lorenzo Ghiberti. Filippo Brunelleschi's Cappella de' Pazzi has impressively strict geometric lines and Agnolo Gaddi's fresco (1338) in the Cappella Baroncelli was the first to depict a night scene (see p. 212).

The turning-point in the life of this scion of Florentine nobility came at the age of nine, when he met the young Beatrice, whom he stylized into an angelic figure. Her early death, and the absence of any physical consummation of his love, kept the relationship "pure", lending it especial value in his eyes. Below, right: *Dante in Exile* (Annibale Gatti, 1854). Below, left: *The Barque of Dante*, painted in 1822 by Eugène Delacroix. Right: The statue of Dante in front of the church of Santa Croce in Florence.

DANTE: LOVE, LUST, AND LONGING

Dante is Florence's most famous son, and yet the basilica at Santa Croce contains only a cenotaph, designed by Stefano Ricci in 1829, with no mortal remains within; Italy's greatest poet was buried on 14 September 1321, but in Ravenna, where he had sought refuge having been first banished from Florence and then condemned to death in his absence in 1302. The "Black" Guelphs, loyal to the pope, who held sway in the city of his birth, had discovered in him a supporter of the "White" Guelphs, loyal to the emperor. Until his flight, the trained lawyer, born in 1265, had held a series of leading political offices in the city, writing several political tracts that had attracted considerable attention; yet it was to be the *Divine Comedy* that secured his place in Western literary history, a 100-canto poem describing a journey through the afterlife: Hell (Dante's famous Inferno), Purgatory, and Paradise are all brought to life in the work. The *Divine Comedy* is the most important work of Italian literature, both in terms of its content and its artistic merit. The central theological and metaphysical concerns of the age are lyrically revisited through the prism of ancient philosophy, and, in writing in demotic Tuscan, Dante did no less than lay the foundations of modern Italian.

THE HIGHLIGHTS: FLORENCE AND SURROUNDINGS

San Miniato is clad inside and out in white and green marble (below and right). Spinello Aretino's frescoes in the sacristy (1387) depict the life of St Benedict (below, right). The tomb of Cardinal Jacob of Lusitania was created by Antonio Rossellino in the 15th century (below, inset left).

INFO Walks

The most pleasing way to reach the basilica is on foot: follow the river from the Ponte Vecchio to the Porta San Niccolò and delicate flights of steps will take you up to the Piazzale Michelangelo. The reward for such effort is a magnificent view of the city of Florence and the Arno valley.

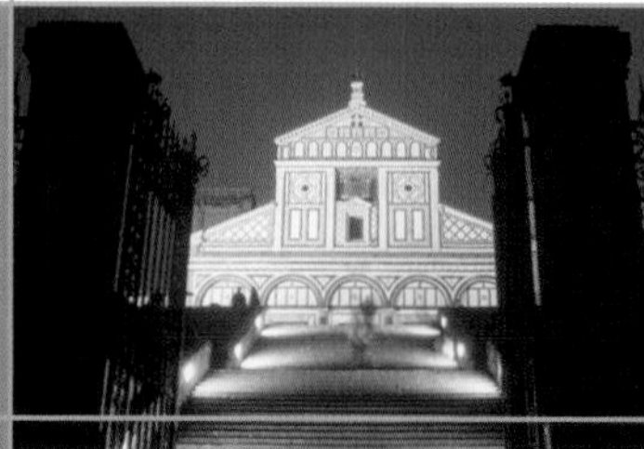

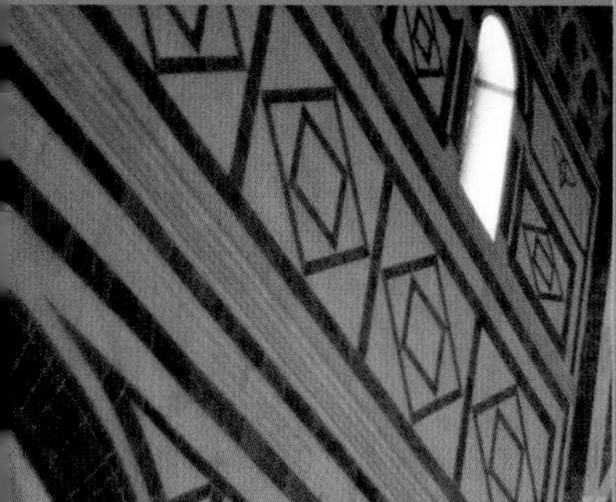

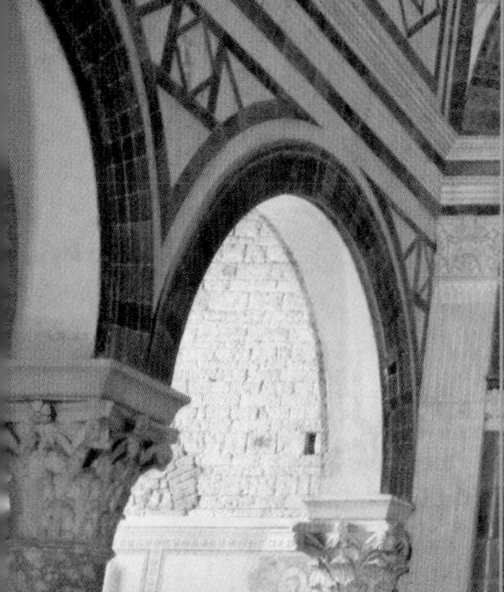

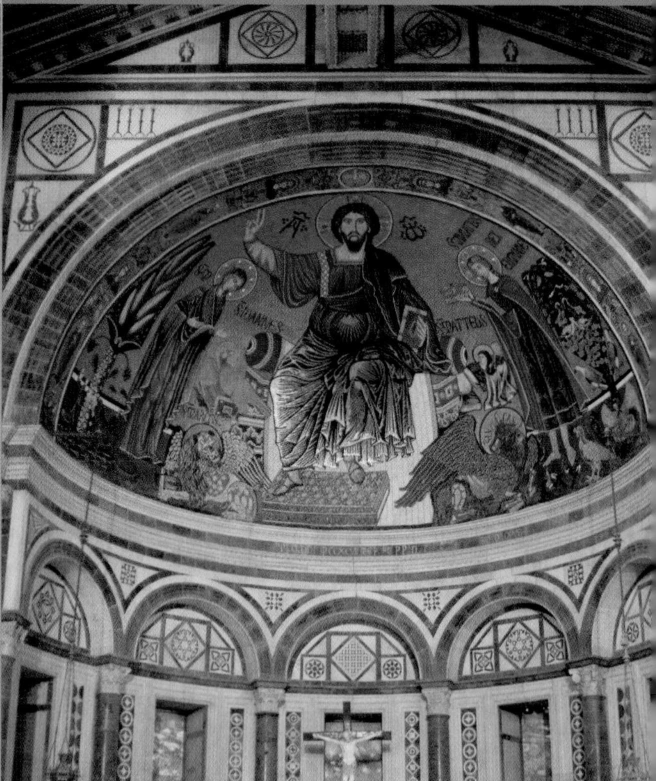

San Miniato al Monte owes its name to St Minias, over whose tomb the building was constructed at the beginning of the 11th century. Part of a Benedictine monastery (it passed to the Olivetan Order in 1373), this three-naved basilica situated high above Florence has an entrancing white Carrara marble and green serpentine façade. In the 15th century a chapel was added on the left-hand side for James of Lusitania, a Portuguese cardinal who died in Florence. The central aisle of the basilica is dominated by the barrel-roofed marble ciborium created by Michelozzo in 1448 for an altar dedicated to St Giovanni Gualberto. The majolica panels are the work of Luca della Robbia and the altarpiece is by Agnolo Gaddi. The entrance to the sacristy, decorated by Spinello Aretino, is adorned with images of saints that are among the earliest frescoes in Florence.

THE HIGHLIGHTS: FLORENCE AND SURROUNDINGS

A good view: Fiesole, with the bell tower of the Duomo San Romolo in the foreground (right). The three naves of this venerable church are marked by Romanesque columns with classical capitals (below, left). Below: The touching depiction of the Virgin in the chapter house of the convent of San Domenico di Fiesole.

INFO Missionary museum

Missionary history: the exciting exhibition in the Museo della Missione Francescana has mementos of missionary journeys from all over the world.

Via San Francesco 13, 50014 Fiesole; Tel (055) 591 75; Tues–Fri 10.00–12.00, 15.00–17.00, Sat 15.00–17.00.

Somewhat removed from Florence and situated high above the city, the little town of Fiesole was settled by the Etruscans and became a separate diocese in 492. There are several extensive archeological sites here, with the remains of a Roman theater, hot baths, and remnants of the Etruscan city wall. Despite later additions, the lines of the cathedral of San Romolo, built in the 11th century but inspired by ancient temples, still reveal the architectural influence of the proto-Renaissance. The Badia Fiesolana, a former monastery located not far from the town, has been the site of the Università Europea, the European University Institute, since 1976. There is a villa on the site, which the great poet Giovanni Boccaccio (1313–1375) is said to have used as inspiration when choosing a location for the frame narrative *Il Decamerone*, his collection of bawdy novellas (see p. 214).

THE HIGHLIGHTS: FLORENCE AND SURROUNDINGS

A place name known to the world, and all because of the creative genius of one man: the beautiful location of Vinci (below). Whether Leonardo was actually born in the simple *casa natale* (below, inset left) is disputed.

INFO Vinci museum

The spirit of Leonardo da Vinci can be felt everywhere within the walls of the castle: inventions such as the bicycle prototype can be admired as scale models.

Castello dei Conti Guidi, 50059 Vinci; Tel (05 71) 93 32 51; Mar–Oct 9.30–19.00 daily, Nov–Feb 9.30–18.00 daily.

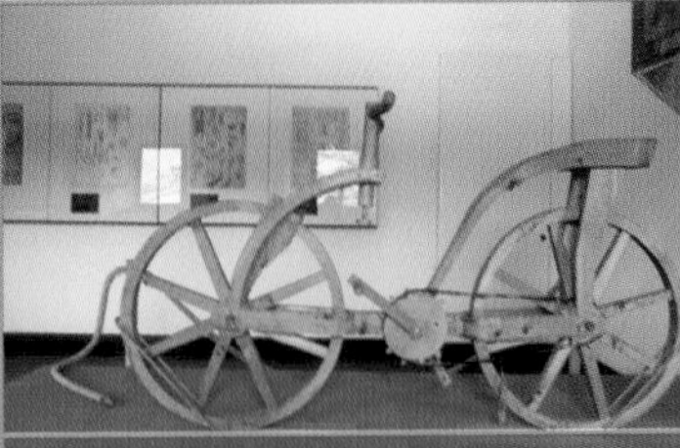

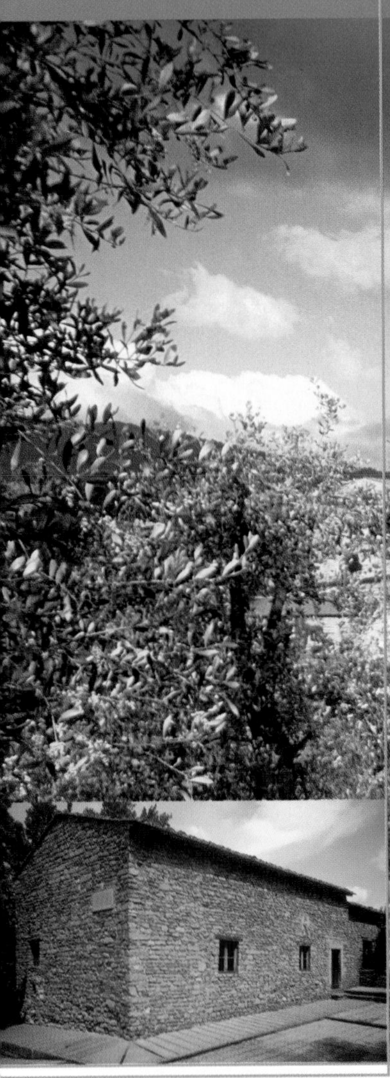

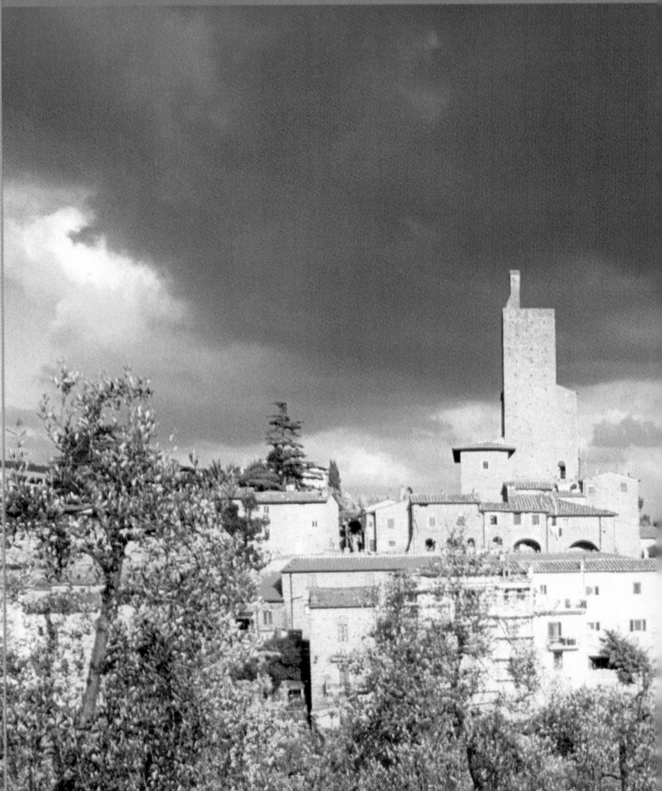

VINCI 26

The little town of Vinci lies half-hidden between vineyards and olive groves on the southern slopes of Montalbano; the famous inventor, scientist, and artist Leonardo da Vinci was born somewhere near here in 1452. The town is dominated by a castle, which first belonged to the counts of Guidi before passing to the city of Florence in 1254. The Museo Leonardiano has been housed here since 1953, displaying models and recreations of Leonardo's inventions such as flying machines, a paddle-driven boat, various siege engines, and a hammer mill. Not every innovation lived up to its creator's expectations. The church of Santa Croce, where Leonardo was christened, stands next to the castle. The Casa di Leonardo, his supposed birth house, is located a little further out of town, in the village of Anchiano, but its authenticity is considered highly doubtful (see p. 214).

Leonardo completed *The Annunciation* (below) at the age of 20, although another artist may have been involved. Right: Design for an invention; cartoon (1512), long considered a self-portrait; *Vitruvian Man* (1492).

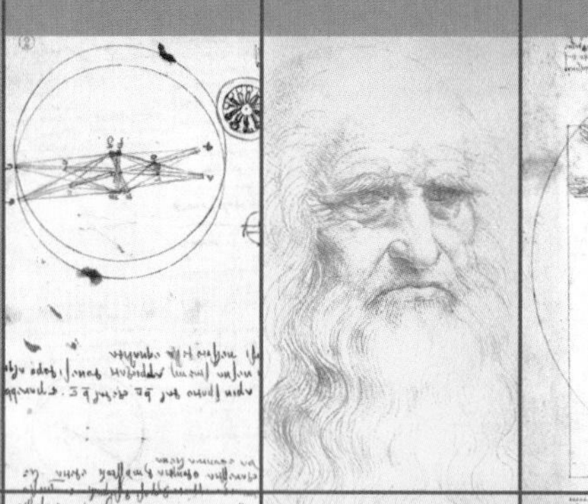

RENAISSANCE MAN: LEONARDO DA VINCI

Hardly any other character in the history of the world is as deserving of the title of "genius" as Leonardo da Vinci. The man "from Vinci" was way ahead of a time that, in Italy especially, was already considered to be exceptionally creative, and his ideas for helicopters, paddle-wheel boats, and diving suits were realized only centuries later. He was one of the first to dissect corpses (secretly – the practice was illegal), gaining an understanding of the intricate workings of the human body; and world-famous pictures such as the *Mona Lisa* (*c.* 1503) have guaranteed him a place in art history. Leonardo (1452–1519), born in Anchiano near the village of Vinci, about 30 km (19 miles) from Florence, was an architect, botanist, meteorologist, biologist, and engineer – among other things. He trained as an artist in Florence under Andrea del Verrocchio until 1482 before entering the service of the Sforza dynasty in Milan, where, in addition to his artistic activity, he wrote and worked as a military advisor. In 1500, Leonardo returned to Florence and by 1512 was working for the pope in Rome. The last two years of his life were spent as a protégé of the French king in Amboise. Sigmund Freud said of him that he was one who "woke too early, in the darkness, when all around him slept".

THE HIGHLIGHTS: FLORENCE AND SURROUNDINGS

Two jewels among the smaller Tuscan towns include San Miniato (below), founded by the Staufer family, and neighboring Empoli, where you can admire the musical angels painted by Francesco Botticini (below, inset) in the Museo della Collegiata di Sant'Andrea.

TIP Truffle festival

Starting in October, the scent gets stronger and stronger in the town of San Miniato as one festival celebrating the truffle follows another; the climax is the great market held in the old town in mid-November.

Info: Piazza del Popolo, 56027 San Miniato; Tel (05 71) 41 87 39 or 427 45.

EMPOLI 27
SAN MINIATO 28

The early prominence of the towns of Empoli and San Miniato rested largely on their location at the junction of two important medieval roads. The 11th-century Collegiata di Sant'Andrea church in Empoli, with its later frescoes by Masolino, and the municipal museum with works by Lorenzo Monaco and Filippo Lippi, among others, are both reminders of its place in the heyday of the Renaissance; just down the road, the Torre di Federico II (the remains of a Staufer castle, named after the emperor Frederick II) has become a symbol of San Miniato. The interior of the 12th-century Romanesque cathedral is decorated with majolica work and has distinct baroque influences. Its *campanile* is named after Margravine Mathilde, who was born in San Miniato in 1046. The Bonaparte family, whose Corsican branch traces its roots to here, built its palace in the town.

THE HIGHLIGHTS: FLORENCE AND SURROUNDINGS

The best time to visit the valley and the River Elsa is in late summer, as the sunflowers in the wide fields are turning their faces to the light (right) and the grape harvest is about to begin. Mist rises from the valley in the early mornings, bringing a welcome freshness (below).

TIP Badia a Coltibuono

This restaurant located in an 11th-century abbey is world-famous. The produce from the vineyards and olive groves of the Stucchi-Prinetti family is among the best in Italy.

53013 Gaiole in Chianti; Tel (05 77) 74 94 24; 1 May–30 Oct daily, 13 Mar–30 April closed Mon, 8 Nov–12 Mar closed.

COLLE DI VAL D'ELSA 29

Heading east from San Miniato, the River Elsa drifts lazily towards Siena through the sparsely populated Elsa valley. Not considered a popular tourist destination, even though it is lined with romantic ruined castles and has great views of the Tuscan hills, the valley is where you will find the little town of Colle di Val d'Elsa, where the warring armies of the Guelphs and the Ghibellines came to blows in 1269. Long overshadowed by Florence, the medieval upper town has a few old churches and a ruined fortress to be explored; but since the 17th century the lower town has also been the internationally renowned heart of Italy's crystal glassware trade and this history is documented in the Museo del Cristallo, with a few select treasures on display. A significant proportion of all the crystal glass produced worldwide still originates from Colle (see p. 215).

THE HIGHLIGHTS: FLORENCE AND SURROUNDINGS

The wine region of Chianti (below), which covers almost a third of the total area of Tuscany, is also a landscape shaped by culture. Temptations to self-indulgence are ever-present in wine merchants' and bars (below, inset) and Greve holds a popular annual wine market.

TIP Castello di Brolio

The noble surroundings of Chianti's home castle is the place to sample and buy the wines produced by the Barone Ricasoli. Tours can be booked in advance.

53013 Gaiole in Chianti; Tel (05 77) 73 02 20; Apr–Oct Mon–Fri 9.00–19.30, Sat and Sun 11.00–18.30, Nov–Mar 9.00–13.00, 14.00–17.30.

Chianti in its narrowest sense refers to a 70,000-ha (173,000-acre) area, located between Florence and Siena, where the red wine Chianti Classico is produced – the bottles are instantly recognizable by the *gallo nero*, the strutting black cockerel on the neck label. As the name is so saleable, six other wine-producing regions in the area have also elected to call themselves "Chianti". The area is best explored in September, when most of the wine festivals are held. The best views of the region are to be found at Montefioralle near Greve; in the mountain village of Radda; in Badia a Coltibuono, with its Romanesque abbey; and in Castello di Brolio, whose fort has been rebuilt as a neo-Gothic castle. Castello Vicchiomaggio near Greve is another 13th-century fortress surrounded by vineyards, and Castello di Verrazzano to the north is even older (see p. 215).

Some of the world's best wines come from Tuscany, which makes wine-tasting a sensuous pleasure (below). John Matta, who produces Vicchiomaggio wine from beautiful dark blue grapes, has been acclaimed several times as Italy's best wine grower (below, inset top right). Many vineyards once belonged to monasteries, and the monastery of Badia a Coltibuono still produces fine wines which age for decades in oak barrels ("barrique" wines), taking on a quite distinct taste from the wood (below, inset bottom right).

CIN CIN AND SALUTE! ITALIAN WINE

Producing and exporting wine has always been an important part of the economy of Italy, the third-largest wine producer in the world after Spain and France; about every sixth bottle of wine consumed today comes from here. The finest Italian wines – with some distinguished Piedmontese exceptions – are also all made in Tuscany. The most popular grape grown in the region is by some margin Sangiovese, literally the "blood of Jove [Jupiter]", a red variety cultivated by the Etruscans before the Romans had even appeared. Successful experiments have also been carried out with Cabernet varieties, giving rise to the "Super Tuscan" appellation. Seven wines from the highest class (DOCG – *Denominazione di origine controllata e garantita*) are local, and most of these are made at the very heart of the region. Brunello di Montalcino, with a minimum four years of barrel age, is considered one of the top red wines; it is sometimes sold with only one year of barrel age as Rosso di Montalcino. Nobile di Montepulciano and Chianti Classico are also popular buys. Another Tuscan wine specialty is *vin santo*, a honey-hued dessert wine made from the Trebbiano and Malvasia grapes that are also popular in the region. The crisp almond biscuits called *cantucci* are traditionally served with this, and these – seriously – are dunked in the wine and then eaten.

THE HIGHLIGHTS

PISA AND THE WEST

The west of Tuscany stretches out from the Arno valley in the north to the Colline Metallifere, south of Volterra, and from Florence in the east as far as the Tyrrhenian Sea in the west. It is the most heavily industrialized part of the region, not least because of its ports. Its scenery is typified by chains of fertile hills that are farmed and where grapes are grown for winemaking. The southern aspects of the hills slope down to the Arno valley, which takes the river to the Ligurian Sea at Marina di Pisa. Aside from its famous Leaning Tower, the city of Pisa has archeological remains dating back to the 5th century BC.

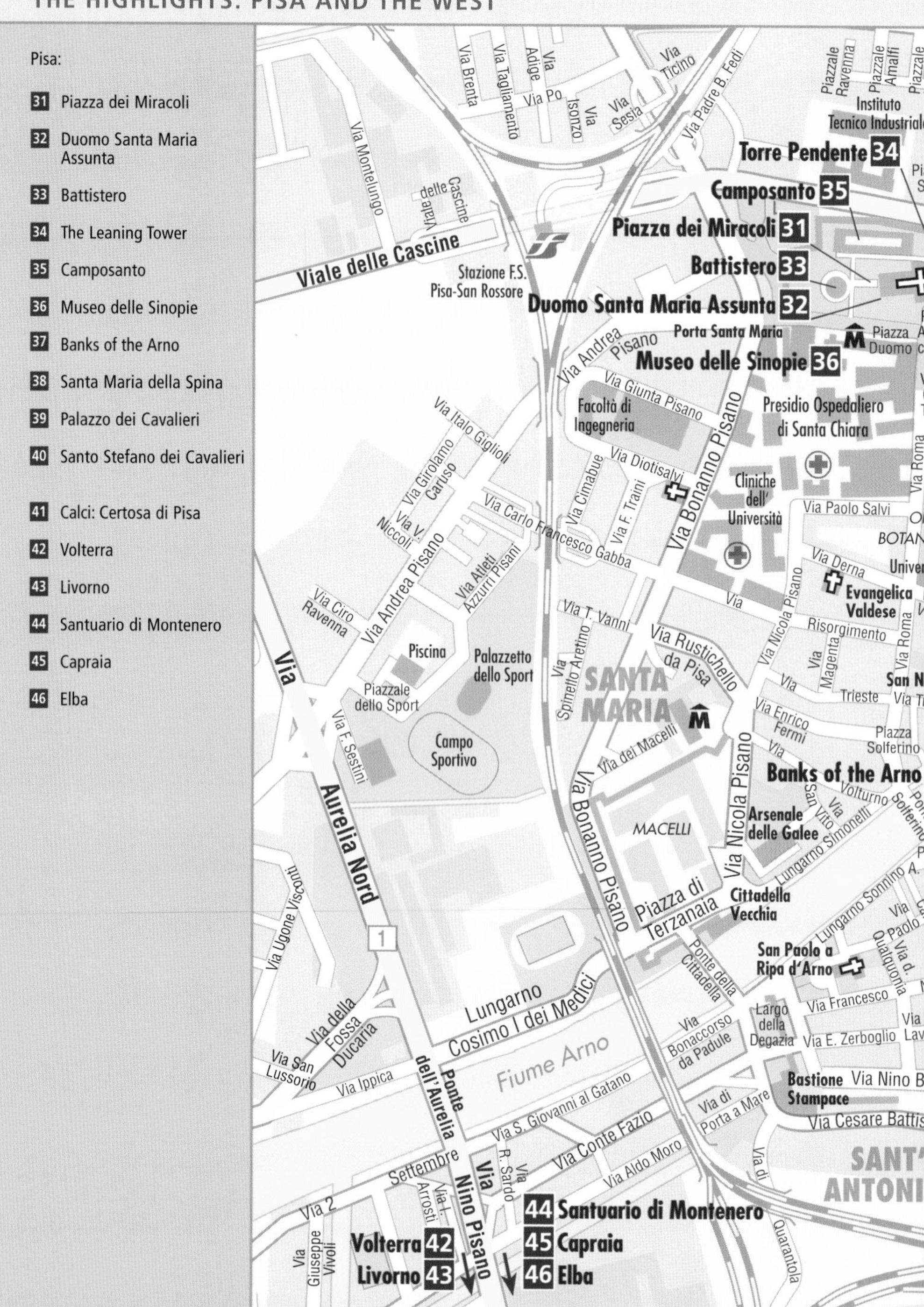
Pisa:
31 Piazza dei Miracoli
32 Duomo Santa Maria Assunta
33 Battistero
34 The Leaning Tower
35 Camposanto
36 Museo delle Sinopie
37 Banks of the Arno
38 Santa Maria della Spina
39 Palazzo dei Cavalieri
40 Santo Stefano dei Cavalieri
41 Calci: Certosa di Pisa
42 Volterra
43 Livorno
44 Santuario di Montenero
45 Capraia
46 Elba
Torre Pendente 34
Camposanto 35
Piazza dei Miracoli 31
Battistero 33
Duomo Santa Maria Assunta 32
Museo delle Sinopie 36
Banks of the Arno
Volterra 42
Livorno 43
44 Santuario di Montenero
45 Capraia
46 Elba
Stazione F.S. Pisa-San Rossore
Viale delle Cascine
Porta Santa Maria
Piazza Duomo
Instituto Tecnico Industriale
Facoltà di Ingegneria
Presidio Ospedaliero di Santa Chiara
Cliniche dell' Università
Evangelica Valdese
Piscina
Palazzetto dello Sport
Piazzale dello Sport
Campo Sportivo
SANTA MARIA
MACELLI
Arsenale delle Galee
Cittadella Vecchia
Piazza di Terzanaia
San Paolo a Ripa d'Arno
Largo della Degazia
Bastione Stampace
SANT' ANTONIO
Fiume Arno
Lungarno Cosimo I dei Medici
Ponte dell'Aurelia
Via Aurelia Nord
Via Bonanno Pisano
Via Nicola Pisano
Via Nino Pisano
Via Andrea Pisano
Via Conte Fazio
Via Aldo Moro
Via Cesare Battisti

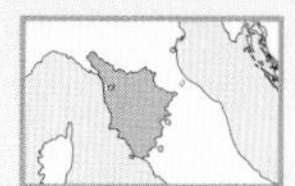

Pisa

PRATALE

SAN FRANCESCO

DON BOSCO

SAN MARTINO

PORTA A PIAGGE

PORTA FIORENTINA

Via Pasquale Galluppi
Via Antonio Rosmini
Campo Sportivo
E. Chiesa
Via di Gello
Via Perugia
Via Bologna
Via Savona
Via Torino
Via Palermo
Via Olbia
Via Firenze
Piazzale Martin Luther King
Via Lucchese
Via Mahatma Gano
Via Fabbricone
Pontecorvo
Via Ippolito Pindemonte
Via Luigi Bianchi
Via Rismondo
Via C.G. Abba
Via Marche Molise
Via Istria
Via Alberto Paparelli
Corte Agonigi
Via dell'Ozeretto
Santo Stefano
Via S. Ansano
Via del Brennero
Largo San Zeno
Via di Pratale
Via Contessa Matilde
12
Abbazia di San Zeno
Calci: Certosa di Pisa 41
Museo dell'Opera del Duomo
Via Cardinale Pietro Maffi
Terme Romane
Via San Zeno
Via Vittorio Veneto
Via Hermada
Via Montello
Via C. Studiati
Via Medaglie d'Oro
Via Vottorio Alfieri
Via Ugo Foscolo
Via Percy Bysshe Shelley
Via Torquato Tasso
Palazzo Arcivescovile
Via C. F. Capponi
Via S. Giuseppe
Via G.B. Pellizzi
Via Battelli
Via Salvatore Quasimodo
Via Spartaco Carlini
Via U. della Faggiola
Piazza S. Caterina
Via G. Carducci
Via S. Apollonia
Sc. Sup. di Studi Universitari
Piazza Martiri della Libertà
Santa Caterina
Via G. di Vittorio
Via Filippo Buonarroti
Università
Via Giorgio Gordon Byron
Piazza Cavallotti
Via E. Filiberto Duca d'Aosta
Via Angelo
Via Silvestro Centofanti
Via Giuseppe Parini
Via San Lorenzo
Palazzo dei Cavalieri
39
40 Santo Stefano dei Cavalieri
Via San Giovanni Bosco
Via San Giov. Bosco
Via Francesco Galdi
San Sisto
P. dei Cavalieri
Via U. Dini
Via G. Oberdan
Via R. Fucini
Via del Ruschi
Piazza S. Francesco
San Francesco
Via San Francesco
Via Oreste Bernardini
Via E. de Amicis
Via Felice Tribolati
Via Mario
Via P. Pao
Via S. Frediano
San Frediano
Domus Mazzinaleana
Piazza San Felice Di Nola
Santa Cecilia
Piazza A. D'Ancona
San Paolo all'Orto
Via Ettore Sighieri
Via G. di Simone
Via Mario Lalli
Via delle Trincer
Via Giovanni D'Achiardi
Via Francesco Flamini
Piazza Dante
Università
Via Tavoleria
Via D. Cavalca
Via Borgo Stretto
San Michele in Borgo
Teatro Comunale "Giuseppe Verdi"
Via del Giardino
Via Ludovico L. Zamenhof
Via Eugenio Donadoni
Canavari
Via Lorenzo Mossa
Via Giovanni Rosini
Piazza Ferrara
Palazzo Upezzinghi
Palazzo Agostini
Piazza G. Garibaldi
Via Palestro
Via G. Giusti
Via S. Bibbiana
Via delle Maioliche
Via Santa Marta
Lungarno A. Pacinotti
Piazza Cairoli
Piazza Repubblica
Via Giuseppe Garibaldi
Lungarno Gambacorti
Via P. Toselli
Ponte di Mezzo
San Pietro in Vinculis
Palazzo Toscanelli
Via L. Gereschi
Prefettura
Via Enrico Betti
38 Santa Maria della Spina
Lungarno Galileo Galilei
Lungarno Mediceo
Museo Nazionale
Via Vincenzo Gioberti
Via Pasquale Landi
Via la Maddalena
Maddalena
Via la Nunziatina
Palazzo Gambacorti (Municipio)
Santo Sepolcro
San Matteo
Piazza S. Silvestro
Via di Concette
Via A. Mario
Via San Martino
Via S. Bernardo
Ponte della Fortezza
Via Sant'
Via G. Mazzini
Corso Italia
Via Kinzica dei Sismondi
Via Pietro Gori
Via la Tinta
Piazza F. del Rosso
Via Silvio Luschi
Via Cisanello
San Martino
Via G. Bovio
Lungarno Bruno Buozzi
Via del Borghetto
Via San Michele degli Scalzi
Via Valentino Baldacci
Via Guido Tizzoni
Carmine
Via del Carmine
Via A. Ceci
Via Bruno
Giardino Scotto
Lungarno Fibonacci
Fiume Arno
Via Manzoni
Piazza M. d'Azeglio
Via G. Pascoli
Via Turati
Via S. Sancasciani
Via Ridolfi
Via C.
Via Antonio
Via G. Mazzini
Via M. d'Azeglio
San Domenico
Via Filippo Turati
Via G.
Bastione del Sangallo e Mura Medioevali
Centro Convegni Palazzo dei Congressi
Via Carlo Matteucci
Sant'Antonio
Piazza Vittorio Emanuele II
Piazza G. Toniolo
Via Benedetto Croce
Via G. Matteotti
Amm. della Provincia
Via G.B. Queirolo
Piazza G.D. Guerrazzi
Via Barattularia
Ponte d. Vittoria
Via Guglielmo Agnelli
Via Mascagni
Via A. Catalani
Viale Francesco Bonaini
Via G. Puccini
Via C. Colombo
Via Amerigo Vespucci
Via della Spina
Corte Braccini
Via Antonio Fratti
Via Francesco da Buti
Via Carlo Cattaneo
Lungarno di Guadolongo
Viale delle Piagge
Via Rainaldo
Piazza della Stazione
Via A.
Viale Filippo Corridoni
Stazione Centrale F.S.
ES/EC

N
0
200 m
600 feet

THE HIGHLIGHTS: PISA AND THE WEST

Pisa's Campo dei Miracoli, the Square of Miracles, always looks magnificent, but different every time, depending on the light. Below, from left to right: The baptistry, the cathedral, and of course the leaning *campanile* tower over the roofs of the city, forming an unmistakable silhouette.

INFO Summer concerts

Musica sotto la Torre, concerts under the Leaning Tower, work their magic on the Piazza each year on summer evenings. Pieces performed usually include contemporary interpretations of the classics.

Tickets (from the beginning of June): Piazza Arcivescovado; Tel (050) 387 22 29.

In his 1910 novel *Forse che si forse che no,* the poet Gabriele d'Annunzio described the unique collection of buildings surrounding the Duomo Santa Maria Assunta, the cathedral at Pisa, as the "Piazza dei Miracoli" – the "Square of Miracles". Construction was begun in 1063, and the work was initially financed with the treasure the Pisans had looted from the Saracens after seizing Palermo from them. A firm and dry location for the cathedral site was sought among the marshland surrounding the city. An old cemetery lying just beyond the city walls was selected – not a happy choice, as the list of the *campanile*, the famous Leaning Tower of Pisa, still demonstrates today. The work took nearly 200 years to complete: the cathedral was consecrated in 1118, the baptistry in 1157, the *campanile* in 1173, and in 1278 the Camposanto was completed (see p. 216).

THE HIGHLIGHTS: PISA AND THE WEST

Unlike other Tuscan cathedrals, the *duomo* at Pisa (right) lies outside the main built-up area of the city, making it appear all the more impressive. The choir mosaic of *Christ Enthroned* was designed by Francesco di Simone and completed by Cimabue (below).

INFO Cathedral museum

The Museo dell'Opera del Duomo exhibits treasures from the building of the cathedral, including sculptures by Pisano and fragments of frescoes from the Camposanto.

Piazza Arcivescovado; Tel (050) 560 547; Apr–Sept 8.00–20.00 daily, Mar and Oct 9.00–19.00 daily, Nov–Feb 10.00–17.00 daily.

The cathedral stands at the focus of the Piazza dei Miracoli. The five-naved basilica is supported by columns and has a three-naved transept and apses on each arm of its cross-shaped floor plan, a design that served as inspiration for many other churches. The dome, decorated with frescoes, was Italy's first crossing cupola. The Romanesque west façade has three portals set in a blind arcade of seven arches on the ground floor, topped with a further four galleries and decorated with sandstone, glass, and majolica ornamentation; there are no less than 52 columns. The gable culminates in a Madonna sculpture by Andrea Pisano. Classical and Arabic influences can be seen in the bronze doors, cast by Bonanus in 1180 for the Porta di San Ranieri; the 24 reliefs depict the life of Mary and Jesus. The most important work of art in the cathedral's interior is the marble pulpit, completed by Giovanni Pisano in 1311 (see p. 216).

THE HIGHLIGHTS: PISA AND THE WEST

The baptistry (below) was built as a separate building, as in theory the unbaptized were not allowed to enter the cathedral. The upper gallery, which is open to the public, has a magnificent view of the font and Nicola Pisano's marble pulpit (below, inset).

TIP Antiques market

The Fiera dell'Antiquariato e Artigianato Artistico, an arts and antiques market, offers a delightful alternative to the souvenir stalls around the Piazza dei Miracoli and is held every second Saturday and Sunday in the month (except July and August) on the Via Santa Maria and Via dei Mille.

PISA: BATTISTERO 33

White Carrara marble was used not only for the cathedral but also for the other buildings on the Campo dei Miracoli. Begun in a Romanesque-Gothic style in 1152, the Battistero with its mighty segmented dome stands 54 m (177 feet) high and has a 107-m (350-foot) circumference, making it the largest baptistry in Italy. The building's highest point is marked with a 3-m (10-foot) 15th-century statue of John the Baptist, whose life is depicted in the panels of the bronze doors at the entrance. An octagonal font, created by Guido Bigarelli in 1246, stands at the exact center of the baptistry, but the artistic highlight is Nicola Pisano's hexagonal pulpit from 1260, with its seven supporting columns and reliefs depicting scenes from the life of Christ. The acoustics of the cylindrical building are also unique, reflecting every sound in a series of echoes (see p. 216).

THE HIGHLIGHTS: PISA AND THE WEST

What a relief: now the foundations have been stabilized, the Leaning Tower of Pisa is once again open to the public. Climbing to the top via the spiral staircase reveals the course of bells on the platform which once served the venerable cathedral.

INFO Climbing the tower

The public are now allowed to climb the 294 steps of the Leaning Tower again. Visitor numbers are restricted and tickets limited to fixed times; these can be ordered online. Booking by telephone is not permitted.

Summer 8.00–20.00 daily,
winter 9.00–17.00 daily.
Bookings: www.opapisa.it

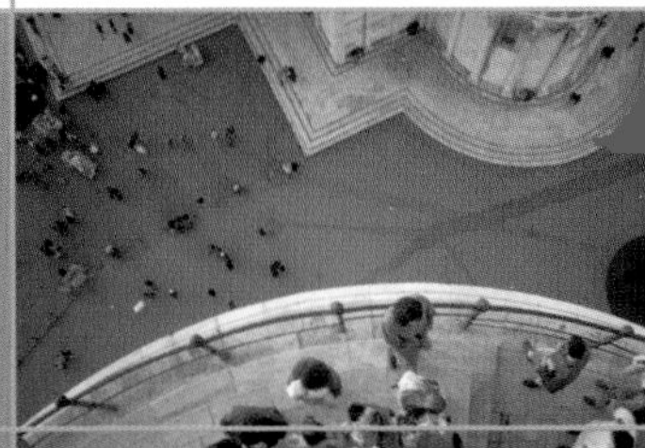

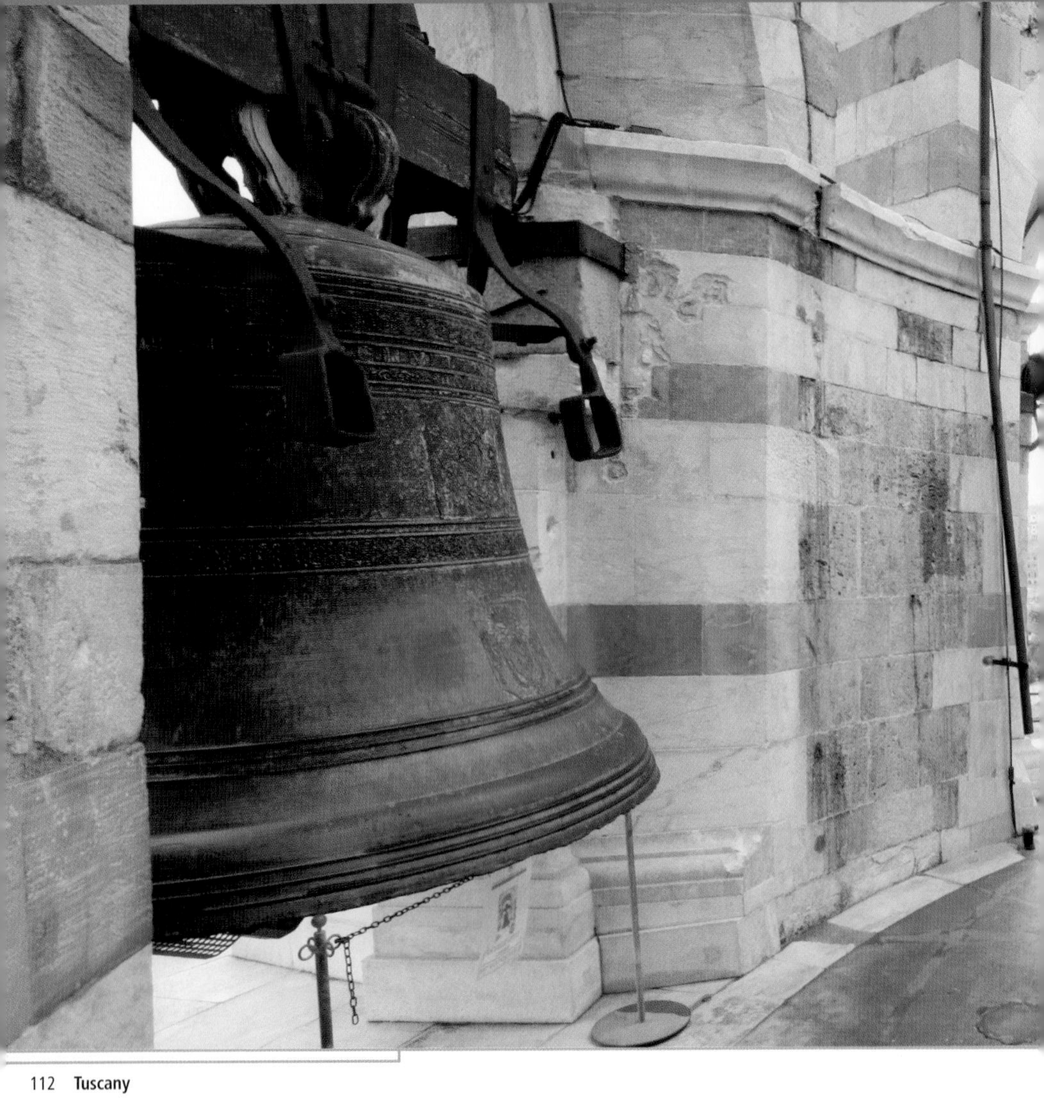

PISA: THE LEANING TOWER 34

The Torre Pendente, intended as the *campanile* (bell tower), was built beside the cathedral choir; in contrast with most Italian church towers, which are square, it has a circular floor plan. Begun in 1173, the "Leaning Tower of Pisa", despite its final weight of 14,200 tons, was literally built on sand, and began to list almost as soon as construction had begun. Its final collapse was anticipated at some point around the year 2000. When an earthquake struck the Pisa area in 1997, the authorities decided to act: the subsoil was compressed, the foundations were injected with concrete, and steel hawsers were used to pull the whole tower 44 cm (18 inches) back toward the vertical. Buildings in its path were temporarily vacated as a precaution. Work was completed in 2001 and the tower reopened to the public – for another three centuries, one can only hope (see p. 216).

The moon Io, casting its shadow on the largest planet (below, right); the four largest satellites of Jupiter are also known as the "Galilean Moons" in commemoration of their discoverer. Below, left: Justus Susterman's 1635 portrait shows Galileo as a 70-year-old. Right: Galileo's house in Arcetri (now a suburb of Florence), where the scholar was monitored by the Inquisition until his death. Far right: Vincenzo Cesare Cantagalli's *Galileo, Dictating Observations to his Secretary* (1870).

THE LAW OF GRAVITY: GALILEO GALILEI

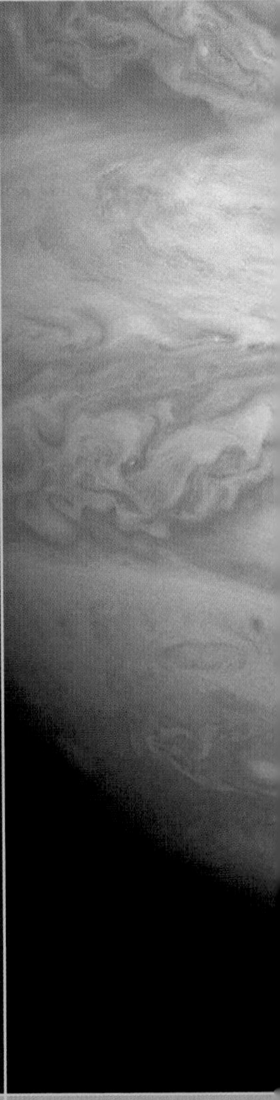

"*Eppur' si muove*" ("and yet it does move"), as Galileo Galilei is said to have murmured as the Inquisition called him to recant his shocking theory that the Earth moved round the Sun. It was another 360 years before the Catholic authorities officially recognized Galileo's theory in 1992 – the Earth had finally moved.

Born in Pisa on 15 February 1564, Galileo always kept science and belief separate. He considered himself a scientist, and, as was so often the case in the Renaissance, looked back to the works of classical thinkers to research the Earth and the stars. His pupil and first biographer, Vincenzo Viviani, reports that Galileo had formulated a theory concerning the isochronicity of pendulum swings as early as 1583, by observing a swinging lamp in the cathedral at Pisa. Viviani further reports that Galileo discovered an equation to describe free fall by dropping items of differing weight and volume from the Leaning Tower of Pisa. Neither anecdote has any more evidence to support it than his remark to the Inquisition quoted above, but Galileo's status as a mathematician, physicist, and philosopher is nonetheless indisputable. There is a plaque at Via Santa Maria 26 (the "Domus Galilaeana") in memory of the scientist, who died on 8 January 1642 at Arcetri (Florence), aged 77.

Below: A unique image from the early Renaissance: in the aftermath of the great plague of 1348, an unknown contemporary master created the monumental *Trionfo della Morte* fresco (*The Triumph of Death*) in the Camposanto. Right: The cloisters.

INFO Museo delle Sinopie

The 1257 fresco sketches in the former hospital of Santa Chiara are considered of great art historical importance. There is an audioguide explaining the artist's techniques.

Piazza del Duomo; Tel (050) 396 22 10; Nov–Feb 10.00–17.00 daily, Mar–Sept 8.00–20.00 daily, Oct 9.00–19.00 daily.

PISA: CAMPOSANTO 35
MUSEO DELLE SINOPIE 36

The Camposanto, Pisa's cemetery, is to be found behind the Baptistry. Construction was begun by Giovanni di Simone in 1278. Legend has it that earth was brought from Jerusalem to the Arno by participants in the First Crusade in order for local residents to be buried on holy ground. The venerable building was completed in the 15th century in the form of a cloister, and its monumental ambulatory is filled with ancient sarcophagi. Many of the frescoes decorating its walls were destroyed in World War II. The Museo delle Sinopie, housed in the old Ospedale di Santa Chiara, may give visitors an idea of their former appearance; so-called *sinopie*, preliminary sketches made for the frescoes in ochre paint and red earth tones, are exhibited here (see p. 216).

THE HIGHLIGHTS: PISA AND THE WEST

The promenade along the Arno, called Lungarno, is lined with magnificent *palazzi.* The church of Santa Maria della Spina (below, to the right of the image) lies next to the river. Appropriately, the Palazzo dei Cavalieri ("Knight's Castle") stands on Piazza dei Cavalieri ("Knights' Square"). Below, inset: The church of Santo Stefano dei Cavalieri.

TIP Osteria dei Cavalieri

Typical local specialties are served here in the ground floor of a 12th-century tower, a few paces from the Piazza dei Cavalieri; the atmosphere is typically Pisan.

Via San Frediano 16; Tel (050) 58 08 58; open for lunch and dinner, Sat lunch only. Closed Sun and all Aug.

PISA: BANKS OF THE ARNO 37 SANTA MARIA DELLA SPINA 38 PALAZZO DEI CAVALIERI 39 SANTO STEFANO DEI CAVALIERI 40

The tiny Gothic church of Santa Maria della Spina lies right on the south bank of the Arno and was built in the 14th century to house one treasure: a thorn (*spina*) from Christ's crown of thorns, no less. Threatened by flooding, the entire chapel was dismantled in 1871 and rebuilt a few meters higher up the bank, and the thorn is now kept in a reliquary in the chapel of the hospital attached to the church of Santa Chiara. Walking from the Arno to the Piazza dei Miracoli takes you through the Piazza dei Cavalieri, the worldly heart of the city. The Palazzo dei Cavalieri, rebuilt in 1562 by Giorgio Vasari, now houses the Scuola Normale Superiore, an elite university founded by Napoleon in 1810. Another creation of Vasari's, the church of Santo Stefano dei Cavalieri, was built nearby between 1565 and 1596, and booty from the Battle of Lepanto (7 October 1571) is still displayed in its interior (see p. 216).

THE HIGHLIGHTS: PISA AND THE WEST

Pisa's "Charterhouse" (below) was built on an enormous scale: there are two cloisters behind the magnificent baroque façade. Right: The bridge linking the Grand Duke's quarters and the monastery. Below, inset: The altar of the now baroque church.

INFO Tours

The Certosa di Pisa (known locally as the Certosa di Calci) offers guided tours every hour in summer. The large geological, botanical, and zoological collection will interest nature fans.

Via Roma 103, 56011 Calci; Tel (050) 93 84 30; Tues–Sat 9.00–19.00, Sun 9.00–13.00.

CALCI: CERTOSA DI PISA 41

The second-largest Carthusian monastery (after Pavia) in Italy is to be found in the very middle of Calci, a small town about 13 km (8 miles) south-east of Pisa in the Valle Graziosa. The monastery buildings were begun in 1366 and given a makeover in the 17th century, during the baroque period, which saw the façade remodeled to resemble a castle. A Napoleonic decree of 1808 dissolved the monastery and the building now houses the Museo di Storia Naturale e del Territorio, the University of Pisa's natural history museum. Calci also has something for art fans: the cupola frescoes in the monastery chapel, created by Stefano Cassini in the 17th century. There are magnificent frescoes in the refectory and the Sala del Granduca in the monastery's guest quarters, a room reserved for the Grand Duke of Tuscany; these can be viewed by appointment.

THE HIGHLIGHTS: PISA AND THE WEST

Seated on a hill, Volterra can be seen from afar along the Cecina valley (below). The Romanesque lines of the cathedral and the original paintwork in the interior have been largely preserved (right). The Palazzo Viti is pure baroque (below, inset).

INFO Etruscan museum

The Museo Etrusco Guarnacci has a fine collection of items from Etruscan culture, including bronzes, coins, jewelry, and over 600 urns, including the famous *Urna degli Sposi.*

Via Don Minzoni 15, 56048 Vol-terra; Tel (05 88) 863 47; mid-Mar–Oct 9.00–19.00 daily, 1 Nov–mid Mar 9.00–14.00 daily.

Positioned high on a hill, the town of Volterra is guaranteed a magnificent view of the Val di Cecina. It is known equally as an important Etruscan settlement and as a base for alabaster manufacture. The ancient walls and the remains of an Etruscan town gate attest to the considerable age of the community, and the ruins of a 1st-century Roman theater can be seen in the north of the town. A large archeological park has been established in the east, located beside a Medici fortress, with the foundations of temples, a water tank, and a fort. A cluster of medieval buildings around the Piazza dei Priori forms the heart of the town: the Palazzo dei Priori, built between 1208 and 1254, and the cathedral of Santa Maria Assunta, whose Romanesque origins are betrayed by the carved *Deposition* among other clues, despite a baroque remodeling of the interior (see p. 216).

More than 50 varieties of alabaster are to be found in the Volterra area, and they are all processed in workshops such as the one below. Rediscovered in the Renaissance, this fine and easily worked material is still used today to make utensils and ornaments (right).

FROM THE DEPTHS OF THE EARTH: ALABASTER

The region surrounding Volterra is one of the principal mining areas for alabaster. The mineral, a hydrous sulfate of calcium, is a variety of gypsum, as its name implies, being derived from the Greek *alábast[r]os*, meaning both gypsum and a vessel made of this material. Alabaster was formed as a limestone deposit over a period of millions of years as prehistoric oceans evaporated. Softer than marble, alabaster can be transluscent when very thin and is easily carved. It is found in various shades, and four varieties are mined at Volterra. The most precious is Agatha, which varies from bright yellow to dark brown. Scaglione, a whitish variant, is more common, and Bardiglio is a kind of whitish-gray. There is also Pietra a marmo, which closely resembles precious Carrara marble, but alabaster feels warm and velvety in comparison with the stone, and is much softer and more easily worked. Because of its translucency it has been popular since Etruscan times for delicate vessels and lamps. "Oriental" alabaster, a calcite considerably harder than "real" alabaster, was used in Ancient Egypt. Classical antiquity made much use of alabaster as a raw material, although in the Middle Ages sculptors seemed to prefer marble and ivory.

The old port of Livorno, the Porto Mediceo (below) is now a marina for luxury yachts and cruise ships. It is a short hop from here to nearby Montenero, with its baroque pilgrim's church and altar dedicated to the Madonna of the Graces (below, inset).

TIP Il Giro del Cane

This agreeable little *osteria* (with garden), run by Daniele Contini, is an ideal spot to sample typical Livorno fish cuisine. The cognoscenti recommend the starters and the homemade desserts.

Borgo dei Cappuccini 314; Tel (05 86) 81 25 60; Mon–Sat open for dinner only, closed in Aug.

LIVORNO 43
SANTUARIO DI MONTENERO 44

Declaring itself a free port in 1657, Livorno soon became one of the most important maritime cities in Italy. Initially belonging first to Pisa and then to Genoa, it was eventually sold to Florence in 1421. The five-pointed city fortifications, which are still clearly visible, and a new port area protected by the mighty Fortezza Vecchia were constructed in the 16th century. The province was to gain fame for its iron-ore mining, and in the 20th century the city became a rallying point for Communism; the PCI, the Italian Communist Party, was founded here in 1921. It was outlawed during the Fascist regime. It is worth taking a short detour from Livorno to the nearby Santuario di Montenero, a place of pilgrimage with a monastery once run by Jesuits and Theatines; the ornate baroque chapel is famed for its 14th-century likeness of the Madonna of the Graces (see p. 217).

The steep and rocky cliffs of the protected island of Capraia lie far out in the Tyrrhenian Sea. The scattered castle ruins almost seem as if they were placed here specifically to enhance the romantic atmosphere of the attractive island scenery.

INFO Island voyage

The motor launch *Margo* sets off for excursions around Capraia every morning and afternoon in good weather. The trips last either two or four hours and include all the island's highlights.

Bookings at Agenzia Viaggi Parco, Via Assunzione 42, 57032 Livorno Capraia Isola; Tel (05 86) 90 50 71.

CAPRAIA 45

The furthest-flung island of the Tuscan Archipelago is 20-sq-km (8-sq-mile) Capraia ("island of the goats"), whose steep volcanic cliffs lie to the northwest of Elba. With the exception of the small town of Porto Vecchio, tucked away in a bay on the eastern side, the entire island is protected as part of the Parco Nazionale dell'Arcipelago Toscano, established in 1989. The island's strategic location between Corsica and the Tuscan coast has meant that Capraia has had a turbulent history, of which the various ruined castles are mute witnesses. The island was first settled in Graeco-Roman times and was briefly a hideout for Saracen pirates before passing into Pisan ownership. After the fateful Battle of Meloria in 1284, which saw the Pisans defeated by the forces of Genoa, the island passed into Genoese control. It has officially been part of Tuscany since 1925.

Tuscany's natural paradise is not confined to the world above sea level: bright gorgonia and corals (below) join strangely shaped beasts like morays, sea slugs (right, from left), and jellyfish in delighting divers.

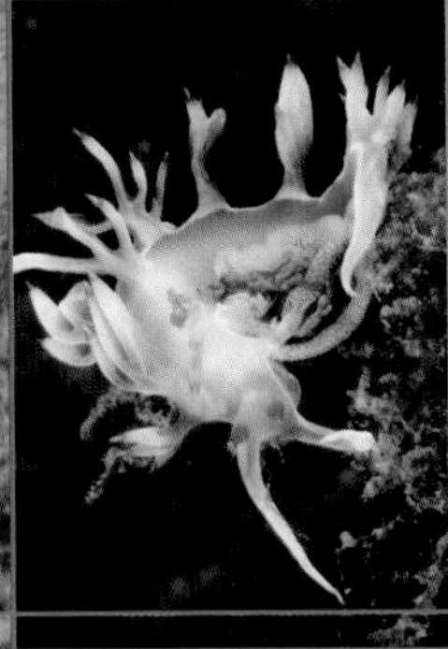

THE UNDERWATER WORLD OF MAR TIRRENO

The Tyrrhenian Sea (Mar Tirreno) is a stretch of the Mediterranean bounded by Corsica and Sardinia to the west, the Ligurian Sea to the north, the Italian coast to the east, and Sicily to the south. The name is derived from the "Tyrrhenoi", seafaring Etruscans. Reaching depths of 3,700 m (12,000 feet), the sea has some idyllic sailing, with island hops possible along the archipelago or across to Corsica or Sardinia, and plenty of ports and marinas to put into on the mainland. The Tyrrhenian Sea is also a very popular destination for divers – its fascinating underwater world of red or black corals and greeny-yellow sea cucumbers is thronged with great shoals of brilliant fish. Monkfish, octopus, and morays live here alongside seahorses and dolphins. The large schools of tuna that visit the Tyrrhenian Sea every spring are a particular attraction. Those wishing to explore the flora and fauna of this biotope without putting on diving gear and taking to the water should visit the Acquario della Laguna in Porto Santo Stefano (Orbetello). Here they have succeeded in keeping creatures such as horn corals and groupers alive at sea level, although they usually live at depths of 50 m (160 feet). There is also an exhibition illustrating underwater volcanic activity.

THE HIGHLIGHTS: PISA AND THE WEST

Now rather built up, the anchorages at Porto Azzurro (below) and Portoferraio (inset, below) have made the island of Elba perennially popular with countless sailing fans. Would-be admirals can relax in the little cafés in the Old Town at Portoferraio.

INFO Villa San Martino

Napoleon had a magnificent summer residence built in leafy grounds next to the rather modest town hall in Portoferraio; the two-floor villa was decorated with frescoes by Ravelli and exotically furnished.

San Martino, 57031 Elba Isola; Tel (05 65) 91 46 88; Tues–Sun 9.00–19.00.

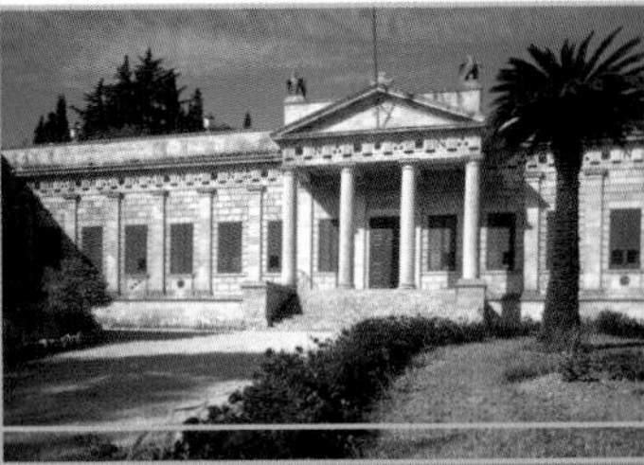

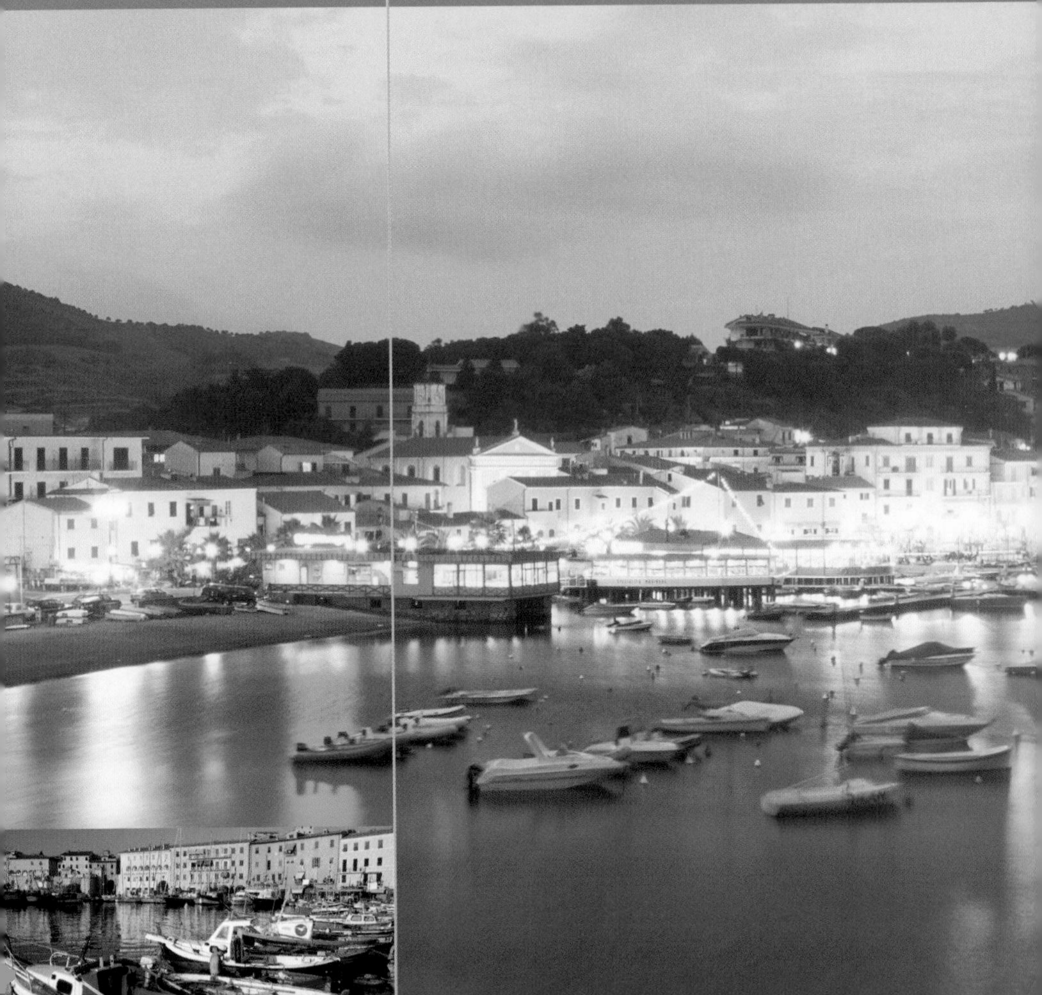

The Etruscans and later the Romans both recognized the beauty of this island, although its deposits of iron were also soon exploited, as the name of the principal town, Portoferraio ("Ironport") attests. The mild climate of the largest island in the Tuscan Archipelago encourages the growth of chestnuts, vines, and olives, as well as the ever-present *macchia*, and agriculture rivals tourism as the most important source of revenue. Bathers will relish the sand and pebble beaches of the coastal resorts in the west (Marciana Marina, Marina di Campo) and the east (Rio Marina, Porto Azzurro), all of which still retain almost a medieval atmosphere. There are even "natural bathtubs" to be found between Fetovaia and Seccheto in the south-west, depressions in the granite rocks that fill with seawater; this is then warmed by the sun, creating a solar-heated spa.

The deposed emperor lived in some style in exile. As governor of the island he had two official residences, the Villa dei Mulini (below, right), as well as the Villa San Martino (below, left). Right: Napoleon's arrival on Elba. Far right: his flight from the island.

NAPOLEON BONAPARTE, EMPEROR OF THE FRENCH

Napoleon Bonaparte (1769–1821), born of Corsican stock, soon made a career for himself in the army and by 1799 he was in a position to take sole control of all of France. Five years later he crowned himself "Emperor of the French" and the ensuing period of his dictatorship saw much of Europe subjugated under French rule. At the peak of his power in 1812 he began his Russian campaign, which whittled away his army (mostly consisting of German troops), and the Battle of Leipzig in 1813 put paid to his dreams of being a world leader. Napoleon was forced to capitulate and was banished to the island of Elba, which he ruled from 4 May 1814 until 1 March 1815. Returning to France, he led a new army against a coalition of European powers, finally being defeated at Waterloo in Belgium. Napoleon spent his last years back in exile on the Atlantic island of St Helena. The Villa San Martino, his summer residence, is proof of the grandeur with which the exiled emperor surrounded himself on Elba. The Egyptian-themed dining room, library, and study are all open to the public. The Chiesa della Misericordia in Portoferraio has a bronze cast of Napoleon's death mask and a memorial mass is held there every 5 May, the date of his death.

THE HIGHLIGHTS

AREZZO AND THE EAST

North-east of the Arno, towards the Apennines, the scenery becomes more rocky and the area less populated; around Mugello and Casentino there are extensive deciduous forests which turn red and gold in the fall. This season also sees the beginning of the hunt for mushrooms and truffles, precious gifts of nature which, along with products like sheep's milk, are local delicacies. The isolation of the mountains and forests here made it the refuge of choice in the Middle Ages for hermits and spiritual dissenters. The city of Arezzo, lying above the flood plain of the Arno, is the birthplace of painter and architect Giorgio Vasari, the great art historian of the Renaissance.

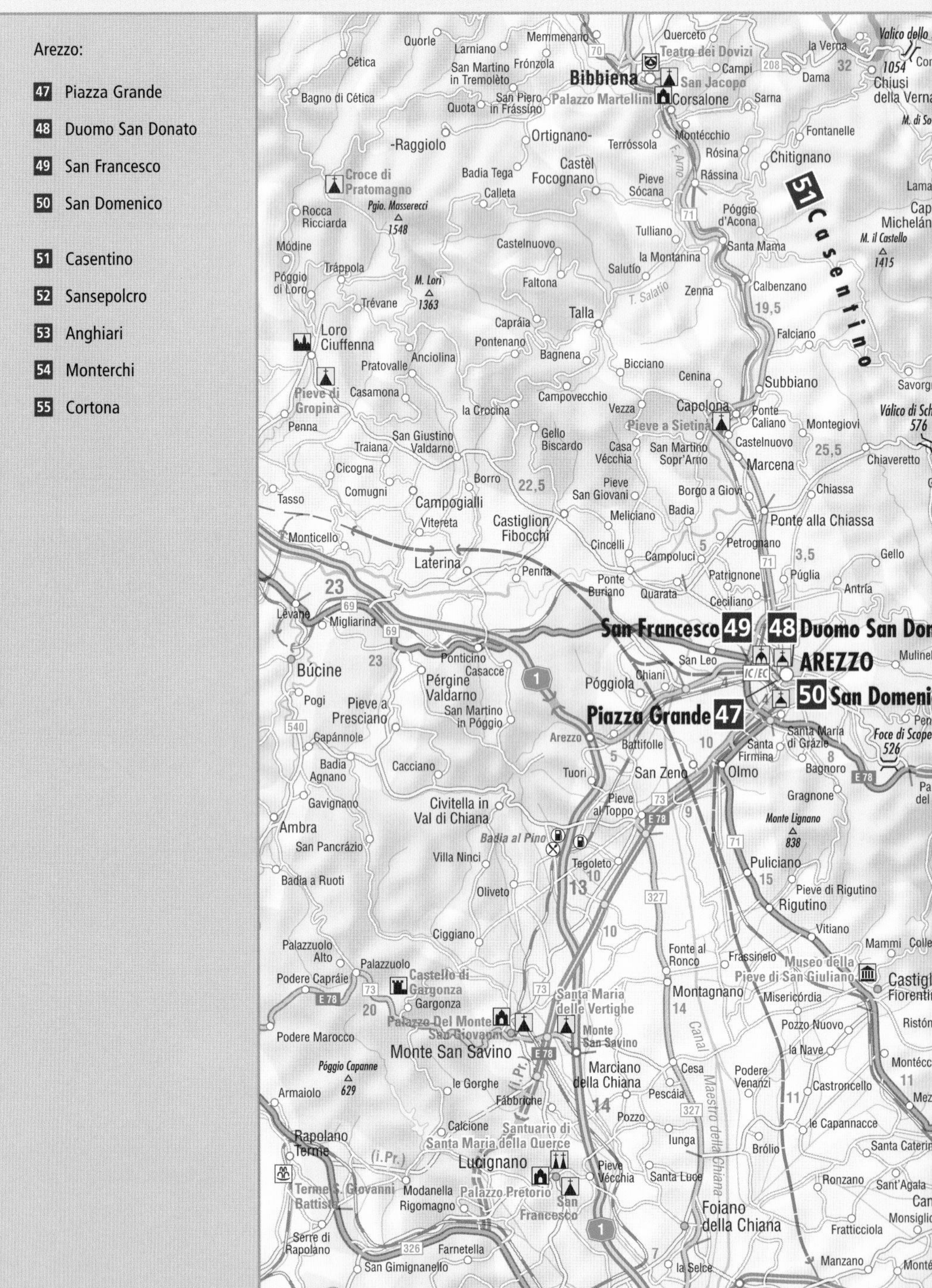
Arezzo:
47 Piazza Grande
48 Duomo San Donato
49 San Francesco
50 San Domenico
51 Casentino
52 Sansepolcro
53 Anghiari
54 Monterchi
55 Cortona
Bibbiena
Teatro dei Dovizi
San Jacopo
Palazzo Martellini
Corsalone
Croce di Pratomagno
Pgio. Masserecci
1548
M. Lori
1363
M. il Castello
1415
Loro Ciuffenna
Pieve di Gropina
Talla
Castèl Focognano
Ortignano-Raggiolo
Subbiano
Capolona
Pieve a Sietina
Castiglion Fibocchi
Laterina
Campogialli
Bùcine
Pergine Valdarno
San Francesco 49
48 Duomo San Don
AREZZO
50 San Domeni
Piazza Grande 47
Civitella in Val di Chiana
Badia al Pino
Monte Lignano
838
Castello di Gargonza
Palazzo Del Monte
San Giovanni
Monte San Savino
Santa Maria delle Vertighe
Marciano della Chiana
Rapolano Terme
Terme S. Giovanni Battista
Santuario di Santa Maria della Querce
Lucignano
Palazzo Pretorio
San Francesco
Foiano della Chiana
Museo della Pieve di San Giuliano
Castiglion Fiorentino
Póggio Capanne
629
Canal Maestro della Chiana
Càsentino

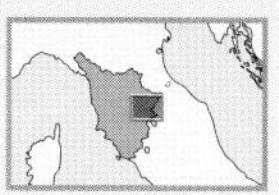

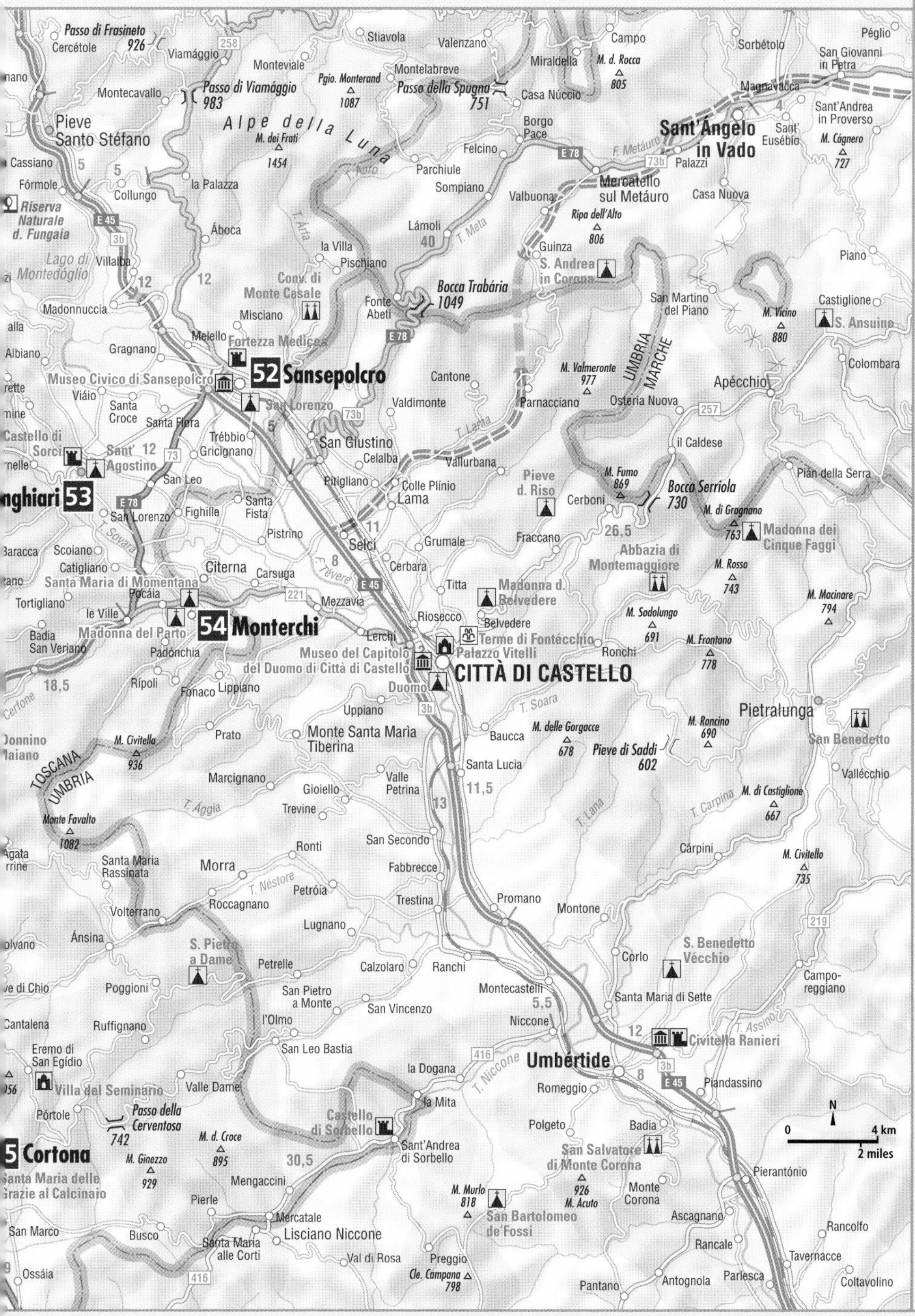

Passo di Frasineto 926
Cercétole
Viamággio
258
Monteviale
Stiavola
Valenzano
Montelabreve
Campo
Miraldella
M. d. Rocca 805
Sorbétolo
Péglio
San Giovanni in Petra
Montecavallo
Passo di Viamággio 983
Pgio. Monterand 1087
Passo della Spugna 751
Casa Núccio
Magnavacca
Sant'Andrea in Proverso
Pieve Santo Stéfano
Alpe della Luna
M. dei Frati 1454
Borgo Pace
Sant'Ángelo in Vado
Sant' Eusébio
M. Cágnero 727
Cassiano
Felcino
F. Metáuro
E 78
73b
Palazzi
Parchiule
Fórmole
la Palazza
Sompiano
Mercatello sul Metáuro
Casa Nuova
Collungo
Valbuona
Riserva Naturale d. Fungaia
E 45
3b
Ripa dell'Alto 806
Áboca
T. Ária
Lámoli
T. Meta
Lago di Montedóglio
Villalba
la Villa
Pischiano
Guinza
Piano
S. Andrea in Corona
Conv. di Monte Casale
Bocca Trabária 1049
Madonnuccia
Misciano
Fonte Abeti
San Martino del Piano
Castiglione
M. Vicino 880
S. Ansuino
Melello
Fortezza Medicea
Albiano
Gragnano
UMBRIA MARCHE
52 Sansepolcro
Museo Civico di Sansepolcro
Cantone
M. Valmerone 977
Colombara
Apécchio
Viáio
Santa Croce
San Lorenzo
Valdimonte
Parnacciano
Osteria Nuova
257
Santa Flora
Castello di Sorci
Trébbio
Sant' Agostino
Gricignano
San Giustino
Celalba
T. Lama
il Caldese
Vallurbana
San Leo
Pian della Serra
Pitigliano
Colle Plínio
Lama
Pieve d. Riso
M. Fumo 869
Bocca Serriola 730
53 Anghiari
San Lorenzo
Fighille
Santa Fista
Cerboni
M. di Gragnano 763
Madonna dei Cinque Faggi
T. Sovara
Pistrino
Selci
Fraccano
Abbazia di Montemaggiore
Baracca
Scoiano
Grumale
Catigliano
Citerna
Carsuga
F. Tévere
Cerbara
M. Rosso 743
Santa Maria di Momentana
Pocáia
Titta
Madonna d. Belvedere
M. Macinare 794
Tortigliano
221
Mezzavia
le Ville
Riosecco
Belvedere
M. Sodolungo 691
Badia San Veriano
Madonna del Parto
54 Monterchi
Lerchi
Terme di Fontécchio
Palazzo Vitelli
Ronchi
M. Frontone 778
Padónchia
Museo del Capitolo del Duomo di Città di Castello
CITTÀ DI CASTELLO
18,5
Rípoli
Fonaco
Lippiano
Duomo
T. Soara
Pietralunga
Cerfone
Uppiano
Prato
Monte Santa Marìa Tiberina
Baucca
M. delle Gorgacce 678
Pieve di Saddi 602
M. Roncino 690
San Benedetto
Donnino
Maiano
M. Civitella 936
Santa Lucia
Vallécchio
TOSCANA UMBRIA
Marcignano
Gioiello
Valle Petrina
11,5
T. Carpina
M. di Castiglione 667
T. Lana
T. Ággia
Trevine
Monte Favalto 1082
13
San Secondo
Ronti
Cárpini
Agata
Santa Maria Rassinata
Morra
Fabbrecce
M. Civitello 735
T. Néstore
Petróia
Volterrano
Roccagnano
Trestina
Promano
Montone
219
Lugnano
Ánsina
S. Pietro a Dame
Petrelle
Calzolaro
Ranchi
Corlo
S. Benedetto Vécchio
Campo-reggiano
Poggioni
San Pietro a Monte
Montecastelli
Santa Maria di Sette
5,5
San Vincenzo
Cantalena
Ruffignano
l'Olmo
Niccone
12
Civitella Ranieri
T. Assino
Eremo di San Egídio
San Leo Bastia
416
la Dogana
T. Niccone
Umbértide
8
3b
E 45
Piandassino
Villa del Seminario
Valle Dame
Romeggio
Pórtole
Passo della Cerventosa 742
la Mita
Castello di Sorbello
Polgeto
Badia
N
0
4 km
2 miles
M. d. Croce 895
Sant'Andrea di Sorbello
55 Cortona
M. Ginezzo 929
30,5
San Salvatore di Monte Corona
Santa Maria delle Grazie al Calcinaio
Mengaccini
926 M. Acuto
Monte Corona
Pierantónio
M. Murlo 818
Pierle
San Bartolomeo de'Fossi
Ascagnano
Mercatale
Rancolfo
San Marco
Busco
Santa Maria alle Corti
Lisciano Niccone
Rancale
Val di Rosa
Preggio
Tavernacce
Ossáia
416
Cle. Campana 798
Pantano
Antognola
Parlesca
Coltavolino

THE HIGHLIGHTS: AREZZO AND THE EAST

The eye-catching and elegant *loggie* designed in the 16th century by Giorgio Vasari for Arezzo's Piazza Grande are just the place to relax with a glass of wine, especially in the early evening, as the light of day begins to fade into dusk.

TIP Antiques market

On the first weekend of every month for the last 40 years, the Piazza Grande and surrounding streets have been filled with antiquities, rarities, and junk of all kinds. The Mercato dell'Antiquariato in Arezzo has over 500 stalls and is the largest in Italy, which makes it worth a trip for any collector.

The area became known for its relief ceramics (Latin: *terra sigillata*, "crested earth") during the time of the Roman empire. In 1289, after the defeat of the local Ghibellines by the Guelphs at Campaldino, Arezzo fell to Florence. The sloping, paved Piazza Grande marks the heart of the town; the great medieval poet Petrarch was born nearby in 1304 and there is a good view of the choir of the church of Maria della Pieve, refashioned in the 16th century by Giorgio Vasari. The Palazzo della Fraternità dei Laici, built next door to the church for a religious lay brotherhood, was used as a civil courthouse from 1786. Its Gothic first floor was completed in 1377 and the upper floors are the early Renaissance work of Bernardo Rossellino. The bell tower of the magnificent Palazzo delle Logge, located on the north side of the square, is yet another of Vasari's creations (see p. 218).

The Casa di Vasari, the house decorated by the master himself on Arezzo's Via XX Settembre (below and top, left), is now a museum. Vasari's painted work adopted a mannerist style (top, middle: the *Allegory of Patience* in the Palazzo Pitti in Florence; top, right: a self-portrait in the Uffizi).

FATHER OF THE HISTORY OF ART: GIORGIO VASARI

Giorgio Vasari (1511–1574) is most closely associated with his encyclopedic biographical work *Lives of the Most Excellent Painters, Sculptors, and Architects*. The book was first published in 1550 and then reissued in a revised and extended edition some 18 years later; it is still considered one of the most important resources in the history of art to this day. Vasari invented the term "Gothic", which he intended pejoratively. He derided the artistic movement described by the term as linked to the barbaric Visigoths and contrasted it with the *Rinascità*, the "rebirth", promoting this as "good" art which took inspiration from nature. Born in Arezzo, he trained as an artist in Florence, where he became a protégé of the Medici, studying alongside Alessandro and Ippolito de' Medici. In Rome he studied the works of Michelangelo, who was to influence his own creations. Among his most beautiful works are the oil and tempera paintings in his house in Arezzo. Vasari was also responsible for the frescoes depicting the life of Pope Paul III in the Palazzo della Cancelleria in Rome. His greatest achievements were as an architect, however: in 1560, work began under his direction on the Palazzo degli Uffizi in Florence, and in 1565 he created the enclosed corridor that bears his name, a connecting passage that crosses the Ponte Vecchio between the Palazzo Vecchio and the Palazzo Pitti on the other side of the Arno.

THE HIGHLIGHTS: AREZZO AND THE EAST

The façade of the Duomo San Donato has never been completed (below, left). The Gothic vaulting within only intensifies the impression of light and space (below, right). The left side chapel holds Piero della Francesca's captivating depiction of Mary Magdalene (below, middle); the fresco cycle in San Francesco is by the same hand (right).

TIP Antica Trattoria da Guido

Classic Tuscan cuisine served in the Stilo family's rustic restaurant, which seats only 40, so it is best to book in advance.

Via Madonna del Prato 85; Tel (05 75) 237 60; open Mon–Sat and first Sun in month for lunch and dinner, closed last two weeks in Aug.

AREZZO: DUOMO SAN DONATO 48 SAN FRANCESCO 49 SAN DOMENICO 50

Construction was begun on the Duomo San Donato in 1277; Pope Gregory X, who had died the year before, was to be buried here and in 1459 Piero della Francesca painted his St Mary Madgdalene fresco for the cathedral. Piero della Francesca was also responsible for a ten-part picture cycle in the church of San Francesco, illustrating the discovery of the True Cross by St Helena, the mother of the Emperor Constantine. The church's unprepossessing exterior would never lead you to suspect that one of the greatest art works in Tuscany lies within. San Domenico, a 13th-century Dominican church, should also not be missed; a painted crucifix by Cimabue from between 1260 and 1270 stands out among the other venerable pictures and frescoes (see p. 218).

Piero's artistic endeavors were to reach their apotheosis in his cycle of frescoes in the church of San Francesco, commissioned in 1452 by the Bacci, one of the richest families in Arezzo at the time (below: *The Adoration of the Holy Wood* and *The Queen of Sheba with King Solomon*); he is still considered one of the greatest perspective artists of his time. The double portrait of Federigo da Montefeltro and his wife Battista Sforza (right), painted around 1470, is one of his most famous works and now hangs in the Uffizi in Florence.

GROUNDBREAKING FRESCOES: PIERO DELLA FRANCESCA

Piero della Francesca was born around the year 1416 in the tiny mountain village of Sansepolcro, which lies to the north-east of Arezzo; he was to die here too, on 12 October 1492 (according to Vasari, he was blind for the last years of his life). Piero trained as a painter under Domenico Veneziano, assisting him in furnishing Sant' Egidio and Santa Maria Nuova in Florence with frescoes, but his later life was to prove unpredictable. He worked in Urbino, Ferrara, Rimini, Rome, and Arezzo, where his greatest work was created in the 1450s: the cycle of frescoes in the church of San Francesco. Piero was one of the greatest early Renaissance exponents of the art of fresco-painting, a technique that demanded speed and accuracy, and involved the application of pigments to wet plaster; he achieved unheard-of levels of three-dimensionality in his art, combining a feel for color with the incorporation of natural light. Piero also prepared the way for painters such as Raphael and the great Dutch masters with theoretical writings in which he formulated his theory of mathematically based perspective. He succeeded in applying this theory in his *Flagellation of Christ*, now hanging in the Galleria Nazionale delle Marche in Urbino, which also demonstrates the artistic maturity of his technique of depicting his subjects against a backdrop of classical or ancient architecture.

THE HIGHLIGHTS: AREZZO AND THE EAST

A procession of monks entering the Chiesa delle Stimmate (below, right), where St Francis is said to have received his stigmata. The church also contains Andrea della Robbia's *Madonna with Saints* in terracotta (below, left). Almost all of Casentino can be seen from Poppi (right).

INFO Castello di Poppi

This well-preserved 13th-century castle belonging to the Counts of Guidi is situated above the town of Poppi. There is a richly decorated banqueting hall and military exhibits.

Piazza della Repubblica 1, 52014 Poppi; Tel (05 75) 52 05 16; Mar–Oct 10.00–18.00 daily, Nov–Feb Thurs–Sun 10.00–17.00.

The wooded hills of what is today the Casentino National Park have always been a little isolated, and proved to be a good place for the settlements of unworldly religious orders. The Carmaldolites founded a monastery near Poppi in the 11th century, and their baroque church contains panels by Giorgio Vasari. Even Francis of Assisi visited Casentino; in 1213 Count Orlando Cattini di Chuisi made him a gift of the mountain of La Verna and it was here the saint is said to have received the wounds (stigmata) of Christ on 14 September 1224. The Chiesa delle Stimmate was founded on this spot in 1263. In 1481 the altar wall was decorated by Andrea della Robbia, who also was responsible for several terracotta works in the Chiesa Maggiore, on which work was begun in 1348. A rock that St Francis supposedly covered with leafy boughs and used as a bed can also be seen at La Verna.

THE HIGHLIGHTS: AREZZO AND THE EAST

Inspired by history and always inspiring: the Piazza Torre di Berta in Sansepolcro is the traditional stage for the *Palio della Balestra*, a crossbow competition held each year in September. Right: The town of Monterchi; below, inset: the equally pretty little town of Anghiari.

TIP Enoteca Guidi

The Guidi family have stocks of the finest wines of the region, which they keep in a 17th-century *palazzo* and serve to accompany tasty Tuscan delicacies; there are also six guest rooms available.

Via Luca Pacioli 46, 52037 Sansepolcro; Tel (05 75) 74 10 86; open for lunch and dinner, Wed, Jul closed.

SANSEPOLCRO 52 ANGHIARI 53 MONTERCHI 54

In 1827 Giulia Buitoni bought a little pasta shop and succeeded in manufacturing noodles that were cooked *al dente*, "with a bite" – the Casa Buitoni, Italy's first pasta manufacturer, was to become the seed of a whole noodle empire. Sansepolcro is also known as the location of the birth and death of the painter Piero della Francesca (*c.* 1416–1492), several of whose works are to be found in the Museo Civico, including the *Madonna della Misericordia* and the *Resurrection*. Another work by Piero, the *Madonna del Parto*, hangs in nearby Monterchi. The Battle of Anghiari took place in 1440 somewhere between here and the little village of Anghiari; this struggle between the Florentines and the Milanese was recorded in a work painted for the Palazzo Vecchio by Leonardo da Vinci, which disappeared in mysterious circumstances some time during the 16th century.

The Martinis are an old Sansepolcro family; their traditional butcher's shop is run by Aldo, the father (below). The Enoteca Guidi in Sansepolcro (right) is the ideal combination of a top restaurant with an excellent wine cellar.

TUSCAN CUISINE: DELICATE AND SUBTLE

Tuscany has long been a much-vaunted destination for gourmets. The region's cuisine is as varied as the landscape: the coast has many fish dishes, of which the fish soup known as *cacicucco* is the best known, while central Tuscany is known for its *pecorino*, a sheep's cheese that is milder than the more well-known Pecorino Romano. The woods of the east supply the ingredients for numerous game dishes prepared with local herbs and truffles. The *bistecca alla fiorentina* is a Florentine delicacy – the thick T-bone steaks used for it, two fingers thick, traditionally come from the white cows kept in the Val di Chiana and the Arno valley. *Lardo di Colonnata*, white ham matured in marble, is the pride of northern Tuscany. The element common to all the specialties produced in the area is the ubiquitous olive oil. To extract the highest quality *olio d'oliva extravergine*, extra virgin olive oil, the olives must be cold-pressed within two days of picking; old, manually driven stone oil presses are often used for this. Tuscan olive oil also has uses beyond the kitchen: blessed by a priest and mixed with chrism, it is used for ritual anointing in the church.

THE HIGHLIGHTS: AREZZO AND THE EAST

An idyllic evening on the Piazza della Repubblica (below). The *Annunciation* (below, right), painted by the Dominican monk Fra Angelico, is one of the treasures of the Chiesa del Gesù (now the Museo Diocesano). Below, inset: The Renaissance interior of the cathedral. Right: A fountain statue on the Piazza Signorelli.

INFO Museo Diocesano

A museum has been established in the oratory of the Chiesa del Gesù with one of the greatest collections of sacred treasures in Tuscany, including Fra Angelico's *Annunciation*.

Piazza del Duomo, Cortona; Tel (05 75) 628 30; 1 Apr–31 Oct 10.00–19.00, 1 Nov–31 Mar 10.00–17.00, closed Mon in winter.

The town of Cortona enjoys a picturesque location on the slopes of Monte Sant'Egidio, not far from the Umbrian border and close to Lake Trasimene. It is one of the oldest towns in Tuscany, as evidenced in the Museo dell'Accademia Etrusca, whose exhibits include a bronze Etruscan lamp dating from the 4th century BC. Surrounded by town walls dating back to the Etruscan era, the main square boasts two churches: the Renaissance-influenced cathedral of Santa Maria, with a baroque high altar by Francesco Mazzuoli, and the Chiesa del Gesù, home of an *Annunciation* (1433/34) by Fra Angelico, who lived in the delightful Dominican monastery at the gates of the town. In the early 13th century the Franciscans founded a monastery in Cortona and another of the town's sons, the Renaissance painter Luca Signorelli, is said to be buried in the monastery chapel (see p. 219).

THE HIGHLIGHTS

SIENA AND CENTRAL TUSCANY

With the last foothills of Chianti somewhere to the north and the bare, moon-like landscape of the Crete to the south, the heart of Tuscany, near the city of Siena, is covered in the red Sienese soil that supports precious vineyards around Montalcino and Montepulciano. Central Tuscany is also famed for its medieval treasures: the towns of Volterra and San Gimignano in the west, or the castles found everywhere, relics of feuds lasting centuries between the *comune* of Florence and Siena as they fought for dominance of this beautiful region. Dating back to the time of the Etruscans, Siena is rich in historic sites – the medieval central part of the city has been designated a UNESCO World Heritage Site.

Siena:

56 Duomo Santa Maria Assunta

57 Libreria Piccolomini

58 Museo dell'Opera Metropolitana

59 Battistero di San Giovanni

60 Ospedale di Santa Maria della Scala

61 Piazza del Campo

62 Palazzo Pubblico

63 San Gimignano

64 Crete

65 Val d'Orcia

66 Montepulciano

67 Montalcino

68 Monteriggioni

69 Abbazia di Monte Oliveto Maggiore

70 Pienza

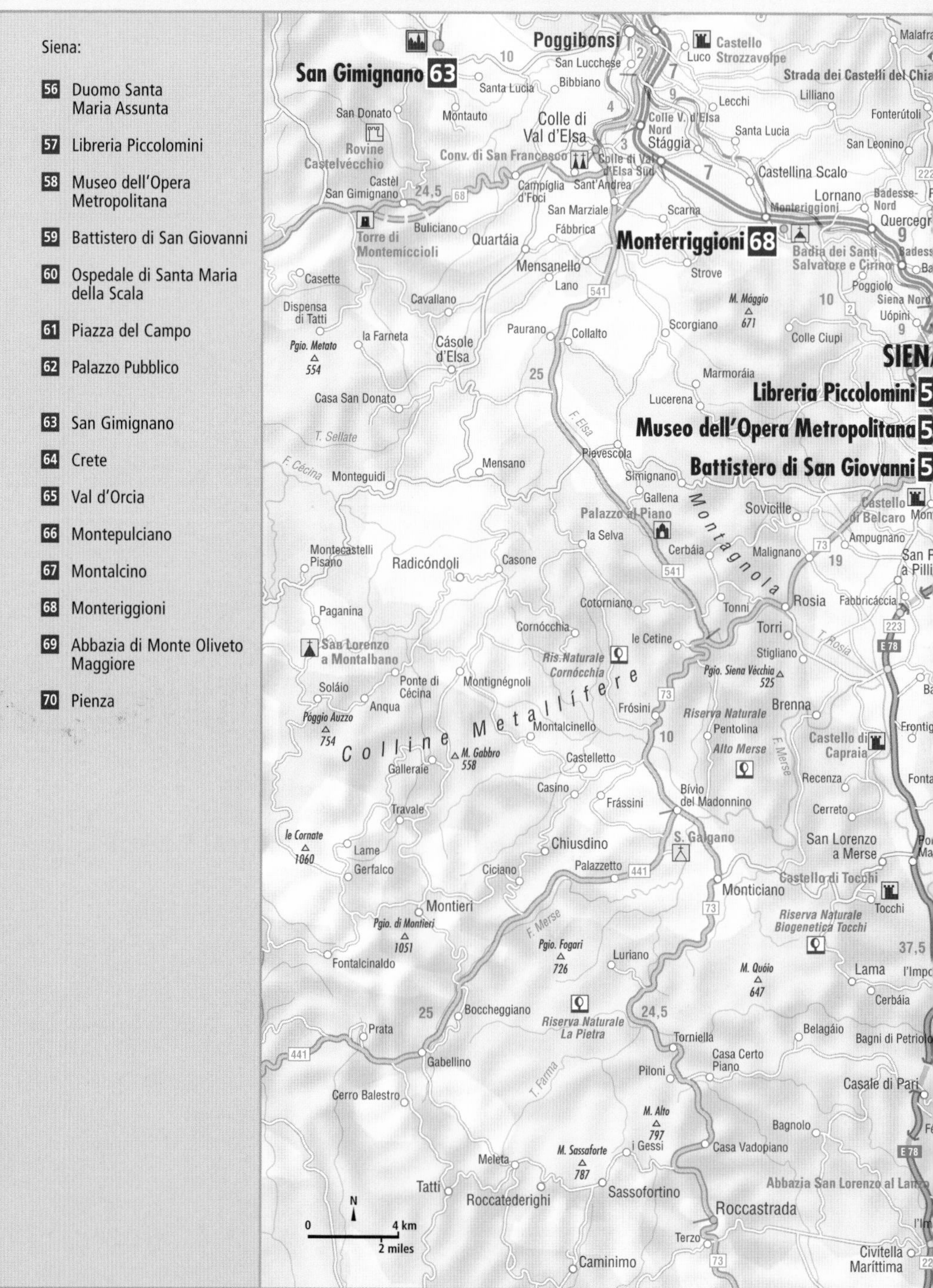

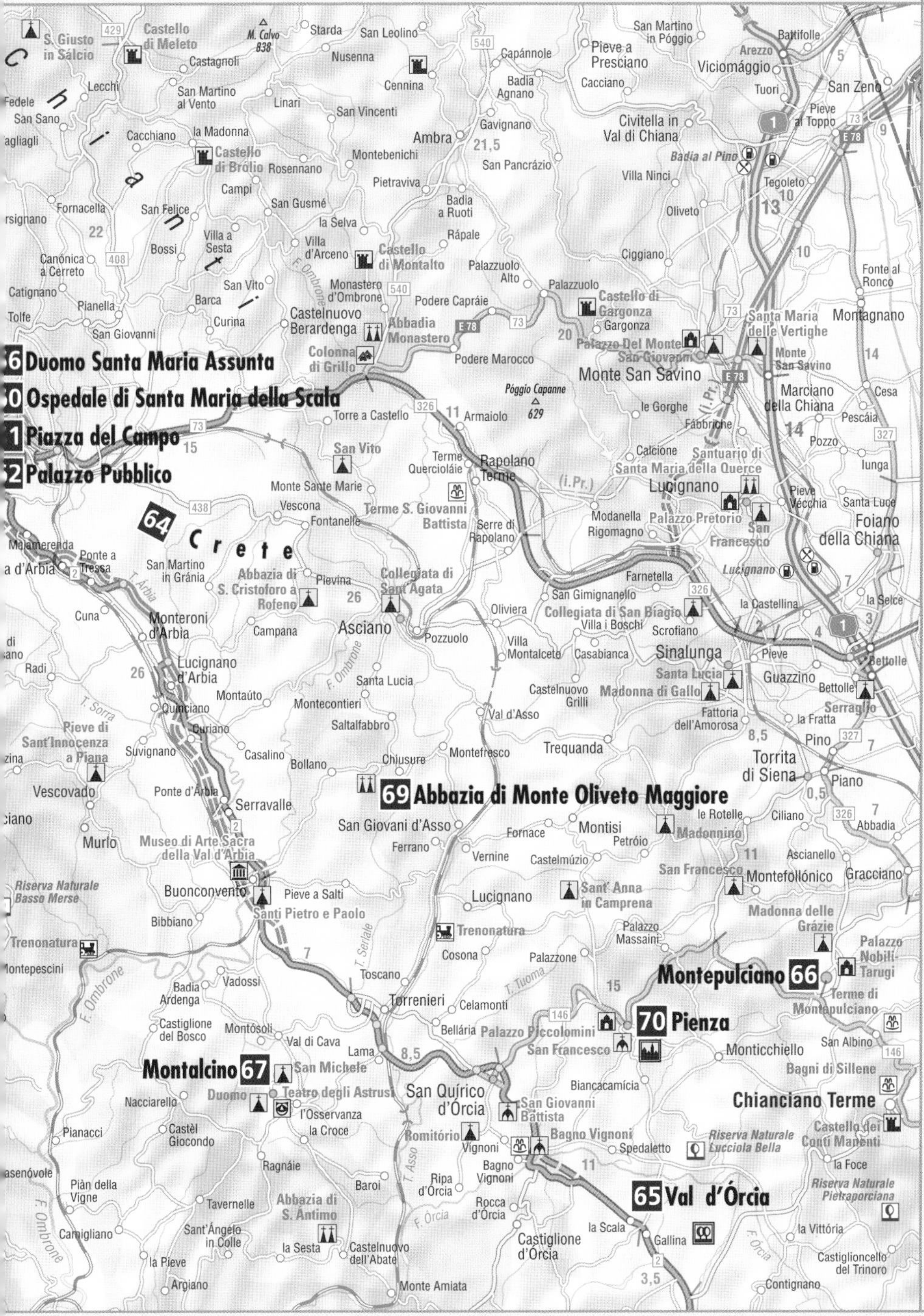

S. Giusto in Sálcio
Castello di Meleto
M. Calvo 838
Starda
San Leolino
Castagnoli
Nusenna
Capánnole
San Martino in Póggio
Pieve a Presciano
Battifolle
Arezzo
Viciomággio
Chianti
Lecchi
San Martino al Vento
Cennina
Badia Agnano
Cacciano
Tuori
San Zeno
Fedele
San Sano
Linari
San Vincenti
Gavignano
Civitella in Val di Chiana
Pieve al Toppo
agliagli
Cacchiano
la Madonna
Ambra
Montebenichi
Castello di Brolio
Rosennano
San Pancrázio
Badia al Pino
Villa Ninci
Tegoleto
Campi
Pietraviva
Fornacella
San Felice
San Gusmé
Badia a Ruoti
Oliveto
rsignano
la Selva
Villa a Sesta
Villa d'Arceno
Rápale
Bossi
Canónica a Cerreto
Castello di Montalto
Palazzuolo Alto
Ciggiano
Fonte al Ronco
San Vito
Catignano
Monastero d'Ombrone
Podere Capráie
Palazzuolo
Castello di Gargonza
Pianella
Barca
Gargonza
Tolfe
Curina
Castelnuovo Berardenga
Abbadia Monastero
Santa Maria delle Vertighe
Montagnano
San Giovanni
Palazzo Del Monte
San Giovanni
Monte San Savino

6 Duomo Santa Maria Assunta

Colonna di Grillo
Podere Marocco
Monte San Savino
Marciano della Chiana
Cesa

0 Ospedale di Santa Maria della Scala

Póggio Capanne 629
le Gorghe
Pescáia

1 Piazza del Campo

Torre a Castello
Armaiolo
Fábbriche
Pozzo

2 Palazzo Pubblico

San Vito
Terme Quercioláie
Rapolano Terme
Calcione
Santuario di Santa Maria della Querce
lunga
Monte Sante Marie
Lucignano
Pieve Vécchia
Santa Luce
Vescona
Terme S. Giovanni Battista
Foiano della Chiana

64 Crete

Fontanelle
Serre di Rapolano
Modanella
Rigomagno
Palazzo Pretorio
San Francesco
Majamerenda
Ponte a Tressa
a d'Arbia
San Martino in Grània
Abbazia di S. Cristoforo a Rofeno
Pievina
Collegiata di Sant'Agata
Lucignano
Farnetella
la Selce
Cuna
San Gimignanello
la Castellina
Monteroni d'Arbia
Campana
Asciano
Oliviera
Collegiata di San Biagio
Villa i Boschi
Scrofiano
Pozzuolo
Villa Montalceto
Casabianca
Sinalunga
Pieve
Bettolle
Radi
Lucignano d'Arbia
Santa Lucia
Santa Lucia
Guazzino
Montaúto
Castelnuovo Grilli
Madonna di Gallo
Bettolle
Quinciano
Montecontieri
Fattoria dell'Amorosa
Serraglio
Pieve di Sant'Innocenza a Piana
Curiano
Saltalfabbro
Val d'Asso
la Fratta
Suvignano
Casalino
Pino
Montefresco
Trequanda
Bollano
Chiusure
Torrita di Siena
Vescovado
Ponte d'Árbia
Piano

69 Abbazia di Monte Oliveto Maggiore

Serravalle
le Rotelle
Ciliano
San Giovani d'Asso
Montisi
Abbadia
Murlo
Fornace
Petróio
Madonnino
Museo di Arte Sacra della Val d'Arbia
Ferrano
Vernine
Castelmúzio
Ascianello
San Francesco
Gracciano
Riserva Naturale Basso Merse
Buonconvento
Pieve a Salti
Montefollónico
Lucignano
Sant'Anna in Camprena
Santi Pietro e Paolo
Madonna delle Grázie
Bibbiano
Palazzo Massaini
Trenonatura
Trenonatura
Palazzo Nobili-Tarugi
ontepescini
Cosona
Palazzone
Montepulciano 66
Vadossi
Toscano
Badia Ardenga
Terme di Montepulciano
Torrenieri
Celamonti
Castiglione del Bosco
Montósoli
Bellária
Palazzo Piccolomini
70 Pienza
Val di Cava
San Francesco
San Albino
Lama
Monticchiello
Montalcino 67
San Michele
Bagni di Sillene
Biancacamícia
Duomo
Teatro degli Astrusi
San Quírico d'Órcia
Nacciarello
San Giovanni Battista
Chianciano Terme
l'Osservanza
Pianacci
Castèl Giocondo
la Croce
Romitório
Bagno Vignoni
Riserva Naturale Lucciola Bella
Castello dei Conti Manenti
Vignoni
Spedaletto
Ragnáie
Bagno Vignoni
la Foce
asenóvole
Piàn della Vigne
Baroi
Ripa d'Órcia
Riserva Naturale Pietraporciana

65 Val d'Órcia

Tavernelle
Abbazia di S. Antimo
Rocca d'Órcia
Camigliano
Sant'Ángelo in Colle
la Scala
Castiglione d'Órcia
la Vittória
Gallina
la Sesta
Castelnuovo dell'Abate
la Pieve
Castiglioncello del Trinoro
Argiano
Monte Amiata
Contignano

THE HIGHLIGHTS: SIENA AND CENTRAL TUSCANY

A symbol of the Christian concept of the world: the decoration of the hexagonal cupola of the cathedral represents the stars in the sky (below). This is one of the few Romanesque elements in an otherwise Gothic edifice adorned with a façade of varying shades of marble, mosaics, and sculptures.

INFO Siena by night

Siena is at its most beautiful in the evenings, when the bustle of the streets moves into the bars and restaurants, and the sparkling city lights are best enjoyed from the square in front of the cathedral, a viewing platform 350 m (1,100 feet) above sea level and Siena's highest point.

The alternation of white and black marble, with the addition of red marble on the façade, gives this 12th-century, three-naved, originally Romanesque basilica a rather distinctive appearance. Giovanni Pisano's impressive Gothic west façade displays clear French influences, with its three high portals and numerous gargoyles. The torso of the so-called "new cathedral" with its great façade stands beside the *campanile*. The striped pillars and the 56 separate marble mosaic images on the floor, all masterpieces of inlay work, immediately strike the eye inside the cathedral, one of the most lavishly decorated churches in the world. There is another sculptural treasure beyond the crossing in the form of Nicola Pisano's octagonal pulpit (1266–68), and Pinturicchio's frescoes in St John's Chapel gaze down upon Donatello's magnificent bronze of the Baptist (see p. 220).

THE HIGHLIGHTS: SIENA AND CENTRAL TUSCANY

Pinturicchio created truly fantastic pictorial worlds for the walls of the Libreria Piccolomini (below). The Battistero di San Giovanni is also richly decorated with frescoes and has a bronze grave marker by Donatello (below, inset).

INFO Museum

The Museo dell'Opera Metropolitana, the cathedral museum, has an exciting cross-section of great art, especially late medieval and early Renaissance panel paintings.

Piazza Duomo 8; Tel (05 77) 28 30 48; Mar–May, Sept, Oct 9.30– 19.00 daily, Jun–Aug 9.30–20.00 daily, Nov–Feb 10.00–17.00 daily.

SIENA: LIBRERIA PICCOLOMINI 57 MUSEO DELL'OPERA METROPOLITANA 58 BATTISTERO DI SAN GIOVANNI 59

The Libreria Piccolomini adjoining the cathedral was built to house Pope Pius II's library and was decorated by Pinturicchio in 1502 with magnificent frescoes depicting his life. A visit to the Battistero di San Giovanni means leaving the cathedral; the three-naved baptistry with its lavish frescoes was constructed as the cathedral choir was extended in the 14th century, and the façade was completed in 1382. The focus of the baptistry is the 1417 font, which stands on a hexagonal pedestal with bronze reliefs by Jacopo della Quercia, Donatello, and Ghiberti. The Museo dell'Opera Metropolitana is to be found on the east side, in the first three arches of the incomplete transept of the Duomo Nuovo, with exhibits by artists of the caliber of Giovanni Pisano, Jacopo della Quercia, and Duccio (see p. 220).

THE HIGHLIGHTS: SIENA AND CENTRAL TUSCANY

The charitable traditions of the Ospedale di Santa Maria della Scala in Siena are depicted in Domenico di Bartolo's frescoes, created around 1440, which allow a fascinating insight into the day-to-day running of an early modern hospital (below).

INFO Archeological museum

The numerous Etruscan (right) and Roman grave finds in the so-called *cunicoli*, which lie beneath the Santa Maria della Scala museum complex, help to bring a long-forgotten world back to life.

Piazza Duomo 2; Tel (05 77) 22 48 28; 10.30–18.30 daily.

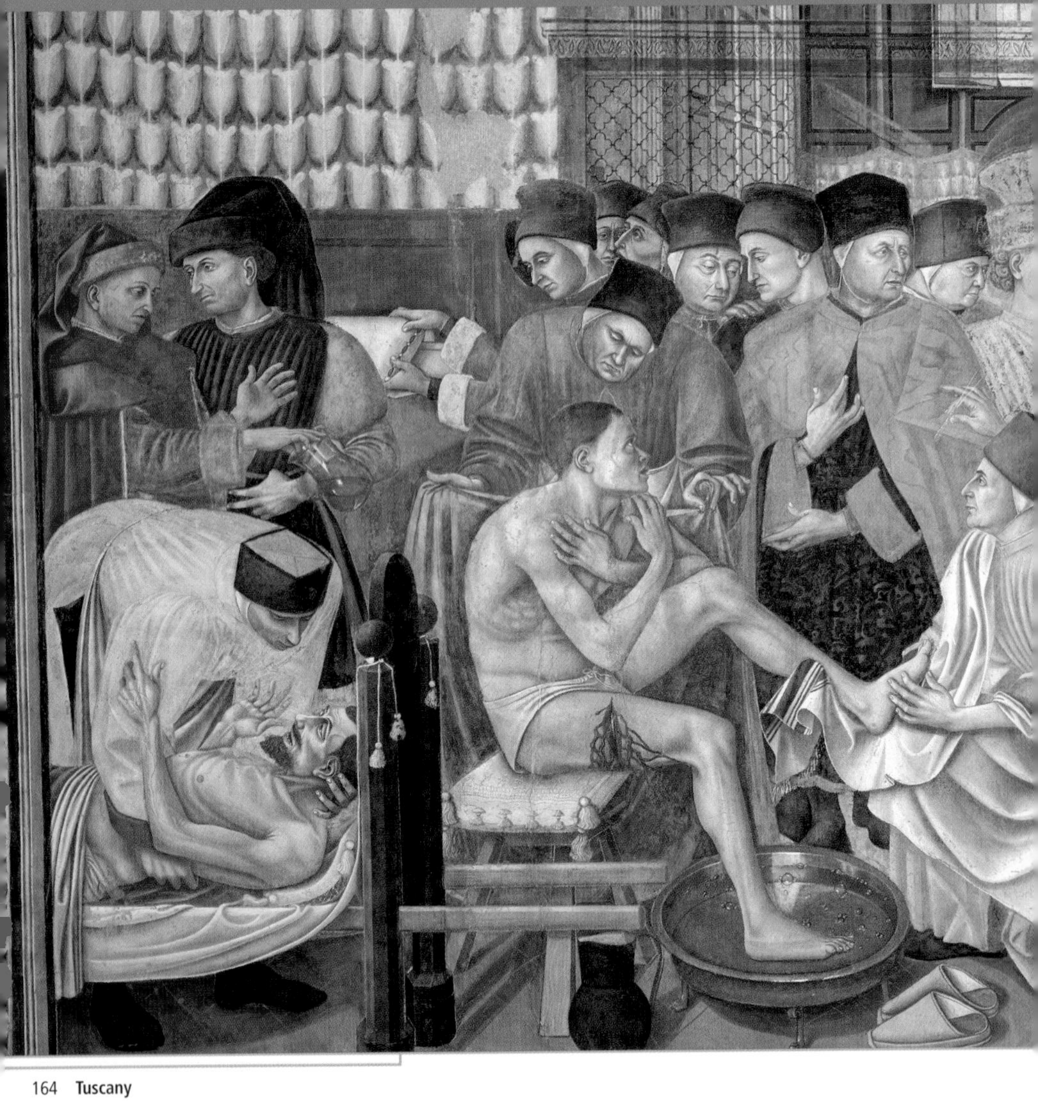

SIENA: OSPEDALE DI SANTA MARIA DELLA SCALA 60

The Ospedale di Santa Maria received the addition of "della Scala" to its name as it stands opposite the cathedral steps. Founded around 1000 by the cathedral canons as a hospital for pilgrims, the imposing building was still being used for the treatment of the sick until only a few decades ago, and this history is recorded in the cycle of frescoes painted between 1440 and 1443 in the Sala del Peregrinaio, the "pilgrim's room", by Domenico di Bartolo from Asciano. The images show workers treating the sick and caring for orphans, a record that makes the frescoes of enormous cultural and historical value without even considering their artistic merit. The Old Sacristy has paintings by Lorenzo Vecchietta, the Cappella del Manto has a lunette by Domenico Beccafumi; the Cappella della Madonna and the church of Santissima Annunziata are also worth seeing (see p. 220).

THE HIGHLIGHTS: SIENA AND CENTRAL TUSCANY

Beside the Palazzo Pubblico, the Torre del Mangia, the second-tallest bell tower in Italy, casts a long shadow across the Piazza del Campo (below). Siena residents are all too aware of the great history of their town. A traditional delicatessen (below, inset); flags with district insignia (right).

TIP Pasticceria Nannini

The legendary Nannini family of pastry chefs has kept the Siena baking tradition alive for 100 years. Local delicacies of excellent quality are to be found here and you can enjoy a homemade espresso in the bar next door.
Via Massetana Romana 56; Tel (05 77) 28 52 08; 7.30–19.30 daily.

SIENA: PIAZZA DEL CAMPO 61
PALAZZO PUBBLICO 62

Radiating out from the Palazzo Pubblico (town hall) and bounded by rich merchants' houses, Siena's central point, the Piazza del Campo, was made Italy's first pedestrianized zone in 1956. Jacopo della Quercia's Fonte Gaia fountain (1419), once part of the municipal water supply, stands on the square opposite the town hall with its imposing 102-m (335-foot) tower, the Torre del Mangia, completed in 1344. Ambrogio Lorenzetti created the allegorical fresco of *The Good and the Bad Regiment* for the Sala della Pace in the Palazzo Pubblico in 1340, an expression of Siena's republican perception of itself. The especial veneration of St Mary after the Battle of Montaperti in 1260 is evidenced by Simone Martini's *Enthroned Madonna* (*c.* 1315) in the Sala del Mappamondo (see p. 220).

Seats at the world-famous Palio on Siena's Piazza del Campo are much sought-after (below). After the keenly fought horse race, which not every rider completes despite making every effort, the streets fill up with people looking to celebrate or commiserate. Right: Historic costumes and proud standard-bearers are an essential part of the race.

THE PALIO: FAST, FURIOUS, AND INTENSE

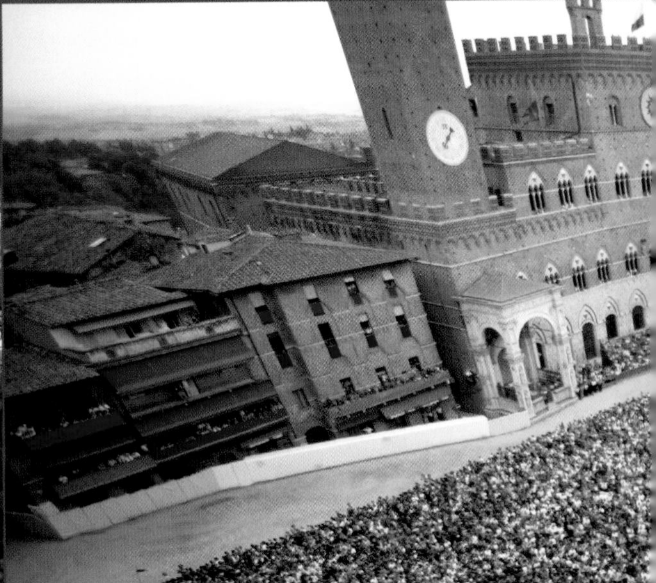

Twice a year since the beginning of the 14th century, the Piazza del Campo has transformed itself into the spectacular stage for a highly traditional festival. The Palio di Provenzano is held every year on 2 July in honor of the Holy Virgin, while the Palio dell'Assunta takes place on 16 August, forming part of the general celebrations of Ascension Day. Ten of the 17 city districts, known as *contrade*, compete in each contest. Professional *fantini* are hired, bareback jockeys who will contest the race on horses assigned to them by lot. The course follows the 300-m (990-foot) perimeter of the Piazza, which must be lapped three times in the space of just a few minutes. As the course is only 7.5 m (25 feet) wide, the race is often won not by the quickest but by the one most able to force his way through his opponents. The use of bull's pizzles as whips is not only permitted, but positively encouraged, and both the horses and the other riders are fair game. The victorious *contrada* receives as a trophy the *pallium*, a victory banner newly created for that year. The Palio di Siena should not be missed: the representatives of each *contrada*, dressed in historic garb, processing through the city, the solemn blessing of the horses and riders, the flag-wavers, and the bands of musicians are all unique highlights of this event.

THE HIGHLIGHTS: SIENA AND CENTRAL TUSCANY

The local aristocracy, mostly a mixture of rich wool, wine, and spice merchants, expressed their political aspirations in the height of their fortified towers: each wanted to build higher than his neighbor. The towers, of which 15 remain from an original 72, also offered protection against external enemies.

INFO Panoramic view

The highest tower in San Gimignano has a view across the whole Val d'Elsa. The 54-m (177-foot) Torre Grossa is accessible from the Museo Civico in the Palazzo del Popolo.

Piazza del Duomo, 53037 San Gimignano; Tel (05 77) 94 00 08; 1 Mar–31 Oct 9.30–19.00, 1 Nov–28 Feb 10.00–17.30.

SAN GIMIGNANO 63

Visible from afar, the unique skyline created by the soaring dynastic towers of San Gimignano have earned the town the nickname of the "Manhattan of the Middle Ages". They were constructed by aristocratic families from the town who had grown rich through trade, for the town was once an important commercial hub. The Frankish road that passes nearby took exporters from northern Europe all the way to Rome. San Gimignano's churches should also not be missed – the 12th-century core of the Collegiata Santa Maria Assunta has been preserved and reveals precious frescoes painted by Benozzo Gozzoli and Taddeo di Bartolo; Domenico Ghirlandaio's work can be seen in the chapel dedicated to St Fina, the town's miracle-working patron saint. There is a 17-part fresco cycle depicting the life of St Augustine (*c.* 1465), also by Benozzo Gozzoli, in the simple church of Sant'Agostino (see p. 220).

THE HIGHLIGHTS: SIENA AND CENTRAL TUSCANY

The mist at dusk envelops the Val d'Orcia (below, left: San Quirico) in mysterious light. The Cappella Vitaletta near San Quirico (below, top right) looks back on a venerable religious tradition. The hills of the Crete (right) are almost bare – a chastening result of logging and overgrazing.

INFO Horti Leoni

Even if somewhat small in dimensions, the Horti Leoni at San Quirico is one of the most beautiful gardens in Italy, with stark geometric lines contrasting with ancient oaks.

Piazza della Libertà, San Quírico; Tel (05 77) 89 72 11; Mar–Sept 10.00–18.00 , Oct–Apr 9.00–17.00.

CRETE 64
VAL D'ORCIA 65

The Italian word *creta* means clay or chalk. The Crete is a whole landscape south-east of Siena, between Vescona and Asciano, consisting of long, bare hills – the result of logging and overgrazing. There are striking ash-gray to yellow hillocks, slowly surrendering to erosion, which resemble the surface of the moon and elicit melancholy feelings in the observer. The fading hills still nurture herbs, which lend their scent to *pecorino*, the spicy sheep's cheese, but the land is too poor to support farming. The area – in particular the Val d'Orcia near San Quirico, further to the south – was to become the first to inspire landscape painters and the idyllic scenery of the Renaissance has its roots here, as does perhaps the desire for a harmonious integration of Man and nature.

THE HIGHLIGHTS: SIENA AND CENTRAL TUSCANY

An avenue of cypresses lines the pilgrim's way through the vineyards to the church of Madonna di San Biagio (below). Below, inset: Taddeo di Bartolo's late Gothic altar triptych (1401) in the cathedral at Montepulciano is as sublime as the nooks and crannies of the Old Town are picturesque (right).

TIP Caffè Poliziano

The famous Antico Caffè Poliziano has stood on the steep main street of the Old Town in Montepulciano since 1868. Federico Fellini used to drink hot chocolate in its welcoming art nouveau ambience.

Via Voltaia del Corso 27/29, 53045 Montepulciano; Tel (05 78) 75 86 15; Thurs–Tues 7.00–24.00.

MONTEPULCIANO 66

Montepulciano is both a festival town and a wine town – there are vintners and subterranean wine cellars everywhere, tempting you in to try the famous Vino Nobile di Montepulciano. The art nouveau Caffè Poliziano holds a jazz festival every July, the same month as the Cantiere Internazionale d'Arte, founded by Hans Werner Henze in 1976, which features both classical and modern music. The Bruscello festival in mid-August stages scenes from the town's history and the Bravio delle Botti at the end of the month is a fun barrel race. Two magnificent *palazzi* and the early baroque cathedral with its unfinished façade are to be found at the heart of the town, the Piazza Grande. Just beyond the city walls lies the yellow travertine of the Madonna di San Biagio pilgrim's church, whose late Renaissance central building is attributed to Antonio di Sangallo the Elder (see p. 221).

THE HIGHLIGHTS: SIENA AND CENTRAL TUSCANY

Times occasionally change for the better: the fort at Montalcino (below) has not been used for military purposes for many years, and now houses an atmospheric wine bar. Below, inset: Many a fine drop of liquid nectar is stored in the town's cellars – and sometimes also even drunk there.

TIP Excellent honey

An insider tip among the countless specialties and wines for sale in the Enoteca La Fortezza is their incomparable honey, which comes in various, sometimes quite quirky flavors.

Piazzale Fortezza, 53024 Montalcino; Tel (05 77) 84 92 11; summer: 9.00–20.00 daily, winter: 9.00–18.00 daily.

MONTALCINO 67

Surrounded by vineyards that can be seen from miles around, the small town of Montalcino is the source of Brunello di Montalcino, one of Italy's finest red wines. The strategic location of the town – it is located on an old trade route with an excellent view of the surrounding area – ensured that it was fortified at an early stage in its history; the La Rocca castle, which dominates the town, dates back to the second half of the 14th century. Monks were also among early visitors to the town; the Abbazia Sant'Antimo, a 12th-century Romanesque masterpiece, lies just beyond the town walls. This Benedictine abbey was at one time one of the richest in Tuscany, but lost its endowment at the end of the Middle Ages. The three-naved chapel, whose many ornamental reliefs and Renaissance frescoes betray French influences, was restored in the early 20th century (see p. 223).

THE HIGHLIGHTS: SIENA AND CENTRAL TUSCANY

Its location in the middle of the Sienese plain offered Monteriggioni no natural protection from its enemies, and so a circular wall with turrets was soon built around the settlement (below). The limited space *intra muros* has allowed the town to retain its historic medieval character.

TIP Cooking school

Signoria Lucia's *Scuola di cucina Toscana* initiates pupils into the art of Tuscan cuisine. Her personalized courses for a maximum of two people at a time will teach you every culinary secret you need to know.

Ristorante Il Pozzo, Piazza Roma 20, 53035 Monteriggioni; Tel (05 77) 30 41 27.

The poet Dante sang the praises of the fortified town of Monteriggioni in the *Inferno* section of his *Divine Comedy*, and the ensuing centuries seem to have left it untouched. The small town is still surrounded by its almost circular, 500-m (quarter-mile) long medieval wall inset with 14 equidistant square towers, although its location on Monte Ala has made it the scene of some military altercations; the town was established between 1213 and 1219 as a military strong point for the Republic of Siena, withstanding Florentine sieges in the 13th and 16th centuries. By a stroke of ill luck, however, Monteriggioni finally fell quite peacefully to Florence in 1554. The town thus passed through this change of regime relatively unscathed, and the Romanesque church and the merchants' houses on the main square, the Piazza Roma, have been preserved to this day (see p. 221).

THE HIGHLIGHTS: SIENA AND CENTRAL TUSCANY

Poor and isolated: the monks of the monastery of Monte Oliveto Maggiore follow the Rule of St Benedict that was laid down hundreds of years ago. The 15th-century choir stalls are the pride of the chapel. Right: The monastery seen from the air.

TIP Monastery estate

Produce from the monastery estate, such as wine and olive oil, can be bought in the cantina. An old cottage nearby houses the monastery's guest rooms.

Azienda Agricola di Monte Oliveto Maggiore, 53041 Asciano; Tel (05 77) 70 72 69.

ABBAZIA DI MONTE OLIVETO MAGGIORE 69

The Benedictine monastery of the "great mount of olives" lies on a hillside in the Crete off the road a little way beyond the town of Buonconvento. The monastery was built in 1313 by Bernardo Tolomei, a Sienese aristocrat who had decided – along with two friends from other noble Sienese families – on a spiritual life of poverty. To this day it is still the home of monks who abide by the original Rule laid down by Tolomei and confirmed by the pope in 1344. The monastery's principal attraction is the two-floor cloister, built between 1426 and 1443, with its cycle of 36 frescoes depicting the life of St Benedict. Ten of the early Renaissance panels were painted by Luca Signorelli from 1495, and 25 further panels (starting in 1505) were created by Giovanni Antonio Bazzi, whose High Renaissance imagery here is reminiscent of no less an artist than the great Leonardo da Vinci.

THE HIGHLIGHTS: SIENA AND CENTRAL TUSCANY

Pope Pius II (1405–1464) had the village of his birth, Corsignano, converted into a "model town", despite its location on a mountainous hillside (right). As the town developed, new buildings were embedded in the steeply sloping land. Pienza's highest point is the bell tower belonging to the 14th-century town hall (below).

INFO The Piccolomini Garden

A jewel of garden design behind the Palazzo Piccolomini: reached from the central courtyard, the view from the garden out over the surrounding countryside is idyllic.

Piazza Pio II, 53026 Pienza; Tel (05 78) 74 83 92; Mar–Oct Tues–Sun 10.00–18.30, Oct–Mar Tues–Sun 10.00–16.30, closed Jan.

Unusually, Pienza did not develop organically – rather, it was commissioned specifically as a model town, and by no less a Christian authority than the Renaissance humanist Pope Pius II, after whom it is named. The main buildings of this "town of humanist ideals", as it might be described, were completed between 1459 and 1462 by the Florentine architect Bernardo Rossellino. Almost from nothing, Rossellino has created a harmonious whole on a quite magnificent scale. The central feature of Pienza is the Piazza Pio II, whose south side faces the two-level blind arcades that form the façade of Santa Maria Assunta cathedral. To the right of the cathedral lies the Palazzo Piccolomini, whose lines are reminiscent of Leon Battista Alberti's Palazzo Rucellai in Florence. The palace was named after the pope's family (he was born Enea Silvio Piccolomini, see p. 222).

THE HIGHLIGHTS

GROSSETO AND THE SOUTH

Southern Tuscany, with Latium to the south, is among the hottest and least densely populated areas of the region. The vegetation here is typified by knee-high evergreen undergrowth interspersed with cactus figs. Cows are grazed here, as are the sheep from whose milk Pecorino Toscano cheese is manufactured. Traces of the Etruscans are to be found everywhere, and Massa Marittima is one of the best-preserved medieval towns in Italy. As a change from the Renaissance art ubiquitous elsewhere in Tuscany, in Capalbio you can admire the bright tones and soft curves of modern sculptures by the French artist, Niki de Saint Phalle.

71 Massa Marittima
72 Grosseto
73 Pitigliano
74 Saturnia
75 The Maremma coast
76 Parco Naturale Regionale della Maremma
77 Monte Argentario
78 Isola del Giglio
Massa Marittima 71
Castiglione della Pescáia
Grosseto 72
Marina di Grosseto
75 The Maremma coast
Parco Naturale Regionale della Maremma 76
Monte Argentário 77
78 Ísola del Giglio
Piàn di Rocca
Roccamare
San Giovanni Battista
Riva del Sole
Badiola
Ris. Nat.
Canale Diversivo
Casotto dei Pescatori
Marrucheto
Diaccia Botrona
Pineta del Tómbolo
Fosso Tanara
Il Poggione
Podere Sterpeto
Fortezza Medicea
San Francesco
Podere San Lorenzo
Tenuta Pingrosso
Santa Maria di Rispéscia
Rosmarina
Principina a Mare
Tráppola
Spergoláia
F. Ombrone
Alberese
Marina di Alberese
Torre di Collelungo
Monti dell' Uccellina
Póggio Lecci 415
San Rabano
Cala di Forno
Póggio Raso 280
Valle Maggiore
Collécchio
Fonteblanda
Talamone
Bengodi
Terme dell'Osa
Golfo di Talamone
Via Aurelia Etrusca
Formiche di Grosseto
Parco Nazionale dell'Arcipélago Toscano
Mar Tirreno
Punta Lividónia
Porto Santo Stéfano
Fortezza Spagnola
Punta Cala Grande
Ísola Argentarola
Cala Píccola
Convento dei Padri Passionisti
Ísola Rossa
Punta di Trorre Ciana
Punta del Fenáio
Punta Faraglione
Gíglio Castello
Gíglio Campese
Gíglio Porto
Póggio d. Pagana 498
Cala delle Canelle
Punta del Capel Rosso
N
0 4 km
2 miles

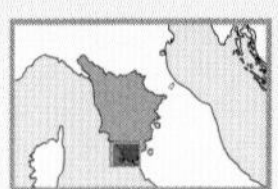

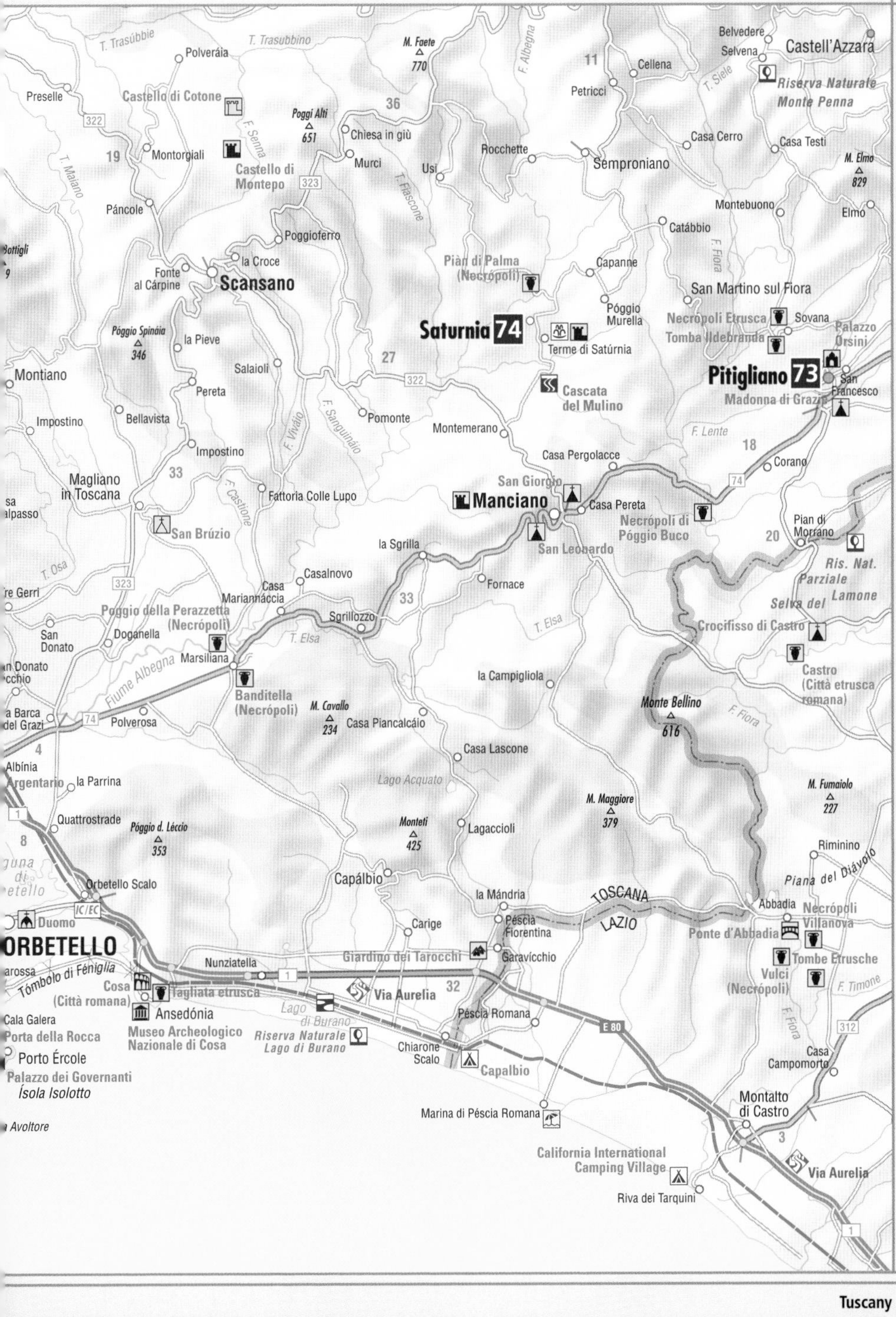

T. Trasúbbie
T. Trasubbino
Polveráia
M. Faete 770
F. Albegna
11
Cellena
Belvedere
Selvena
Castell'Azzara
T. Siele
Riserva Naturale Monte Penna
Preselle
Castello di Cotone
322
Poggi Alti 651
36
Petricci
Chiesa in giù
Casa Cerro
Casa Testi
T. Maiano
19
Montorgiali
Murci
Rocchette
Semproniano
M. Elmo 829
Castello di Montepo
323
Usi
T. Fiascone
Páncole
Montebuono
Elmo
Catábbio
Poggioferro
F. Fiora
la Croce
Capanne
Piàn di Palma (Necrópoli)
Fonte al Cárpine
Scansano
San Martino sul Fiora
Póggio Murella
Necrópoli Etrusca
Sovana
Tomba Ildebranda
Palazzo Orsini
Saturnia 74
Terme di Satúrnia
Póggio Spinàia 346
la Pieve
27
Montiano
Salaioli
Pitigliano 73
San Francesco
Madonna di Grazie
Pereta
Cascata del Mulino
Impostino
Bellavista
F. Sanguináio
Pomonte
F. Vivàio
Montemerano
F. Lente
18
Impostino
Casa Pergolacce
Corano
33
Magliano in Toscana
F. Castione
San Giorgio
Fattoria Colle Lupo
Manciano
Casa Pereta
74
San Brúzio
Necrópoli di Póggio Buco
Pian di Morrano
20
San Leonardo
la Sgrilla
Ris. Nat. Parziale Selva del Lamone
T. Osa
Casalnovo
323
Fornace
Casa Mariannáccia
33
Poggio della Perazzetta (Necrópoli)
Sgrillozzo
T. Elsa
Crocifisso di Castro
San Donato
Doganella
T. Elsa
Marsiliana
Fiume Albegna
Castro (Città etrusca romana)
la Campigliola
Banditella (Necrópoli)
M. Cavallo 234
Casa Piancalcáio
Monte Bellino 616
F. Fiora
Polverosa
74
4
Albínia
Casa Lascone
Argentario
la Parrina
Lago Acquato
M. Fumaiolo 227
1
Quattrostrade
M. Maggiore 379
8
Póggio d. Léccio 353
Monteti 425
Lagaccioli
Riminino
Orbetello Scalo
Capálbio
Piana del Diávolo
la Mándria
TOSCANA
LAZIO
Abbadia
IC/EC
Duomo
Pèscia Fiorentina
Carige
Necrópoli Villanova
ORBETELLO
Ponte d'Abbadia
Nunziatella
Giardino dei Tarocchi
Garavícchio
Tombe Etrusche
Tómbolo di Fenìglia
1
Vulci (Necrópoli)
Cosa (Città romana)
Tagliata etrusca
Via Aurelia
32
F. Timone
Ansedónia
Lago di Burano
Péscia Romana
F. Fiora
Cala Galera
Museo Archeologico Nazionale di Cosa
Riserva Naturale Lago di Burano
E 80
312
Porta della Rocca
Chiarone Scalo
Capalbio
Casa Campomorto
Porto Ércole
Palazzo dei Governanti
Ísola Isolotto
Montalto di Castro
Marina di Péscia Romana
3
California International Camping Village
Via Aurelia
Riva dei Tarquini
1

THE HIGHLIGHTS: GROSSETO AND THE SOUTH

Daring hairpin bends must be negotiated on the road up to Massa Marittima (below). You can see the sea from here in good weather. Right: A view of the Duomo San Cerbone and the Piazza Garibaldi with its street cafés.

INFO Palazzo Pretorio

This elegant 13th-century, travertine *palazzo* conceals one of the greatest works by an artist of the Sienese school, Ambrogio Lorenzetti's *Maestà*, as well as other paintings of a more Gothic style.

Piazza Garibaldi, 58024 Massa Marittima; Tel (05 66) 90 22 89; Tues–Sun 10.00–12.30, 15.00–19.00.

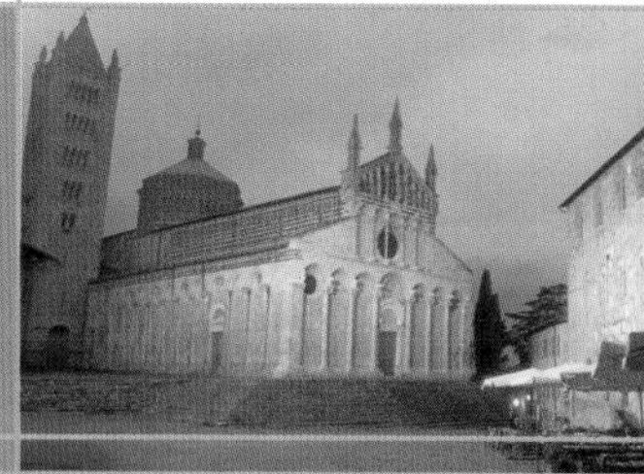

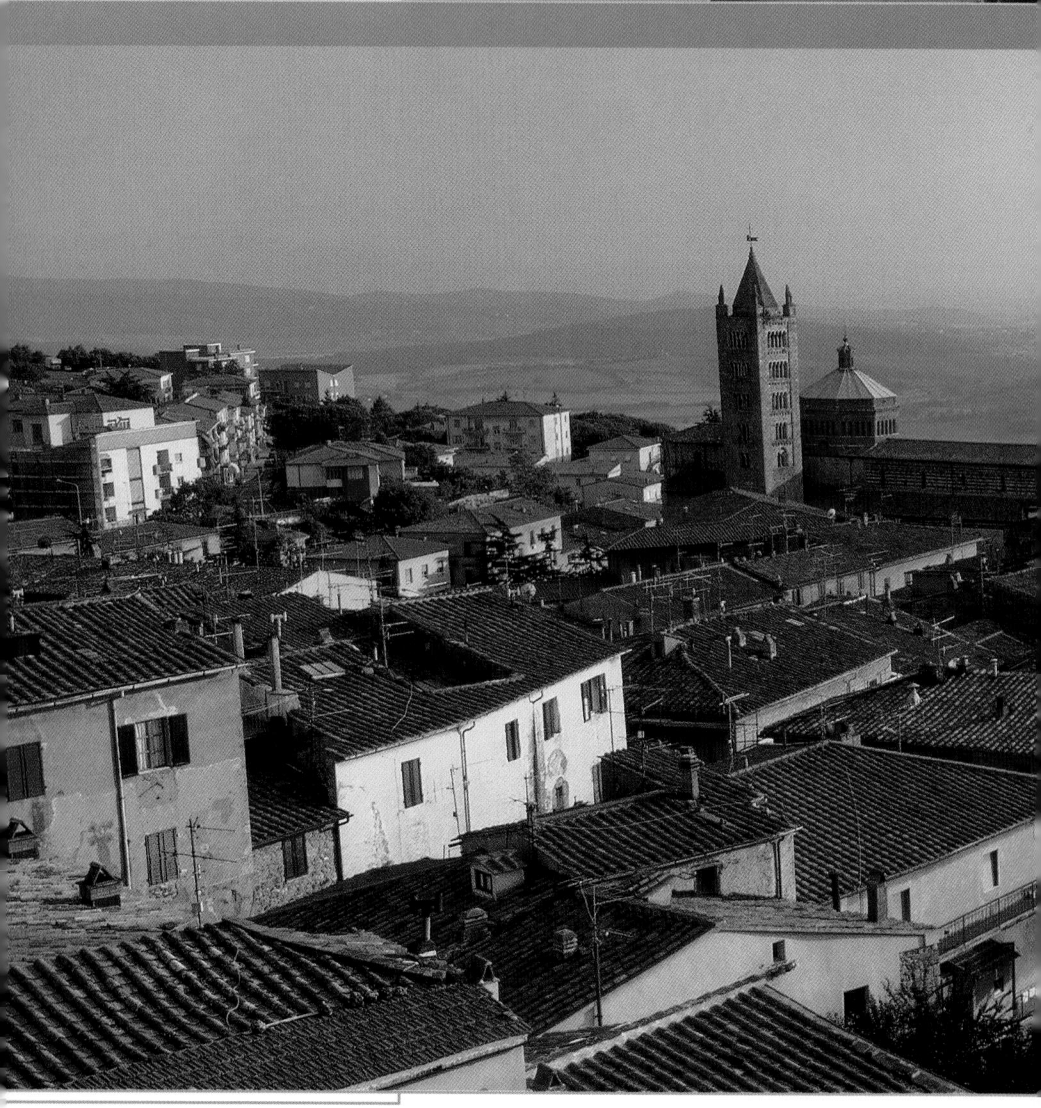

The cathedral of San Cerbone, constructed in the 13th century with obvious Pisan as well as some Sienese influences, is situated on a terrace on Piazza Garibaldi in Massa Marittima's Old Town. Giovanni Pisano designed the façade of the building, which incorporates both Romanesque and Gothic elements, with a total of 12 blind arcades culminating in a gable topped with a series of further arcades. The fascinating interior of the church reveals a font dating from 1380, carved from a single block of travertine by Giroldo da Como, and the crypt houses the sarcophagus of St Cerbonius, the patron saint of Massa Marittima, who was once the bishop of Populonia. The town was conquered by Siena in the 14th century and a fortress built by occupying Sienese troops lies at the heart of the new town, offering excellent views over the surrounding countryside (see p. 224).

THE HIGHLIGHTS: GROSSETO AND THE SOUTH

Grosseto is probably the sleepiest provincial capital in Tuscany. Certainly, very few tourists stray here; they come mostly to visit the Romanesque cathedral (below). The welcome is warm, however, for perhaps this very reason, and the town is well known for its pleasures of the vine (below, inset).

INFO Archeological Museum

The Museo Archeologico e d'Arte della Maremma has interesting Etruscan finds from Roselle and Vetulonia, as well as prehistoric and Roman exhibits.

Piazza Baccarini 3, 58100 Grosseto; Tel (05 64) 48 87 50; May–Sept Tues–Sun 10.00–13.00, 17.00–20.00, Oct–Apr 10.00–13.00, 16.00–19.00.

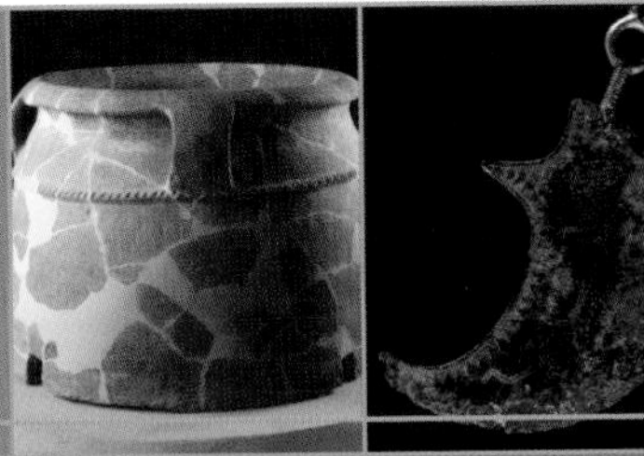

Grosseto, the largest town in southern Tuscany, is located in the Maremma region and is surrounded by a massive fortified ring wall with defensive bastions, begun in 1574 by Francesco I de Medici and completed 19 years later. A decree of 1138 by Pope Innocent II elevated the town to a diocese, a status previously held by nearby Roselle. The ruins of the ancient city of Rusellae, one of the mightiest members of the Etruscan league of 12 towns, are preserved some 10 km (6 miles) north of Grosseto in an archeological park. At Vetulonia, still further to the north, there is an Etruscan necropolis with multi-level grave structures where artfully made gold artifacts have been discovered. The neo-Gothic town hall (Palazzo della Provincia) and the cathedral of San Lorenzo with its brick *campanile* on the Piazza Dante form the twin central points of Grosseto's Old Town (see p. 224).

The Etruscans, a mysterious people, created a very early advanced civilization. They laid roads and built bridges, were excellent potters, metalworkers, and goldsmiths, and passed on the art of writing to the Romans. Evidence of their culture is principally to be seen in the rich finds of the necropolises (cities of the dead) of Populonia (below, left) and Sovana (below, right). The Etruscan museum in Volterra holds sculptures from various periods (right) to illustrate the various phases of Etruscan culture.

THE ETRUSCANS: FROM THE MISTS OF HISTORY

Even today, the exact origins of the Etruscan civilization are uncertain. It is known, however, that they settled parts of the regions known today as Tuscany, Umbria, and Latium in about 1000 BC: study of their language and the oldest discovered artworks, combined with modern genetic research, would suggest that immigrants from Lydia in Asia Minor (the region around modern Izmir on the Turkish coast) intermarried with the local population of this part of Italy, thereby founding an advanced civilization – the heyday of the society in about 600 BC is evidenced by numerous first-class works of art found in Tuscany. By this time, the Etruscans had taken command of all central Italy, although no coherent national structure emerged; instead, a league of 12 cities was formed, based on economy and religion, ruled by the nobles. One of the pillars of Etruscan prosperity was the mining and refining of metal ores in Tuscany and on the island of Elba, and the other was seafaring: there was initially brisk sea trade with the Greek world, which then led to war and the defeat of the Etruscan fleet by the Greeks. Skirmishes with the Celts and Romans were to follow. Weakened by such warring, the Etruscans sought a treaty with the Romans and their culture was gradually absorbed by the empire around 100 BC.

THE HIGHLIGHTS: GROSSETO AND THE SOUTH

Below: The crush of houses on the tufa cliff at Pitigliano. Right: Saturnia, known to the Etruscans thousands of years ago as Aurinia, lies on an isolated outcrop of travertine beside the ancient Via Clodia.

INFO Hot springs

A trip to the public sulfur baths at Saturnia is a popular diversion. A little further down from the town, near the spa facility, there is the waterfall of Cascate del Molino, which has created a natural pool in the tufa. If it is less crowded you can just take a dip in the Gorello, the river above the waterfall.

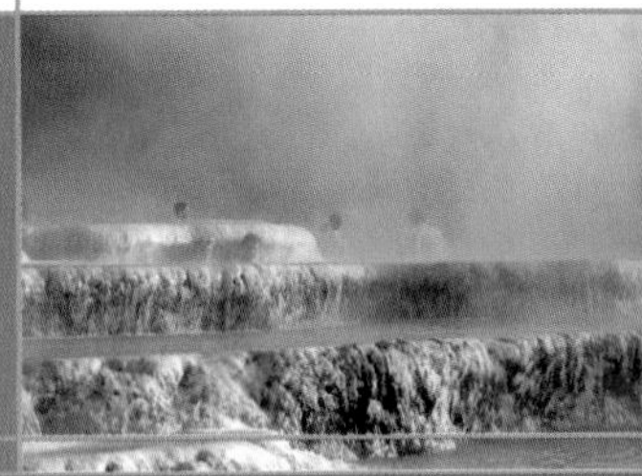

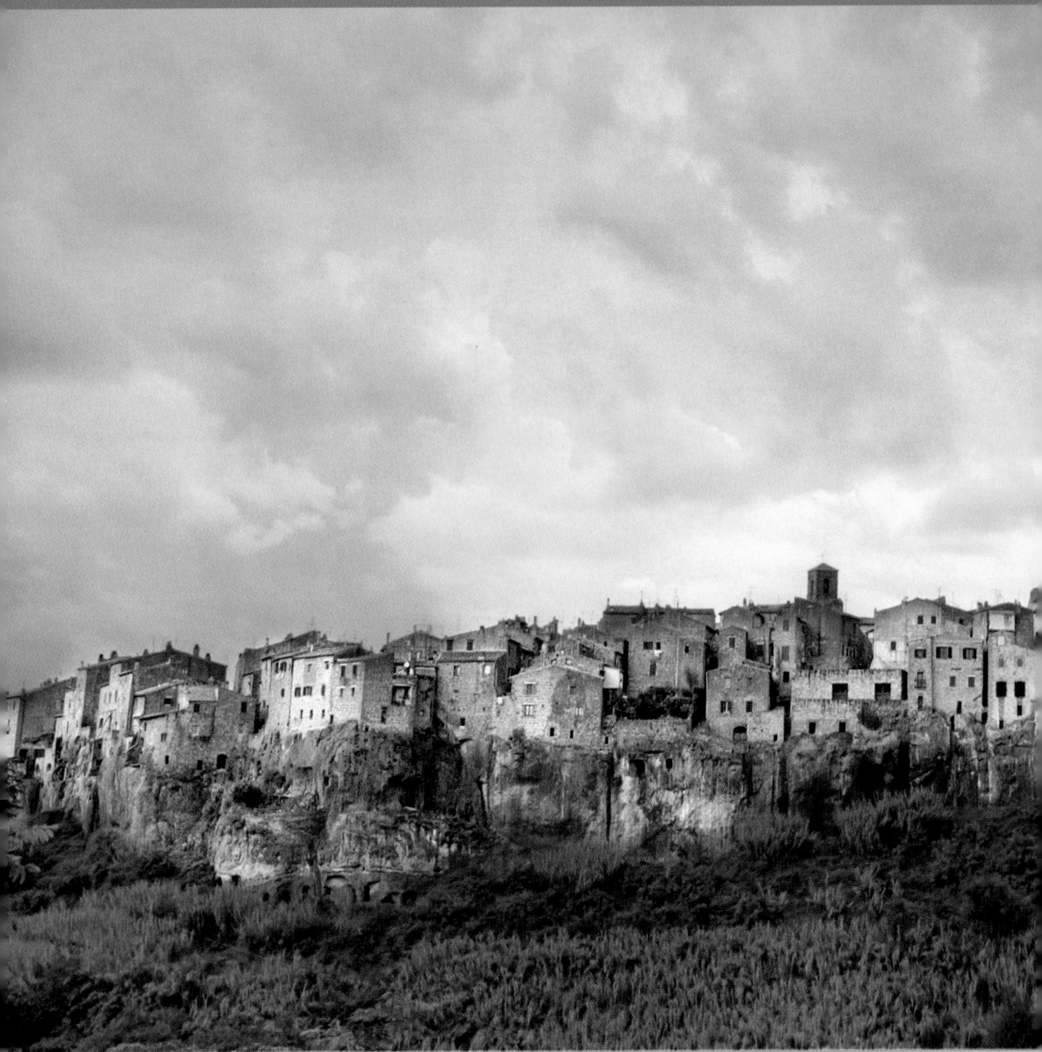

PITIGLIANO 73
SATURNIA 74

The town of Pitigliano was founded on a plateau of steep tufa cliffs once settled by the Etruscans. The 14th-century *palazzo* of Count Orsini holds magnificent works by Francesco Zuccarelli, who was born in Pitigliano in 1702 and who also created works for the cathedral. The nearby synagogue, dating from the late 16th century and recently restored, is evidence of the former size of the Jewish community, which perished in the terrors of the 20th century. According to legend, the village of Saturnia, one of the oldest Etruscan settlements in Italy, was founded by Saturn, the Roman god of agriculture. The warm springs here have always been prized for their healing and remission of asthmatic and rheumatic conditions. The water flows from the extinct volcano of Monte Amiata into the earth, where it is enriched with sulfur, returning to the surface at Saturnia (see p. 224).

THE HIGHLIGHTS: GROSSETO AND THE SOUTH

The coastal villages of Talamone (below) and Castiglione (right) lie in the far south of Tuscany, on the border with Latium. The villages still support themselves principally from fishing, even if their marinas have since become popular berths for immaculate touring yachts.

INFO Pineta del Tombolo

The most beautiful beach on the Maremma stretches for miles along the Pineta del Tombolo between Castiglione and Marina di Grosseto; it is an ideal location in fall and winter for a long stroll close to nature.

THE MAREMMA COAST 75

The Maremma region follows the south-west coast from Piombino to the Monte Argentario peninsula. Sparsely populated and flat, the landscape features long, sandy beaches alternating with pine groves that extend out to the *macchia* of the interior. The long and sometimes troubled history of the seaside resort of Castiglione della Pescaia is evidenced by the hilltop castle with its three fortified towers built by the Pisans from the 10th century (before the town eventually fell to Florence in 1406). The neighboring town of Talamone has also had a chequered past: in 225 BC the Battle of Campo Regio took place here, with the Roman legions defeating the Gauls. Some 2,000 years later, on 6 May 1860, it became a resting-place for the hero of Italian independence, Giuseppe Garibaldi, and his "Expedition of the Thousand" en route to conquering Sicily and Naples.

THE HIGHLIGHTS: GROSSETO AND THE SOUTH

Agriturismo is an environmentally friendly, nature-based kind of tourism which is particularly encouraged by the nature parks in Tuscany. Planting crops (right) and rearing animals (longhorn cattle are shown below) are essential elements of this style of vacation, which is growing ever more popular.

INFO Maremma nature park

As visitor numbers are restricted in the park, it is worth avoiding peak times such as Easter or mid-August. Tickets can be purchased at the entrance at Alberese, where you can also book a guide or a tour on horseback.
Information: Via del Fante, 58100 Alberese; Tel (05 64) 40 70 98.

PARCO NATURALE REGIONALE DELLA MAREMMA 76

The Maremma National Park, founded in 1975, is an idyllic location for nature fans and supporters of *agriturismo*. Stretching north from Talamone to the estuary of the Ombrone, the park is prized by ornithologists – and others – for the variety of its birdlife, although it has also become a refuge for both a local species of horse and other endangered species such as wild cats and the stone marten. Hikers prefer the huge holm oaks and the *macchia* vegetation on the heights of the Monti dell'Uccellina. The Maremma was originally a completely inaccessible swamp, rife with malaria-bearing mosquitoes, until the creation of drainage channels in the 19th century made the region both healthier and agriculturally viable. The longhorn cattle (*Maremmana*) reared here are famous, and the local *butteri* – Tuscan cowboys, who ride in distinctive saddles – test their skill with these at popular rodeos (see p. 225).

THE HIGHLIGHTS: GROSSETO AND THE SOUTH

The wealth of luxury yachts and fine fish restaurants at Porto Ercole (below, inset) would give any of the marinas on the French Côte d'Azur a run for their money. The bathing beaches, situated between steep cliffs, are often difficult to reach but are worth the effort for the pure relaxation they offer (below).

TIP | Pescatori

The fishing collective at Orbetello owns its own restaurant located in the fortress. In the summer it is run almost as a fast-food establishment, and the prices and the food in the closed season are still very reasonable.
Via Leopardi 9, 58010 Orbetello; Tel (05 64) 86 06 11.

MONTE ARGENTARIO 77

In the ancient world, Monte Argentario was still an island lying off the southern coast of the Maremma. However, silting up has resulted in the creation of two narrow causeways (*tomboli*) to the mainland and the modern peninsula is now a tempting mixture of wooded hills and shallow bays, which are excellent for swimming, as well as large yacht marinas. The view from the highest point, Monte Telegrafo (635 m/ 2,080 feet), can extend to the island of Corsica when the weather is good. The massive fortifications in the two main towns of Porto Santo Stefano and Porto Ercole are reminders of Monte Argentario's 16th-century role as a Spanish stronghold. A 19th-century causeway links the peninsula with the town of Orbetello, which was fortified a century earlier. The main attraction in this coastal town is the 14th-century, three-naved cathedral with its simple Gothic travertine façade.

Many of the sculptures in the Giardino dei Tarocchi are not just fascinating from the outside; the giant figures have passageways inside, such as the *Empress* (right: exterior detail) and the *Temperance Chapel* (below). Below, inset, from left: Representations of the *Sun*, the *World*, and the *Hierophant* from the major arcana.

NIKI DE SAINT PHALLE: THE POWER OF IMAGINATION

The town of Capalbio, dominated by a massive, crenellated tower, lies on a hillside a little way to the north of Lago di Burano in the Monteti foothills. The French-born artist Niki de Saint Phalle (1930–2002) and her husband Jean Tinguely (1925–1991), also an artist, spent their summer months here from 1979, and the Giardino dei Tarocchi (Tarot Garden) created by these early classical modernists has been open to the public as a sculpture park since 1998. The garden is populated with 22 fabulous creatures, inspired by the tarot pack and created by Niki de Saint Phalle. The sculptures, which reach heights of 15 m (50 feet) and have passageways inside, are made of brightly painted, cement-covered steel armatures and have been decorated with bespoke tiles made from stained Murano glass or fragments of mirrors. The lush garden surrounding these creations has artificial lakes and was intended by the artist to be a place where nature and art would meet. Many of the figures, such as the *Empress*, are reminiscent of the *Nanas*, the generous female forms clad in bright garments which first made Niki de Saint Phalle famous in 1964 and which are now to be found in many great cities throughout the world. The Giardino dei Tarocchi is one of her masterpieces.

THE HIGHLIGHTS: GROSSETO AND THE SOUTH

The best way to reach Giglio, the second-largest island in the Tuscan Archipelago, is by boat. The ferry from Monte Argentario docks at Giglio Porto (below). From the fortress of Giglio Castello there is a superb view of the sea, especially at sunset (right).

INFO Hiking

Apart from the divers, visitors preferring dry land are also well looked after: there are plenty of hiking trails across the island, although the thorny *macchia* make long trousers a wise choice. Hiking maps can be purchased at the tourist office.
Proloco Isola del Giglio, 58013 Giglio Porto; Tel (05 64) 80 94 00.

ISOLA DEL GIGLIO

Isola del Giglio, the "Island of Lilies", lies off the southern Tuscan coast near the Monte Argentario peninsula. No lilies grow here, however – the name is in fact derived from the Latin word *aegilium*, meaning "goat". Apart from supporting animal husbandry, Giglio has been a mining center for iron ore and other minerals since the end of the Stone Age; combined with its strategic location, this has made the island hotly contested property over the centuries, and almost every significant Italian sea power has owned it at one point or another. Construction of the fortified town of Giglio Castello began under the Pisans and the port of Giglio Porto with its striking tower was completed under the rule of the Medici in the 16th century. The Isola del Giglio is now part of the maritime park, the Parco Nazionale dell'Arcipelago Toscano, and its underwater treasures are a big attraction for divers.

TUSCANY EXPLORER

COMPACT TUSCANY

Tuscany is considered to be the cradle of modern culture. Groundbreaking developments in art, science, and commerce began here during the Renaissance and relics from this great period are ubiquitous, although particularly concentrated in Florence. Earlier cultures have also left their mark in the area: excavations have unearthed many great Etruscan and Roman works of art. Although much of Tuscany's cultural wealth is found in its major cities, there is many a beautiful church, delightful piazza, and fine work of art in the region's small towns and villages, and sampling traditional dishes and local wine in a romantic *osteria* is pure pleasure!

Carrara

(See p. 24.)

Cava Museo
The Fantiscritti quarries at Carrara have a private open-air museum exhibiting tools and a fully furnished miner's hut, laid out as it would have been until the 20th century.
Admission free.
Tel 05 85/709 81;
Easter to Oct 9.00–19.00 daily.

Museo Civico del Marmo
The five sections of this municipal museum devoted to the famous stone quarried in Carrara has displays outlining the formation of marble, mining in the past, and modern uses of the stone.
Viale XX Settembre 85;
Jul–Aug Mon–Sat 10.00–20.00, May–Jun and Sept Mon–Sat 10.00–18.00, Oct–Apr Mon–Sat 8.30–13.30, closed Sun.

Club Alpino Italiano
If you want to find out about outdoor pursuits in the Apuan Alps, this is the place for information on hiking tours, which can also be booked here.
Via Giorgi 4;
Tel 05 85/63 2519.
www.aptmassacarrara.it

VAMA S.A.S.
If you have some cash to spare and would like to smarten up your bathroom with some marble from Carrara, this firm has a huge selection of tiles, flagstones, and even furniture inlaid with marble, though it could be somewhat chilly to the touch on a cold day.
Via Campo d'Appio 126;
Tel 05 85/503 93.
www.vamamarmi.it

Colonnata di Carrara Ditta R.L.
Luigi Rolla, a local butcher, produces not only Italian sausages and meats but also one of the most famous specialties from the Apuan Alps, *lardo di Colonnata* – fine white ham which has been pickled for at least ten months in marble containers containing herbs, garlic, and other spices.
Via della Fontana 21;
Tel 03 39/080 48 55.
www.drldicolonnata.com

Ninan
This tiny gourmet restaurant specializes in light regional dishes. Booking is certainly recommended.
Via Lorenzo Bartolini 3;
Tel 05 85/747 41;
closed Sun.

La Tavernetta da Franco
A well-known restaurant in the picturesque heart of the town serving excellent fish dishes, which are a specialty, though meat dishes are on the menu too.
Piazza Alberica 10;
Tel 05 85/77 77 82;
closed Mon.
www. ristorantelatavernetta.it

Hotel Radar
A small but charming hotel located on a hillside about 2 km (a mile) outside Carrara. There is a fantastic view of the coastal plain and of the Apuan Alps, where the quarries are clearly visible. Guests will be delighted to discover that the restaurant on the ground floor of the hotel serves regional dishes with the emphasis on fresh local produce.
Via delle Macchiacce 13;
Tel 05 85/84 28 40.
www.italiaabc.it/h/radar

Michelangelo
Prospective guests should not be put off by the hotel's exterior; a stay here is really very pleasant. Each room is furnished with accessories from a different period.
Corso Fratelli Rosselli 3;
Tel 05 85/77 71 61.

Colonnata

Da Venanzio
A gourmet restaurant serving exquisite regional cuisine. Try wafer-thin slices of *lardo di Colonnata*, the justly famed white ham of the region; the homemade antipasti are also delicious.
Piazza Palestro 3;
Tel 05 85/75 80 62.
closed Thurs and Sun.

Viareggio

Ecotour
Take the two- to three-hour boat trip down the canal to Lago Massaciuccoli, a peaceful stretch of water that is all that remains of a vast deltaic lagoon, and watch Viareggio and its hinterland slip by. Giacomo Puccini, the famous opera composer, had a villa at Torre del Lago, on the lake, and the house is now open as a museum.
Tel 05 84/484 49;
summer months only.
www.burlamacca.it

Al Porto
A traditional fish restaurant, situated right on the side of the quay. From the large terrace there is a great view in summer.
Via M. Coppino 118c;
Tel 05 84/38 38 78;
closed Sun.

Da Romano
A small but intimate venue for gourmets and foodies, considered to be one of the best fish restaurants on the west coast of Italy. Extremely popular, so booking ahead by telephone is essential.
Via Mazzini 120;
Tel 05 84/313 82;
closed Mon.

Plaza e de Russie
Of all the *belle epoque* palaces that have been converted into hotels in Viareggio, this is the oldest, the smallest, and also the most elegant. About 20 of the 50 rooms have an excellent sea view. Breakfast and dinner are served on the rather exclusive roof terrace.
Piazza d'Azeglio 1;
Tel 05 84/444 49.
www.plazaederussie.com

Principe di Piemonte
Often used by directors as a luxurious film set, and previously known (since the 1920s) as the Select Palace Hotel, this elegant building with its views of the Tyrrhenian Sea reopened in 2004 after a complete renovation. Both the interior and the exterior have been beautifully refurbished. There is a nice spa area, a gym, a swimming pool, a terrace on the fifth floor, and a restaurant with an excellent panoramic view.
Piazza Giacomo Puccini 1;
Tel 05 84/40 11.
www.principedipiemonte.com

From left: Oval in shape like an amphitheater, the Piazza del Mercato in Lucca; a lone farmhouse in the Orecchiella Park at Garfagnana; the wild and steep Apuan Alps; Viareggio: the dining room of the Plaza e de Russie hotel.

LUCCA AND THE NORTH

The insider tips listed here refer to the sights described in the Highlights chapter (pp. 16–43).

Orecchiella Park Garfagnana

Hiking

A nature reserve north of Lucca with a variety of plant life, such as the petite globe daisy (*Globularia incanescens*) and animals such as the recently resettled mouflons (species of wild sheep). From the summit of Pania al Corfino, there is an excellent view of the Serchio valley.
Orecchiella Park Information Office;
Tel 05 83/61 90 18.
www.ingarfagnana.it

Parco Naturale delle Alpi Apuane

(See p. 23.)

Hiking

The dramatic karst scenery of these limestone peaks, with a natural stone arch visible from miles around, is in the far north-west of Tuscany, near Lucca. Species of Alpine crow, short-toed eagles, and spectacled salamanders have made the Apuan Alps their home, along with clumps of horse chestnut trees.
Visitors' Center:
55047 Seravezza,
Via Corrado del Greco 11;
Tel 05 84/75 61 44.
www.parks.it

Lucca

(See p. 30.)

Museo del Fumetto

A museum for fans of comic book art and the graphic novel. There are computer-controlled booths and all kinds of multi-media presentation, life-size figures, and comic book rarities.
Piazza San Romano 4;
Tel 05 83/563 26;
Tues–Sun 10.00–19.00.
www.museoitalianodelfumetto.it

Museo Nazionale di Villa Guinigi

The museum is housed in Villa Giunigi, built outside the city walls by Paolo Giunigi, lord of Lucca, in the 15th century. The extensive grounds have garden sculptures dating back to 1788. There is an archeological collection of Roman statues, as well as medieval and modern sculptures; on the upper floors of the house is an exhibition of precious sacred objects – church furniture, gold artifacts, fabrics, and paintings, including some by Fra Bartolomeo and Pompeo Batoni. The *Portrait of the Young Alessandro Medici* is a highlight.
Via della Quarquonia;
Tel 05 83/49 60 33.

Palazzo Mansi and Pinacoteca Nazionale

Dating from the 16th/17th century, this palace, whose public rooms were substantially refitted in the 18th century, houses a collection of paintings donated by Grand Duke Peter Leopold II of Tuscany. It features Medici portraits and Florentine, Venetian, and Flemish paintings, not to mention masterpieces woven in silk.
Via Galli Tassi 43;
Tel 05 83/58 34 61.

Teatro del Giglio

The most important theater in the city is this 19th-century neo-classical building that once hosted a concert by Niccolo Paganini, the greatest violin virtuoso of his age. Operas by the great Italian composers Puccini and Rossini also premiered here.
Piazza del Giglio;
13.00–15.00;
Tel 05 83/46 75 21.
www.teatrodelgiglio.it

Camiceria Cerri

A wide selection of shirts and matching ties. If you decide to buy, your purchase can be further distinguished with a monogram, for a touch of distinctive Italian elegance.
Via Fillungo 178;
Tel 05 83/49 11 80;
closed Sun.
www.cerricamiceria.com

Cioccolateria Caniparoli

This chocolatier uses the highest quality Belgian chocolate with which to manufacture its tempting creations. Chef Piero Caniparoli is famed for his divine, melting praline fillings.
Via San Paolino 96;
Tel 05 83/534 56.

Gioielleria e Antiquariato Carli

The oldest jeweler's in the city (established 1655) is just the place if you are looking for vintage jewelry, smart clocks, or fine silver cutlery.
Via Fillungo 95;
Tel 05 83/49 11 19.

Pasticceria Taddeucci

Gourmets, foodies, and locals are in agreement that this baker's produces the best *buccellato di Lucca* for miles around – a tasty sponge cake made with orange peel, aniseed, and raisins.
Piazza San Michele 34;
Tel 05 83/49 49 33;
Fri–Wed 8.00–13.00, 15.00–20.00, closed Thurs.

Agli Orti di Via Elisa

If you are in need of some peace and quiet, you can enjoy a pizza a little removed from the bustle of the city in this traditional *trattoria* and pizzeria, which also has a pleasant courtyard.
Via Elisa 16;
Tel 05 83/49 12 41.

Antica Locanda dell'Angelo

A family-owned bar established in 1414. Mamma runs the kitchen with great efficiency, producing all kinds of regional classics to the delight of the hungry who come here.
Via Pescheria 21;
Tel 05 83/477 11;
closed Sun evening and all day Mon.
www.locandadellangelo.it

Gelateria Veneta

One of the best ice cream parlors in Lucca, set in a quiet location not too far from the city walls.
Via Vittorio Veneto 74;
Tel 05 83/46 70 37.
www.gelateriaveneta.net

Puccini

Not exactly cheap, but the food is good in this smart and elegant fish restaurant. Ask for a table on the terrace, which is very pleasant.
Corte San Lorenzo 1;
Tel 05 83/31 61 16;
closed Tues and Wed lunchtime.

La Luna

This charming hotel is located in the heart of the Old Town, only a short walk from the Piazza Anfiteatro.
Corte Compagnie 12;
Tel 05 83/49 36 34.
www.hotellaluna.com

Palazzo Alexander
How about staying in an elegant 12th-century *palazzo*? All the guest rooms are tastefully furnished and have satellite TV, a minibar, a safe, and an internet connection.
Via Santa Giustina 48;
Tel 05 83/58 35 71.
www.palazzo-alexander.com

Bagni di Lucca

Spa
Bagni di Lucca is a small town about 30 km (19 miles) from Lucca proper, and its hot springs have been attracting visitors since the 19th century – Napoleon's younger sister, Pauline, for example, after whom a grotto (Paolina) is named, and the German poet Heinrich Heine, who wrote movingly about the Baths of Lucca. The sick are still treated here, and the able-bodied can still enjoy some pampering. Bagni di Lucca's unique selling point is the damp air in the two grottos (Grandale and Paolina), which helps treat skin problems and rheumatism.
Tel 05 83/872 21.
www.termebagnidilucca.it

Massaciucoli

Oasi Lipu Massaciucoli
This cooperative institution organizes trips through local watercourses and marshy areas. You can hire canoes and kayaks here and take advantage of the guides' excellent local knowledge to see the area from a different vantage point.
Tel 05 84/97 55 67.
www.oasilipumassaciucoli.org

Montecatini

(See p. 36.)

Montecatini Golf
An extensive 18-hole course in a charming area of gentle, rolling hills, with a swimming pool and a restaurant in the clubhouse.
Loc. Pievaccia, Via dei Brogi;
Tel 05 72/64 06 92;
closed Tues.
www.montecatinigolf.com

The puppet who became a boy: Parco di Pinocchio in Collodi.

Spa
The healing power of the springs at Montecatini has been known since the 15th century. The four springs (Rinfresco, Leopoldina, Regina, and Tettuccio) are particularly effective for digestive complaints and liver or gall bladder problems. The healthy can also take the waters or treat themselves to massages or fango treatments (where mud is used to cleanse the body and remove toxins) in the magnificent architectural setting of one of the oldest health spas in Italy.
Viale Verdi 41;
Tel 05 72/77 81.
www.termemontecatini.it

Grand Hotel Tettuccio
This art nouveau hotel offers elegance, charm, and excellent service. The spa facilities and the famous hot springs are just a few steps away and the magnificent terrace is an excellent vantage point from which to observe the bustle on the Viale Verdi, the resort's main thoroughfare.
Viale Giuseppe Verdi 74;
Tel 05 72/780 51.
www.hoteltettuccio.it

Hotel Torretta
A four-star establishment whose fame has spread far beyond Tuscany, the hotel is situated beside the spa's extensive grounds and commands an excellent view of the town. There is an inviting swimming pool in the well-tended garden with a salt-water hydro pool and various spa treatments.
Viale Bustichini 63;
Tel 05 72/703 05.
www.hoteltorretta.it

Seravezza

Antro del Corchia
Monte Altissimo conceals one of the largest cave complexes in Italy. Tours and cave visits where you can explore galleries of stalactites are available and are an excellent way to escape the heat of the Tuscan day.
Visitors' Center Alpi Apuane
Via Corrado del Greco 11;
Tel 05 84/758 21.
www.parcapuane.toscana.it

Pistoia

(See p. 38.)

Ospedale del Ceppo
The entrance to this hospital, which was founded in the 13th century as a hostel for pilgrims, is decorated with a majolica frieze from the workshop of the della Robbia family. The medicine museum in the hospital will tell you all you need to know about the slightly gory history of the collection of surgical instruments on display.
Tel 05 73/35 22 20;
advance telephone bookings only.

Palazzo del Comune
The ground-floor arcade and matching triptych windows in the upper floors give the town hall and its coat of arms a medieval feel. A stone staircase in the courtyard leads up to the municipal museum on the upper floors, where you can learn about Pistoia's place in the history of art, and the adjoining Giovanni Michelucci documentation

From left: Atmospheric and scenic: Carmignano lies on a hillside; the ornate arcades of the Ospedale del Ceppo in Pistoia; Bagni di Lucca is good for you; Terme Tettuccio in Montecatini.

LUCCA AND THE NORTH

The insider tips listed here refer to the sights described in the Highlights chapter (pp. 16–43).

center has a wealth of fascinating information about the work of one of the most important Italian architects of the 20th century.
Piazza Duomo;
Tues–Sat 10.00–19.00, Sun 9.00–12.30.

Merceria Vannucci
Housed in the medieval Palazzo del Capitano, this haberdasher's stocks everything you might need for needlework, from buttons to thread, needles, braid, and edging. A handy haunt for seamstresses who would like to lend an Italian feel to their homemade garments.
Via di Stracceria 5/7;
Tel 05 73/217 95.

Pelletteria Andreini
A small shop selling leather goods, including all kinds of smart handbags, luggage, and suitcases, as well as an extensive range of both small and large umbrellas.
Via degli Orafi 31;
Tel 05 73/233 87.

La Bottegaia
This *osteria* is always full and serves tasty antipasti, starters, and main courses at reasonable prices. There is an inviting terrace for *alfresco* dining.
Via del Lastrone 17;
Tel 05 73/36 56 02;
closed Mon and Sun lunchtime.

Lo Storno
Situated right behind the Piazza Sala in the heart of the city, this traditional *osteria* serves dishes with an authentic Tuscan heritage.
Via del Lastrone 8;
Tel 05 73/261 93;
closed Sun.
www.lostorno.it

San Jacopo
This cozy restaurant, named after Pistoia's patron saint, serves generous portions at very reasonable prices. The place is always packed, so it is worth booking ahead.
Via Crispi 1;
Tel 05 73/277 86;
closed Mon.

Leon Bianco
A traditional hotel in the pedestrianized zone near the cathedral. The rooms are furnished in a modern style and there is parking for guests.
Via Panciatichi 2;
Tel 05 73/266 75.
www.hotelleonbianco.it

Collodi

(See p. 40.)

Parco di Pinocchio
A stroll round the Pinocchio Park reveals life-sized statues that are all related to the famous children's story, but which are far from Disneyesque in character. There are also demonstrations, shows, and exhibitions, and a puppet laboratory. Children can let off steam in the maze in "Toyland", in the pirate grotto, or even on a corsair ship.
Via San Gennaro 3;
Tel 05 72/42 93 42;
8.30–18.30 daily.
www.pinocchio.it

Prato

(See p. 42.)

Museo del Tessuto
The textile museum is housed in an old factory building and has an interesting collection of fabrics, machines, and related historical documents. There are even a few fabric samples from the ancient world (*c.* 400 BC).
Via Santa Chiara 24;
Mon and Wed–Fri 10.00–18.00, Sat 10.00–14.00, Sun 16.00–19.00, closed Tues.

Palazzo Datini
The walls and ceilings in the former house and offices of this rich Prato family are decorated with paintings. The cloth merchant Francesco di Marco Datini (1335–1410) had business connections in over 200 cities, from Stockholm to Beirut, and is credited as being the inventor of a currency exchange system and double-entry book-keeping. History enthusiasts with an interest in economics can view the extensive archives.
Via Mazei;
Mon–Sat 9.00–12.00, 16.00–18.00, closed Sun.

Arts & Crafts
This workshop is a good source of art objects made of glass, glazed door panels, decorated mirrors, and ornaments for staircases and walls.
Via Pomeria 15;
Tel 05 74/44 82 48.
www.artsecrafts.com

Ellebi Italia Srl
Shawls and scarves in linen, cotton, wool, silk, and knitted cashmere are all available from this boutique, as well as matching accessories.
Via Gora del Pero 33–35;
Tel 05 74/665 70;
Sept–Jan Mon–Fri 10.30–18.00, also Oct–Dec Sat 10.30–12.30 and Dec Sun 10.30–12.30, Feb–Jul Mon–Fri 10.30–12.30, 13.30–17.00.
www.ellebisrl.it

Oro Etrusco
This goldsmith's workshop uses an ancient Etruscan granulation technique similar to filigree. The varied range of items offered here includes necklaces with set stones, bracelets, and rings, as well as quirky objects such as gold and silver bookmarks.
Via Santa Trinita 65;
Tel 05 74/427 26.
www.oroetrusco.it

La Vecchia Cucina di Soldano
Traditional regional Tuscan cuisine served in a very cozy – and very popular – *trattoria*, at reasonable prices.
Via Pomeria 23;
Tel 05 73/346 65;
closed Sun.

Enoteca Barni
Here you can choose between tasty full meals, a self-service Barni lunch, or other Tuscan delicacies.
Via Ferrucci 22;
Tel 05 73/60 78 45;
closed Sat lunch and Sun, Mon, dinner.

Flora
An extremely pleasant three-star hotel in the historic heart of town. The rooms are elegant and tastefully furnished.
Via Cairoli 31;
Tel 05 74/335 21.
www.hotelflora.info

Carmignano

Fattoria Ambra
The cellars of this estate south-west of Prato are stocked with some of the very best wines in the region, such as the elegant Carmignano and the smooth Barco Reale.
Via Lombarda 85;
Tel 055/48 64 88.

Florence

(See p. 48.)

Auditorium Flog
First opened in 1972, Auditorium Flog can accommodate around 1,000 fans and holds rock, pop, and blues concerts performed by local and international stars, although as a cultural initiative Flog (Fondazione Lavoratori Officine Galileo) also tries to give less well-known musicians their big break.
Via Michele Mercati 24b; Tel 055/422 03 00. www.flog.it

Casa Buonarroti
Michelangelo's house holds several early works by the master, such as the *Battle of the Centaurs*, a marble relief created by the artist when he was 17, and the somewhat later *Madonna and Child*, as well as another marble relief sometimes known as the *Madonna of the Steps* (*Madonna della Scala*). There are also cartoons, architectural sketches, and other works by the immensely talented Michelangelo, together with works by other artists such as Bugiardini, Venusti, and Pontormo.
Via Ghibellina 70; Wed–Mon 9.30–14.00.

Jazz Club
Both Italian and international stars (and newcomers too) get to perform at this venue, which is considered an institution by jazz fans and has a reputation that extends much further than the banks of the Arno.
Via Nuova dei Caccini 3; 21.30–2.00 daily. www.jazzitalia.net

La Dolce Vita
A bar and an art gallery combined, with a cool terrace; this is also a hip meeting place for the Florentine club scene. Good live music on Wednesdays and Thursdays.
Piazza del Carmine; Tel 055/28 45 95; 17.00–1.30 daily. www.dolcevitaflorence.com

Museo del Bargello
Originally constructed as mayoral offices, this *palazzo* is a hoard of real treasures, with statues such as Donatello's famous bronze, *David*, the first free-standing nude sculpture to be created since ancient times. There are other pieces by Donatello, as well as works by Verrocchio, Michelangelo, Benvenuto Cellini, and Giambologna.
Via del Proconsolo 4; Tel 055/238 86 06; 8.15–14.00 daily.

Museo di Storia della Scienza
The focus in this museum is on astronomy, alchemy, and medicine. A particular highlight is the telescope with which the Renaissance genius Galileo Galilei discovered the four largest moons of Jupiter.
Piazza dei Giudici 1; Mon and Wed–Sat 9.30–17.00, Tues 9.30–13.00, closed Sun.

Museo Firenze Com'era
Florence "as it was" – the city's long history is brought alive with illustrations, paintings, art prints, and city maps dating back from several eventful centuries.
Via dell'Oriuolo 24; Fri–Wed 9.00–14.00, closed Thurs.

Museo Marino Marini
The old church of San Pancrazio has been converted into a museum dedicated to the Tuscan sculptor, painter, and graphic artist Marino Marini (1901–1980), with sculptures, paintings, and sketches from every creative period of this master of classical modernism.
Piazza San Pancrazio; Mon and Wed–Fri 10.00–17.00, Sat and Sun 10.00–13.00, closed for 2 weeks in Aug.

Museo Stibbert
An interesting collection, now filling 60 rooms, of weapons, clothing, art, and everyday objects from various ages, which once belonged to collector Frederick Stibbert – his mother was Italian and his father English. The collection is housed in the villa that was once Stibbert's home.
Via Frederico Stibbert 26; Mon–Wed 10.00–14.00, Fri–Sun 10.00–18.00, closed Thurs.

Palazzo Davanzati
If you want to know what a Florentine *palazzo* once looked like, the Casa Fiorentina is the place for you. Three floors of furniture, carpets, ceramics, drawings, sculptures, and everyday objects bring the Middle Ages, the Renaissance, and the baroque period to life.
Via Porta Rossa 13r; Tel 055/238 86 10; 8.15–13.50 daily.

Palazzo della Crochetta
The Etruscan museum (Museo Archeologico Centrale dell'Etruria) houses the largest collection of Etrurian artifacts in Tuscany, with many finds from Etruria, including a brightly painted sarcophagus from Larthia and the famous bronze of the Chimera of Arezzo, unearthed in 1555. There are also some remarkable reconstructions of tombs, with typical Etruscan molded sarcophagus lids, and a coin collection.
Via della Colonna 38; Mon 14.00–19.00, Tues, Thurs 8.30–19.00, Wed and Fri–Sun 8.30–14.00.

Palazzo Rucellai
The Fratelli Alinari photography museum is situated on the ground floor. There are countless historic photos of the city and its inhabitants, forming a comprehensive picture of recent history. The *palazzo* itself, built in the 15th century to designs by Leon Battista Alberti for the Rucellais, a rich merchant family, is considered one of the most important Renaissance townhouses in Florence.
Via della Vigna Nuova; Tues–Sun 10.00–19.30.

Teatro Communale
Florence's largest opera house and theater seats 2,000 and has stalls, boxes, and a gallery based on an amphitheater. The basic design was completed in the 19th century, but it was damaged by fire shortly after its opening and again in World War II; it was subsequently modernized in the early 1960s.
Corso Italia 16; Tel 055/21 11 58; Sept–Feb.

Teatro della Pergola
The best acting companies in Italy perform in this traditional theater between October and May. The original 17th-century

Impressions of Florence (from left): the Arno, flowing peacefully through the city into the sunset; the baptistry of San Giovanni; Museo del Bargello; antiques on sale to collectors.

IN AND AROUND FLORENCE

The insider tips listed here refer to the sights described in the Highlights chapter (pp. 44–101).

wooden construction was replaced in stone a century later. The current design dates back to the premiere of Verdi's Macbeth in 1847. The first performances of Mozart's operas in Italy were staged in the Teatro della Pergola.
Via della Pergola 18; Tel 055/226 41. www.pergola.firenze.it

Teatro Saschall
This venue holds a mixture of rock and pop concerts, cabaret, and various political functions. Saschall was founded in 1978 and was originally under canvas, before moving in 2002 to its current, slightly more solid, surroundings with seats for 1,700 patrons.
Lungarno Aldo Moro 3; Tel 055/650 41 12. www.saschall.it

Teatro Verdi
A mixed schedule of classical concerts, ballet, drama, musicals, and pop concerts with seating for 1,500 people. Founded in 1854, its orginal name was Teatro delle Antiche Stinche after the Trecento prison on the site of which it was constructed. (Several cells are still visible on the underground levels of the theater.)
Via Ghibellina 99; Tel 055/21 23 20. www.teatroverdifirenze.it

CAF Tours
City tours and regular excursions by coach to towns such as Fiesole, Pisa, Lucca, San Gimignano, and Siena; all trips must be booked in advance.
Via S. Antonino 6r; Tel 055/21 06 12. www.caftours.com

The historic Palazzo Davanzati.

Costoli
Florence's largest swimming baths are open throughout the year, with an additional outdoor pool available in summer.
Viale Paoli; Tel 055/623 60 27; 10.00–20.00 daily.

I Renaioli
Take a relaxing boat tour on the Arno in a restored historic barge. The mooring is between Ponte Vecchio and Ponte delle Grazie.
Lungarno Diaz; Tel 34 77 98 23 56; May–Oct 9.00–12.00, Jul–Aug 9.00–11.00, 18.00–24.00. www.renaioli.it

Mondo Bimbo
An veritable institution for children, where bambini between the ages of two and ten years can climb about for hours on inflatable apparatus, clamber over various animals, trampoline their way around bouncy castles, and play a whole range of games.
Via Ponte Rosso; Tel 055/553 26 46; 10.30–19.30 daily.

Parco delle Cascine
This beautiful and extensive park area with its swimming pool and racecourse is a popular weekend destination for Florentine families, joggers and picnickers alike. There is also an amphitheater in the park which acts as a venue for concerts during the summer months.
Piazza Vittorio Veneto.

Piscina le Pavoniere
Florence's largest and most beautiful open-air swimming pool is located in the Parco delle Cascine.
Viale della Catena 2; Tel 055/36 22 33; Jun–Sept 10.00–20.00 daily.

Zoologia 'La Specola'
Visitors are greeted by strange, 18th-century wax figures from the zoological museum's collection, some of which (such as the anatomically correct reproductions of dissected animals) might not be recommended for people with delicate dispositions.
Via Romana 17; 9.30–16.30 daily, closed first and last Mon of every month.

Busatti
An interior decor firm with an enormous selection of precious, handmade fabrics and textiles in various shades and patterns. The majority are still made using traditional methods. If you would like to add a touch of Italian luxury and elegance to your home, this is the place to come.
Lungarno Torrigiani 11r; Tel 055/263 85 16. www.busatti.com

Farmacia di Santa Maria Novella
The most famous apothecary's in Florence, and one of the oldest in Europe (it was officially established in 1612), tempting locals and tourists alike with fragrant items to take home.
Via della Scala 16;
Tel 055/21 62 76.
www.smnovella.com

Ferragamo
Fans of simple elegance buy their shoes, fashionwear, and accessories here. At the workshop where it all began (house no. 2 in the same street) there is a shoe museum dedicated to the firm's founder, Salvatore Ferragamo (1898–1960), who was considered to be the "King of the Shoemakers", providing footwear for film stars such as Sophia Loren and Audrey Hepburn.
Via Tornabuoni 16r;
Tel 055/27 11 21.
www.salvatoreferragamo.it

Giulio Giannini & Figlio
Handmade marbled paper (every sheet of which is unique), writing paper in attractive boxes, and other writing paraphernalia, including many stylish items, are all available from this printer's and bookbinder's.
Piazza dei Pitti 37r;
Tel 055/21 26 21.
www.giuliogiannini.it

Al Trebbio
This restaurant with its cozy outdoor tables, located on a quiet square right behind the church of Santa Maria Novella, serves a range of Tuscan specialties at really reasonable prices.
Via delle Belle Donne 47r;
Tel 055/28 70 89;
12.00–14.30, 19.00–23.00 daily.
www.trattoriaaltrebbio.com

Sostanza
A popular traditional *osteria*, once frequented by Marc Chagall and John Steinbeck, with excellent traditional dishes on the menu. Start, if you can, with a simple *tortina* (omelette) with seasonal fillings such as artichokes or ceps, and finish off with a *bistecca alla Fiorentina.*
Via del Porcellana 25r;
Tel 055/21 26 91;
closed Sat–Sun.

Roman colonnades in the Duomo San Romolo in Fiesole.

ZàZà
Once a market bar and now a *trattoria* popular with both locals and tourists. Imaginatively prepared Florentine cuisine is served here and bookings are essential.
Piazza del Mercato 26;
Tel 055/21 54 11;
closed Sun.
www.trattoriazaza.it

Il Guelfo Bianco
A comfortable hotel located in a renovated 18th-century merchant's house, with rooms decorated in a pretty, Florentine style.
Via Cavour 29;
Tel 055/28 83 30.
www.ilguelfobianco.it

Fiesole

(See p. 88.)

Teatro Romano
A venue steeped in history: every summer the Roman amphitheater (with reconstructed seating for up to 3,000) achieves its original purpose as part of the Estate Fiesolana festival, hosting classical, folk, and jazz concerts or ballet and theater performances.
Via Portigiani 1;
Tel 055/59 87 20;
Jun–Sept.

Bencista
This pension in a charming 15th-century villa offers rooms with an excellent view of Florence and a mixture of traditional and modern decor. There is also a restaurant with a terrace and an extensive garden in which to stroll.
Via Benedetto da Maiano 4;
Tel 055/5 91 63.
www.bencista.com

Vinci

(See p. 91.)

Tourist information
It will come as no surprise to learn that the town is geared almost entirely toward its most famous son. Leonardo da Vinci's birth house and museum is a little way out of town and the church of Santo Stefano still houses the font where he was baptized. The old fortress has been turned into the Museo Leonardiano, with information about Leonardo's scientific work and inventions in particular.
Via della Torre 11;
Tel 05 71/56 79 30.
www.comune.vinci.fi.it

Impruneta

Terme di Firenze
If you find yourself needing a rest from the wealth of cultural treasures that Florence has to offer, take a short excursion to Impruneta, less than 20 km (12 miles) away. The hot baths here date back to classical antiquity and retained their popularity into the Middle Ages, coming back into vogue in the 19th century. The hot springs, Fonte Antica and Fonte Celeste, are now housed in a modern 1990s building, and their healing waters, containing bromine, sulfur, and iodine, are used in treating breathing, skin, and kidney complaints. Spas and massages are also available.
Via Cassia 217;
Tel 055/202 01 51.
www.impruneta.it/terme.html

From left: A typically Tuscan landscape of tall cypresses and undulating hills; Vinci is a reminder of the great Leonardo and his many and varied inventions; a room at the Hotel Il Guelfo Bianco; dining at the hotel.

IN AND AROUND FLORENCE

The insider tips listed here refer to the sights described in the Highlights chapter (pp. 44–101).

Terracotte Mario Mariani

A small pottery which produces vases, jugs, and plant pots in various sizes, as well as tiles and decorative terracotta figures.
Via di Cappello 29;
Tel 055/201 19 50;
closed Sun.

Colle di Val d'Elsa

(See p. 96.)

The town

This little town located in the Elsa valley comprises a modern new suburb, where several companies produce crystal glass, and the Old Town. Colle Alta has partially preserved town walls and two churches worth visiting, Sant'Agostino and Santa Caterina. Several of the older palazzi have been converted into museums.
Via Francesco Campana 18;
Tel 05 77/91 21 11.
www.comune.colle-di-val-d-elsa.si.it

Greve in Chianti

Castello di Uzzano

Although you have to pay to get into these wonderful castle grounds, once inside there are mazes to explore, and statues, picnic areas, and sculptures dotted about between the cedars and sequoias. The gardens are located about 1.5 km (1 mile) north of Greve.
Castello di Uzzano;
8.00–12.00 and 13.00–18.00 daily, closed Sun.

Enoteca del Chianti Classico

Considered one of the best outlets in the whole region for Chianti wines, this *enoteca* also stocks vin santo, olive oil, balsamic vinegar, and much, much more.
Piazzetta Santa Croce 8;
Tel 055/85 32 97;
closed Wed.

Macelleria Falorni

This butchery is considered by locals and tourists alike to be the only place in Greve to buy the best regional cured specialties, including wild boar ham, salami flavored with Chianti Classico, or *finocchiona* (fennel salami).
Piazza Giacomo Matteotti 69–71;
Tel 055/85 30 29.
www.falorni.it

Mangiando Mangiando

A typical local *osteria* serving down-to-earth cuisine in a cheerful, family-orientated atmosphere. There are outdoor tables on the terrace in the main square during the summer months.
Piazza Matteotti 80;
Tel 05 58/54 63 72;
closed Mon.

Albergo del Chianti

A small cozy hotel with a leafy courtyard and a large swimming pool, located right in the heart of town. In summertime you can eat on the hotel terrace and perhaps sample a glass or two of delicious Chianti.
Piazza Matteotti 86;
Tel 05 58/85 37 63.
www.albergodelchianti.it

Castellina in Chianti

The town

This little town is surrounded by Chianti vineyards, and so it comes as no surprise that eating and drinking are popular pastimes here: there are two Michelin-starred restaurants in a town of only 3,000 people. Along with the medieval castle and the old church of San Salvatore, look out for the Via delle Volte, a cloistered passage that runs along the town wall.
Via Ferruccio 40;
Tel 05 77/74 13 92.
www.castellina.com

Gallopapa

Located in the historic heart of town in a rustic vaulted cellar, this was previously an elegant gourmet restaurant but is now an attractive wine bar offering a superb list of Tuscan and Italian wines.
Via delle Volte;
Tel 05 77/429 39

Scarperia

Autodromo Internazionale del Mugello

A must-see for auto fans: Formula 1 and other motor races are held at this racetrack located in a beautiful rural setting just outside the gates of Scarperia, about 20 km (12 miles) north of Florence. Ferrari also conduct their test drives here.
Tel 05 58/49 92 51.
www.mugellocircuit.it

Poggio dei Medici

An extremely well-tended 18-hole golf course in the middle of the Mugello region; one of the top courses in Italy, it offers five different playing routes. It is part of the Sonesta Resort and Country Club; there is a hotel on site too.
Via San Gavino 27;
Tel 05 58/43 04 36;
booking recommended.
www.poggiodeimedici.com

Olmo

La Panacea

A down-to-earth restaurant about 8 km (5 miles) north of Fiesole, serving tasty homemade Tuscan food and fish specialties. The inviting terrace can be used by guests in good weather.
Via Bosconi 58a;
Tel 05 55/489 72;
closed Mon.
www.la-panacea.it

Panzano

Oltre il Giardino

If you visit this restaurant, you must try the homemade pasta and the cheese selection. Classic dishes are served alongside original creations, and in summer you can eat surrounded by flowers on the beautiful terrace.
Piazza Buciarelli 42;
Tel 05 58/85 28 28;
closed Mon.
www.ristoranteoltreilgiardino.it

Relais Fattoria Valle

A magnificent country house with a pool, set in the woods at the edge of town, with a splendid view of the valley. Pets welcome.
Tel 05 58/85 24 82.
www.fattoriavalle.com

San Leonino

Hotel San Leonino

Constructed in a rural Tuscan style, this hotel is located a stone's throw from Castellina in Chianti. The 30 rooms are stylishly furnished, the garden is well maintained, and a refreshing dip in the pool is just the thing on hot days.
Belvedere di San Leonino;
Tel 05 77/74 08 87.
www.hotelsanleonino.com

Pisa

(See p. 106.)

Arsenali Medicei
A permanent exhibition located in the old shipyard, a large red-brick building, presenting finds from the Navi Romane excavation site of boats from the ancient Roman period. There are displays of coins, amphorae, and ceramic work, as well as oriental artifacts and Celtic gold jewelry.
Lungarno Simonelli;
Tues–Fri 10.00–13.00, 14.00–19.00, Sat–Sun 11.00–13.00, 14.00–22.00.

Museo dell'Opera del Duomo
The old cathedral chapter house now houses original statues (copies have been inserted to replace these on the exteriors of the cathedral and baptistry) by Nicola and Giovanni Pisano, an ivory Madonna by the latter, and treasures from the cathedral, including liturgical apparatus, mass vestments, and old paintings.
Piazza Arcivescovado;
Tel 050/56 05 47;
Apr–Sept 8.00–20.00, Mar and Oct 9.00–19.00, Nov–Feb 10.00–17.00.
www.opapisa.it

Museo Nazionale di San Matteo
Located a short way upstream, this 13th-century former Benedictine monastery has an exhibition principally composed of artworks from the time of its construction, including numerous Madonnas, several early depictions of the Crucifixion, a beautiful polyptych of the Madonna by Simone Martini, Masaccio's *St Paul the Apostle* (all that remains of an altarpiece), and and Gentile da Fabriano's early Renaissance *Madonna.*
Piazza San Matteo;
Tel 050/54 18 65;
Tues–Sat 8.30–19.00, Sun 8.30–13.30.

Navi Romane
Construction work in 1998 at Pisa/San Rossore rail station uncovered parts of the old Pisan municipal port and remnants of 16 ships from the Roman period, including a warship and still-laden cargo vessels. The excavation site is unfortunately only partly open to the public.
Tel 050/321 54 46;
only by appointment, book at least one week before visit.
www.navipisa.it

The Botanical Gardens
The world's oldest botanical gardens were laid out in 1543 by Cosimo I, who situated them only a short stroll from the Leaning Tower. Admission is free and you can relax and admire the palm trees, Mediterranean vegetation, and more exotic growths. You might even see some theatrical performances here in the summer months.
Via L. Ghini 5;
Mon–Sat 8.30–13.00.

Dream Bike
Both conventional and electrically assisted cycles can be hired here, along with mountain bikes and scooters for excursions. Be careful if you venture out on to busy roads – Italian driving habits are notorious.
Via del Borghetto 21;
Tel 050/57 98 58.

Il Navicello
Cruises on the River Arno to the estuary or to Calci can be booked here; the night cruises in particular are rather special.
Tel 050/54 01 62.
www.ilnavicello.it

De Bondt
Chocolate lovers from all over the world come to worship at this producer of fine artisan chocolate. Handmade bars, plain or with dried fruit, or spiced up with chili, and the finest pralines ensure Paul de Bondt and Cecilia Iacobelli rank among the world's best chocolatiers.
Lungarno Pacinotti 5;
Tel 050/316 00 73.
www.debondt.it

Ego Concept Store
A boutique where you can browse for hours, according to the cognoscenti, with reliably stylish clothes by well-known Italian designers and many fine accessories.
Lungarno Gambacorti 25;
Tel 050/220 14 71.
www.egoconceptstore.com

Paradiso del Pane
As the name implies, this is the store for specialty Tuscan bread. They also have various pastas from the region, olive oil, salami, and wines.
Piazza delle Vettovaglie 32.

Pasticceria Salza
A good place to meet among the arcades of the Old Town for a coffee, a chat, or an evening aperitif. They also sell every Piedmontese cake the heart could desire, and a few savory specialties.
Via Borgo Stretto 44;
Tel 050/58 01 44;
closed Mon.

Parco Regionale di Migliarino, San Rossore e Massaciuccoli

Hiking
A 24-sq-km (9-sq-mile) park located near Versilia, which boasts ancient pine groves, spruce forests, wild boar, and fallow deer.
Pisa
Tel 050/53 92 17;
open weekends from 8.30 until sunset.
www.parks.it/parco.migliarino.san.rossore

Volterra

(See p. 122.)

Museo Etrusco Guarnacci
One of the largest Italian museums dealing with Etruscan history. It provides an insight into the everyday life and culture of this race of mysterious ancient peoples. The exhibits include funerary urns with lids decorated with alabaster or terracotta figures, bronze artifacts, jewelry, and ancient coins.
Via Don Minzoni 15;
mid-Mar–Oct 9.00–19.00 daily, 1 Nov–mid Mar 9.00–14.00 daily.

Museo Storico dell' Alabastro
The splendid private collection of work exhibited in the museum, which is located in a medieval tower, includes local ornamental vases, busts, and small statues dating from the 18th to the 20th centuries, as well as a selection of furniture decorated with alabaster.
Piazza XX Settembre;
9.30–12.30, 14.30–18.30 daily.

From left: The Tuscan sun beats down on Cecina Mare; alabaster objects in Volterra; Castello di Rocca, San Silvestro; the baroque pilgrim's church of Santuario di Montenero at Livorno.

PISA AND THE WEST

The insider tips listed here refer to the sights described in the Highlights chapter (pp. 102–135).

Palazzo Minucci-Solaini

A beautiful Renaissance building housing both the Pinacoteca – a collection of painted masterpieces from Florence, Siena, and Volterra, with works by Signorelli and Ghirlandaio, among others – and the municipal museum. The highlight of the collection is Rosso Fiorentino's 1521 *Descent from the Cross*, one of the masterpieces of Florentine mannerism.
Via dei Sarti 1;
Mar–Oct 9.00–19.00 daily,
Nov–Apr 9.00–14.00 daily.

ALI Alabastri Lavorati Italiani

A family-run firm founded in 1920, producing a range of decorative items in alabaster, such as lamps, vases, sculptures, chess sets, jewelry boxes, and picture frames, as well as bathroom fixtures which can be delivered to your home for a fee.
Piazza Martiri della Libertà 5–9;
Tel 05 88/860 78;
workshop tours by appointment.
www.alialabastro.it

Pasticceria Migliorini

A baker's with a particular regional specialty: *cavallucci* are honey cakes with nuts, candied fruit, and aniseed. Other specialties available include *ricciarelli, cantuccini,* and *ossi di morto.*
Via Gramsci 21;
Tel 05 88/907 35.
www.pasticceriamigliorini.com

Hotel San Lino

This 15th-century building was originally a convent, only becoming a hotel in 1982. The hotel's central location makes it an ideal base from which to explore Volterra. Relax in the small garden, either on the sun terrace or in the swimming pool, or enjoy the Tuscan cuisine served in the La Monarche restaurant or the little courtyard.
Via San Lino 26;
Tel 05 88/852 50.
www.hotelsanlino.com

Villa Nencini

A rustic hotel building located a little way outside Volterra, which promises peace and relaxation by the pool in the grounds. The center of town is only a 15-minute stroll away and many of the rooms have a commanding view of the surrounding area.
Borgo Santo Stefano 55;
Tel 05 88/863 86.
www.villanencini.it

Livorno

Museo Civico Giovanni Fattori

The city museum behind the Villa Mimbelli has works by the 19th-century Macchiaioli group which formed around the Tuscan impressionist Giovanni Fattori. The group looked to nature for inspiration, rebelling against the strict rules and convention of the Italian academies.
Via San Jacopo, Acquaviva 65;
Tues–Sun 10.00–13.00, 16.00–19.00.

Scama

Interesting city tours along Livorno's network of narrow lanes, canals, and quaysides. The canals were constructed to link the port to the city's storehouses.
Via dei Cordai 15;
Tel 05 86/403 28.

Mercato Centrale

The stalls in this vast, typical early 20th-century steel-framed market hall, and those on the square outside, sell locally produced fruit and vegetables, as well as a whole range of ingredients necessary for authentic Tuscan cooking.
Via del Cardinale;
Tues–Sat 9.00–13.00.

Ristorante da Gennarino

The Mercato Centrale, a classic market hall, is well-known for its extraordinary selection of seafood, and the Gennarino is considered one of the best seafood restaurants in town. Livornese specialties and local wine are served on two floors.
Via Santa Fortunata 11;
Tel 05 86/88 80 93;
closed Wed.

Boston

If you're going to be taking one of the ferries for Corsica, Sardinia, or Sicily, this hotel located just round the corner from the quayside is a practical place to stay. Car park with attendant.
Piazza Mazzini 40;
Tel 05 86/88 23 33.
www.bostonh.it

Cecina Mare

Aquavillage

Four waterslides, pools for ball games, a whirlpool, and a large pool with a wave machine should be enough for any water enthusiast, but there is also a go-kart course, quiet areas, and an area for toddlers.
Via Tevere 25;
Tel 05 86/62 25 39.
www.acquavillage.it

Montenero

Santuario di Montenero

Ardenza is exactly 193 m (633 feet) above sea level and the view from the summit is breathtaking. The chapel here, erected in tribute to the miraculous Madonna di Montenero, is considered an important pilgrimage shrine and can be reached by car, funicular railway, or on foot.
7–12.30, 14.30–18.30 daily.

Peccioli

Parco Preistorico

Children keen on dinosaurs will have a great time here – there are models of dinosaurs of all kinds, from T. Rex to the brontosaurus, as well as mammoths, cave-dwelling bears, and Stone Age humans. A great day out for Jurassic Park fans of all ages.
Via dei Cappuccini;
Tel 05 87/63 60 30;
9.00 to dusk daily.
www.parcopreistorico.it

San Silvestro

Parco Archeologico Mineraio

The park has learning trails with information about the long local history of metalwork, and the visitors' center also has an exhibition. You can get to grips with the subject at the ruins of the ancient mining town of Rocca San Silvestro, which was commercially viable until the Middle Ages, and there is a tour down a 360-m (1,200-foot) mine gallery.
Tel 05 65/22 64 45;
Jun–Aug 10.00–19.00,
Sat–Sun 10.00–18.00.
www.parchivaldicornia.it

Arezzo

(See p. 140.)

Tourist Information

The fourth-largest city in Tuscany has a history stretching right back to the Etruscans. Its most important buildings are medieval or Renaissance, and include the cathedral, the church of San Francesco with its unique cycle of frescoes by Piero della Francesca, and several *palazzi* once belonging to the aristocracy. There are museums dedicated to the life of the poet Petrarch (Casa del Petrarca) and the painter and architect Giorgio Vasari (Casa di Giorgio Vasari), among others.
Emiciclo Giovanni Paolo II;
Tel 05 75/182 27 71;
9.00–19.00 daily.
www.arezzoturismo.it

Casa Museo di Ivan Bruschi

Once belonging to Ivan Bruschi (1920–1996), this house now contains 500 objets d'art in many different styles. Bruschi, a passionate and knowledgeable antiques collector, was also the founder of Italy's biggest antiques market, held annually in Arezzo since 1968.
Corso Italia 14;
Tues–Sun 10.00–13.00, 15.00–19.00.

Sansepolcro's cathedral.

Palazzo Bruni-Ciocchi

This early Renaissance building now houses a museum of medieval and modern art, with a good selection of paintings from Arezzo up to the end of the 16th century. The collection includes works by Margaritone d'Arezzo, Spinello Aretino and his son, Parri, as well as Bartolomeo della Gatta and more modern Tuscan artists.
Via San Lorentino 8;
Tues–Fri 8.30–19.30, Sat–Sun 9.00–13.00.

Fiera Antiquaria

Arezzo is a real magnet for antiques enthusiasts – the biggest antiques and flea market in Tuscany is held on the first weekend in the month in its large market square, the Piazza Grande, and overflows into the surrounding streets.
First weekend in month.

Antica Osteria l'Agania

A popular bar and restaurant in the heart of town, serving Arezzo specialties such as *scottiglia*, a chicken, rabbit, and lamb stew; more adventurous gourmets may enjoy *grifi e polenta* (a calves' cheek ragout served with polenta).
Via Mazzini 10;
Tel 05 75/29 53 81;
closed Mon.
www.agania.com

Lancia d'Oro

Pick a warm evening to dine here under the picturesque arches beside the Piazza Grande. The prices in this stylishly appointed restaurant are rather steep, however.
Piazza Grande 18–19;
Tel 05 75/29 58 94;
closed Mon.

Casa Volpi

This beautiful villa is set in grounds on the edge of town, about 2 km (1 mile) from the center. The guest rooms are comfortably furnished and the in-house restaurant has a solid range of Tuscan food, which is sometimes served outdoors in summer.
Via Simone Martini;
Tel 05 75/35 43 64.
www.casavolpi.it

Patio

If your wallet can take it, even the most demanding guest will find every conceivable comfort in this luxury hotel. Living in regal style in an 18th-century palace comes at a price, of course.
Via Cavour 23;
Tel 05 75/40 19 62.
www.hotelpatio.it

Parco Nazionale delle Foreste Casentinesi, Monte Falterona e Campagna

Hiking

Only a third of this national park in the Apennines is actually in Tuscany; visit the protected beech and pine forests and on Mount Falterona you will find the source of the River Arno, which flows through Florence.
www.parcoforestecasentinesi.it

Sansepolcro

(See p. 150.)

Tourist information

Controlled at one time by the ubiquitous Medici family, the town has numerous 14th- and 15th-century towers, the remains of city walls, and an imposing castle. Apart from this, Sansepolcro is geared toward its most famous son, the painter Piero della Francesca. The Museo Civico has a good selection of his works, including the famous fresco of the Resurrection. The master was certainly influenced by local treasures such as the Romanesque cathedral, remodeled in the Gothic period, and the various beautiful *palazzi*. Sansepolcro is also the home of Buitoni pasta, founded by Giulia Buitoni in 1827.
Tel 05 74/74 05 36.
www.comune.sansepolcro.ar.it

Pinacoteca Comunale

A municipal gallery with works by Luca Signorelli. Santi di Tito and Piero della Francesca, who were both from Sansepolcro, are well represented here, with the latter being largely responsible for the collection's international fame.
Via Matteotti 10;
Jun–Sept 9.00–13.00, 14.30–19.30 daily, Oct–May 9.30–13.00, 14.30–18.00 daily.

Da Ventura

The eponymous restaurant in this hotel is famed for its excellent cuisine, serving tasty regional dishes with seasonal ingredients, especially ceps and truffles.

From left: The densely forested mountains of the Passo della Consuma; the Guidi castle in the small town of Poppi; the grounds of the Casa Volpi; the Emperor of China Suite in the very smart Hotel Patio.

AREZZO AND THE EAST

The insider tips listed here refer to the sights described in the Highlights chapter (pp. 136–155).

Via Aggiunti 30;
Tel 05 75/74 25 43;
closed Mon all day and Sun lunchtime.

Borgo Palace

This modern, five-floor hotel is located about 2 km (1.5 miles) beyond the city limits. Don't be deceived by the hotel's rather sober-looking exterior – there is a cozy, warm atmosphere inside and the rooms are elegantly furnished.
Via Senese Arentina 80;
Tel 05 75/73 60 50.
www.borgopalace.it

Anghiari

Tourist information

This *comune* is mostly associated with the painting *The Battle of Anghiari* by Leonardo da Vinci, lost in the mid-16th century and the subject of much speculation since that time. Hugging the hills, the town is almost completely surrounded by a wall with only three gates allowing access: Sant'Angelo, San Martino, and Fiorentina. Picturesque – and at times extremely steep – streets wind their way up to the Palazzi Marzocco and Taglieschi (which are both now museums) and there are several viewing points with a panoramic view over the valley of the River Tiber.
Tel 05 75/74 92 79.
www.anghiari.it

Locanda Castello di Sorci

You have to eat just whatever is put in front of you in this inn – there is only one choice available on the menu each day. However, everything is homemade and very tasty. The set menu, including a starter, soup, pasta, and a meat dish (either duck, chicken, rabbit, beef, or pork), is very good value.
Tel 05 75/78 90 66;
closed Mon.
www.castellodisorci.it

Monterchi

The town

The name Monterchi is said to have been derived from the Latin *Mons Herculis.* While not exactly located on a mountain as the name implies, the town is set on a small hill. The main attraction, housed in its own Museo della Madonna del Parto, is a Piero della Francesca painting of the Virgin Mary in later stages of pregnancy.
Tel 05 75/700 92.
www.comunemonterchi.it

Cortona

(See p. 154.)

Tourist information

As with many towns in Tuscany, Cortona was founded by the Etruscans, although it now has a decidedly more medieval or Renaissance air. The old city walls transport visitors back through the centuries, the streets are lined with numerous *palazzi*, and there are plenty of churches to visit: the 16th-century cathedral, the 13th-century church of San Francesco and, a little further out of town, the 15th-century church of Santa Maria delle Grazie. The museums and churches conceal considerable treasures within, such as Fra Angelico's *Annunciation* in the Museo Diocesano, and there are even a few Etruscan tombs. Of these, the best preserved and most well known is the Tanella di Pitagora.
Via Nazionale 42;
Tel 05 75/63 03 53.
www.cortonaweb.net

Museo dell' Accademia Etrusca

The main hall of this museum is dedicated to local archeological finds dating from the Etruscan period, and highlights of the collection include several bronze statuettes and the bronze *Hanging Lamp of Cortona*, found in 1840, which is decorated with fantastic mythological figures. There is also a collection of finds from ancient Egypt and the Roman period as well as works by the Cortona artist Gino Severini (1883–1966).
Piazza Signorelli 9;
Tel 05 75/63 72 48;
Apr–Oct Tues–Sun 10.00–19.00, Nov–Mar Tues–Sun 10.00–17.00.
www.accademia-etrusca.org

La Grotta

A *trattoria* which is popular with locals and tourists alike. During the summer months, the tables located outside on the terrace are of course the most sought-after. You have to try the specialty wild boar dishes here, including the papardelle served with a wild boar sauce.
Piazzetta Baldelli 3;
Tel 05 75/63 02 71;
closed Tues.

Osteria del Teatro

A popular restaurant situated in rooms belonging to a small 16th-century *palazzo.* Delicious regional cuisine is on offer here, with dishes such as ravioli filled with zucchini (courgette) flowers.
Via Maffei 2;
Tel 05 75/63 05 56;
closed Wed.
www.osteria-del-teatro.it

Athens

The spacious rooms in this reasonably priced hotel are simply furnished and the terrace has a good view of the Old Town.
Via Sant'Antonio 12;
Tel 05 75/63 05 08.

San Luca

The upper floors of the hotel have a good view of the Old Town and about half the rooms have their own balcony. The large terrace has a view of the Lago di Trasimeno, famed for the battle fought on its shores in 217 BC, during the Second Punic War.
Piazza Garibaldi 1;
Tel 05 75/63 04 60.
www.sanlucacortona.com

Poppi

Ristorante Parc Hotel

The restaurant in this 3-star establishment in Poppi's lower town serves fine food from Tuscany and further afield. The house special is homemade pasta or frequently a fish dish, but you can also order a simple pizza if you like.
Via Roma 214;
Tel 05 75/52 99 94.
www.parchoTelit

Chiusi della Verna

Monte Penna

There is a signposted path to the summit of Monte Penna (1,282 m/4,200 feet above sea level) near the entrance to the Santuario della Verna, where St Francis of Assisi once lived.

Siena

(See p. 160.)

Palazzo Chigi-Saracini
Constructed in the 14th century and later extended, this building now houses the Accademia Musicale Chigiani, the city's music academy founded in 1932, which stages classical concerts here during the summer months.
Via di Città 89, Accademia; Tel 05 77/220 91; ticket bookings: Tel 333/938 55 43; Mon–Tues 9.30–12.30. www.chigiana.it

Museo d'Arte per Bambini
A museum for children under the age of 11, which introduces them to local art and art history through the use of theater performances and workshops. Please note that these are suitable for Italian speakers only.
Via dei Pispini 164; Tel 05 77/465 17.

Ferrovia Val d'Orcia
Old steam locomotives pull the carriages along this historic railway through the delightful countryside around Siena. The route follows the Orcia valley, crossing the Crete, before looping round Monte Amiata and entering the Ombrone valley.
Tel 05 77/20 74 13. www.ferrovieturistiche.it

Antichità Monna Agnese
A wide range of antiques is available at this store. There is a second store in the same street (no. 45) selling all kinds of old-fashioned decorative objects and jewelry.
Via di Città 60; Tel 05 77/28 22 88.

Cortecci
A collection of designer fashionwear by Armani, Gucci, Versace, Burberry, and Missoni. The boutique has a second branch at Piazza del Campo 30.
Via Banchi di Sopra 27; Tel 05 77/28 00 96. www.corteccisiena.it

La Nuova Pasticceria
This *pasticceria* has a wide selection of Sienese baked goods, such as *panforte* (a traditional desert containing fruit and nuts) and *ricciarelli* (orange-flavored almond paste cookies) in a charming shop located in the historic heart of Siena.
Piazzale Maestri del Lavoro 9; Tel 05 77/413 19. www.lanuovapasticceria.com

La Stamperia
Along with photo albums, writing paper, and other stationery goods, La Stamperia also offers a reasonably priced and speedy visiting card printing service which is popular with tourists.
Via delle Terme 80; Tel 05 77/28 04 43.

La Speranza
Situated in a fine old house in the heart of the city, the ambience in this restaurant is suitably refined to match its surroundings. Weather permitting, it is very pleasant to sit outside on the terrace and watch the bustle of the people on the Campo while enjoying well-made Tuscan dishes washed down with a good choice from the well-selected wine list.
Piazza del Campo 32/36; Tel 05 77/28 01 90. www.ristoranteallasperanza.it

Medio Evo
The name of this restaurant immediately sets the atmosphere (Medio Evo means "Middle Ages") – the building dates back to the 13th century and the owners try to do it full justice. The menu is traditional also, and patrons can choose from a classic selection of Sienese and Tuscan dishes.
Via dei Rossi 40; Tel 05 77/28 03 15. www.medioevosiena.it

Hotel Garden
This hotel complex located on the edge of Siena comprises a magnificent old villa as well as two more modern annexes, all set in beautiful grounds. The rooms, some of which are furnished with antiques, have all modern comforts and promise a relaxing and restorative stay.
Via Custoza 2; Tel 05 77/56 71 11. www.gardenhoTelit

Hotel Santa Caterina
A well-restored merchant's house with welcoming rooms. Breakfast here is a real treat, served *alfresco* in summer and under glass in a winter garden when the weather is less clement.
Via E. S. Piccolomini 7; Tel 05 77/22 11 05. www.hscsiena.it

Hotel Villa Liberty
This converted 19th-century villa is located just outside the old city walls, so the hotel is easily accessed by car but is only a short walk from the Piazza del Campo in the historic center. The decor and furnishings of the rooms retain the ambience of its origins as a private residence. The hotel has recently undergone extensive renovations, and a charming virtual tour of the accommodation can be viewed on the website.
Viale Vittorio Veneto 11; Tel 05 77/449 66, www.Villaliberty.it

Piccolo Hotel Il Palio
This hotel is housed in an attractive 19th-century villa located on the edge of the Old Town and an easy walk from the Piazza del Campo. The generous breakfast buffet is served in a magnificent vaulted dining room.
Piazza del Sale 18; Tel 05 77/28 11 31. www.piccolohotelilpalio.it

San Gimignano

(See p. 170.)

Museo della Tortura
For those with strong stomachs only: this private collection of medieval instruments of torture offers detailed descriptions (in Italian and English) of their use.
Via del Castello; summer 10.00–20.00 daily; winter weekends.

Azienda Agricola Casale-Falchini
A wine estate near Casale, situated right beside San Gimignano, and famous for its excellent Vernaccia. The old estate house sells red and white wines, grappa, and olive oil.
Via Casale 40; Tel 05 77/94 13 05. www.falchini.com

From left: Picture postcard pretty: much of the Crete is bare, but this picture shows a less inhospitable part; Monteriggioni; the towers of San Gimignano; the Hotel Santa Caterina in Siena.

SIENA AND THE HEART OF TUSCANY

The insider tips listed here refer to the sights described in the Highlights chapter (pp. 156–183).

Dorandò
Just a few paces from the Piazza Duomo, this small restaurant serves good food and delicious wine, and you can admire the work of local artists on the walls.
Vicolo dell'Oro 2;
Tel 05 77/94 18 62;
closed Mon.
www.ristorantedorando.it

Hotel Bel Soggiorno
Many of the rooms in this hotel on the outskirts of San Gimignano have a breathtaking view of picturesque Tuscan countryside. The 13th-century building also houses an excellent restaurant.
Via San Giovanni 91;
Tel 05 77/94 03 75.
www.hotelbelsoggiorno.it

Hotel Da Graziano
Located just a short walk from the historic heart of San Gimignano, the rooms in this hotel, which has been recently refurbished, are modern and comfortable. The pleasant restaurant terrace is candle-lit in the evenings.
Via G. Matteotti 39/a;
Tel 05 77/94 01 01.
www.hoteldagraziano.it

Montepulciano

(See p. 174.)

Spa
The healing springs of Montepulciano were first documented in the 16th century. The waters are piped through to the treatment and therapy areas from 120 m (394 feet) below ground. The sulfur and iodine in the water is thought to be particularly effective for those suffering from respiratory complaints. Along with the medicinal benefits, there is a whole series of spa treatments on offer, such as Kneipp hydrotherapy, various massages, hydro massages, steam baths, as well as beauty and relaxation programmes, and much more.
Via delle Terme 46;
Tel 05 78/79 11.
www.termemontepulciano.it

Azienda Agricola Crociani
This store in the Old Town sells wine, grappa, and olive oil from its own estate, and you can sample all of them. The Azienda also has guest rooms.
Via del Poliziano 15;
Tel 05 78/75 79 19.
www.crociani.it

Consorzio del Vino Nobile di Montepulciano
A wine-growers' consortium based in a stylishly appointed cellar in the Palazzo del Capitano, selling wine and other local produce.
Piazza Grande 7;
Tel 05 78/75 78 12;
Mon–Sat 13.00–17.00, closed Sun, Nov–Apr phone ahead for an appointment.
www.consorziovinonobile.it

Osteria dell' Acquacheta
There is a family atmosphere in this *osteria* in the center of the town of Montepulciano. Great emphasis is placed on the quality of the ingredients to produce delicious dishes.
Via del Teatro 22;
Tel 05 78/75 84 43;
closed Tues.
www.acquacheta.eu

Agriturismo San Gallo
This beautifully restored farmhouse, which is surrounded by vineyards, is located just off the road to Pienza, about 2 km (1.5 miles) from the historic heart of Montepulciano. The estate has a swimming pool and its own lake, as well as lush orchards, olive groves, and vineyards.
Via delle Colombelle 7;
Tel 05 78/75 83 30.
www.agriturismosangallo.com

Hotel Granducato
A modern building located on the outskirts of Montepulciano with well-appointed rooms and ample parking (garage and parking lot). There is a playroom to keep younger guests entertained.
Via delle Lettere 62;
Tel 05 78/75 86 10.
www.hotelgranducato.it

Monteriggioni

(See p. 178.)

The town
With no less than 14 towers, the impressive 13th-century city wall, mentioned in Dante's *Divine Comedy*, is visible from afar. The town is especially worth visiting during the medieval festival held here every summer. Surrounded by horsemen, craftsmen, musicians, acrobats, falconers, and market traders, all dressed in medieval costume, it feels as though you have been sent back in time.
Località Badesse;
Tel 05 77/30 66 56.
www.comune.monteriggioni.si.it

The Palazzo Chigi-Saracini in Siena was built around 1320.

Hotel Il Piccolo Castello
Set in extensive grounds, this elegant hotel has exquisitely furnished modern rooms which conjure up stylish Tuscan living in the 19th century. Two restaurants serving regional specialties, a café, and a spa equipped with a gym, sauna, swimming pool (with its own bar), and jacuzzi help to make a stay here luxurious and relaxing.
Via Colligiana 8;
Tel 05 77/30 73 00.
www.ilpiccolocastello.it

Hotel Monteriggioni
Swim some lengths of the pool in the hotel's pretty garden and as you climb out your gaze will alight on the medieval walls of Monteriggioni – this is Tuscany straight out of a picture book. Each of the rooms is individually furnished in traditional style but with modern levels of comfort and facilities.
Via 1 Maggio 4;
Tel 05 77/30 50 10.
www.hotelmonteriggioni.net

Pienza

(See p. 182.)

Museo Diocesano
This museum, housed in the Palazzo Borgia, is well stocked with diosecan treasures including paintings and sculptures. The focal point of the collection is a richly decorated 15th-century chasuble worn by Pope Pius II (Enea Silvio Piccolomini, the founder of Pienza).
Corso il Rossellino 30;
Tel 05 78/74 99 05;
Mar–Oct Wed–Mon
10.00–13.00, 14.30–18.30,
Nov–Feb Sat, Sun
10.00–13.00, 14.30–18.00.

Calzoleria Pientina
Here, you can commission finely crafted handmade shoes, bags, and wallets, all traditionally made by artisans of the best Italian leather. A simple commission is ready in a couple of days; anything taking longer can be sent to your home.
Via Gozzante 22;
Tel 05 78/74 90 40.

Fiera del Cacio
The "capital city of *pecorino*", as Pienza is known, stages a great festival at the end of each summer which is really a trade fair dedicated to *pecorino*, the hard cheese made from ewe's milk. You can sample various cheeses from the region, all of which are quite delicious, to your heart's content.
Piazza Pio;
first Sun in Sept.

Trattoria La Chiocciola
A family-run *trattoria* with a rustic feel located right in the heart of the model town of Pienza. Simple Tuscan rustic cuisine is served pepped up here to cater to sophisticated modern tastes.
Via M. Mencatelli 2;
Tel 05 78/74 86 83;
closed Wed.
www.trattorialachiocciola.it

Hotel Relais Il Chiostro di Pienza
Guests are welcomed in a former 16th-century monastery. No two rooms are furnished alike, with decorative styles ranging from the romantic to classically elegant and coolly understated. The adjoining restaurant has a large terrace with a view of the Orcia valley for *alfresco* dining on warm days.
Corso Rossellino 26;
Tel 05 78/78 84 00.
www.relaisilchiostrodipienza.com

Chianciano

Museo Civico Archeologico delle Acque
Opened in 1997, this museum is housed in an elegant late 19th-century building. The exhibits in the museum are mainly from the Etruscan period and include objects such as statues, beakers, and jewelry, the majority of which were unearthed in the immediate vicinity of Chianciano. Some of the holdings on display are on loan from private collections.
Viale Dante;
Tel 05 78/304 71;
Apr–Oct Tues–Sun
10.00–13.00, 16.00–19.00.
Nov–Mar Sat, Sun
10.00–13.00, 16.00–19.00,
www.archeochianciano.it

Sensory Spa
The brand new spa situated in the Hotel Continentale and created by Terme di Chianciano is much more than the now quite commonplace spa area you would expect in any hotel of this standard. Four different treatments are offered: purification, relaxation, strengthening, and balancing. The facilities include saunas, hydro-massages, a Turkish bath, aromatherapy, color therapy, music therapy, and mud baths, as well as various water cures based on the water from the Acquasanta spring, one of Chianciano's five springs (the others are called Acqua Santissima, Acqua Fucoli, Acqua Sillene, and Acqua Sant' Elena). The springs are reputed to offer relief from gastro-intestinal, liver, gallbladder, kidney, respiratory, and circulatory complaints.
Piazza Italia 56;
Tel 05 78/632 72.
www.chiancianoterme.com/en/sensory_spa.html

Patry
This is a place for fish lovers: the menu in this restaurant is heavily skewed toward fresh seafood dishes. If you're not so keen on fish, you can opt for a plate of their excellent homemade pasta instead. During the summer months you can eat outside on the pleasant terrace.
Via di Vittorio 80;
Tel 05 78/630 14.
www.ristorantepatry.it

Grand Hotel Excelsior
Guests are welcomed in a luxurious atmosphere that would be familiar to 19th-century spa visitors. The hotel is still family-owned despite the overtures made by various hotel chains. The 72 rooms and 6 suites combine modern comforts with classically elegant furnishings. There are grounds, a sauna, and a swimming pool.
Viale Sant'Agnese 6;
Tel 05 78/643 51.
www.grandhotelexcelsior.it

Hotel Lory
The rooms are modern and elegantly furnished. The Hotel Lory has been family-owned for 50 years and staff take great pains to accommodate guests' wishes. There is a lovely panoramic view of Val di Chiana and Lago di Trasimeno from the hotel.
Viale G. di Vittorio 286;
Tel 05 78/637 04.
www.hotellory.net

From left: Red-brown bricks are common in Siena, where the cathedral is the highest point; Abbazia di Sant'Antimo, Castelnuovo dell'Abate; in Montalcino: Hotel dei Capitani and the pool at the Vecchia Oliviera hotel.

SIENA AND THE HEART OF TUSCANY

The insider tips listed here refer to the sights described in the Highlights chapter (pp. 156–183).

Castelnuovo dell'Abate

Azienda Mastroianni

This wine estate near Montalcino was established in 1975 and is well known for its fruity and soft Brunello di Montalcino, which you can sample and buy here.
Poderi Loretto di San Pi;
Tel 05 77/83 56 81;
Mon–Fri 9.00–12.30, 14.30 –17.00.

Montalcino

(See p. 176.)

Azienda Agricola Pian dell'Orino

This estate is on the Castelnuovo dell'Abate road near Montalcino. Its organic wine, made exclusively from Sangiovese grosso grapes fermented by naturally occurring yeasts, is justly famous. The owners have thoughtfully included a braille translation on their bottle labels.
Loc. Piandellorino 189;
Tel 05 77/84 93 01.
www.piandellorino.it

Castello Banfi

A top-class wine estate and one of the pioneers of organic viticulture in Italy. The adjoining restaurant serves excellent Tuscan cuisine and of course first-class wine. Booking ahead is definitely recommended here. The restaurant closes during the winter.
Castello di Poggio alle Mura;
Tel 05 77/87 75 32.
www.castellobanfi.it

Hotel dei Capitani

The 18th-century rooms in this hotel are nonetheless modern and comfortable. The windows at the front open out onto the bustling life of this little town, while at the rear there is a captivating view across the Orcia and Arbia valleys. There is a swimming pool in the large, panoramic garden.
Via Lapini 6;
Tel 05 77/84 72 27.
www.deicapitani.it

Hotel Vecchia Oliviera

This is surely a Tuscan dream! Where else can you feel as close to the unspoilt countryside as in the (unfortunately all too few) rooms of this hotel, situated at the gates of Montalcino in a building that once housed an old oil press. There is, of course, a large garden, which has a swimming pool with the added pleasure of hydro-massage.
Porta Cerbaia, corner of Via Landi 1;
Tel 05 77/84 60 28.
www.vecchiaoliviera.com

Paganico

Giovanni Nannoni

The grappa produced at this distillery not far from Montalcino is sold not under the company name but under the name of each individual wine-maker: Atesino, Gabbiano, Nittardi, and Verrazzano, for example.
Aratrice 4;
Tel 05 64/90 52 04.
www.nannoni.it

Chiusi

Museo Nazionale Etrusco

The Etruscan Museum on the square in front of the cathedral has a comprehensive collection, including clay and alabaster funerary urns, ornately decorated sarcophagi, wall frescoes, photos of finds from tombs, and much more. Chiusi was one of the 12 city states in the pre-classical Etruscan League (6th century BC).
Via Porsenna 93;
Tel 05 78/22 44 52;
9.00–20.00 daily.

Tombe Etrusche

The road to Lago di Chiusi is lined with Etruscan grave sites which can be visited as part of a guided tour. The Tomba della Scimmia (early 5th century BC), named after a dancing monkey (*scimmia*) depicted in a fresco in the tomb, is just one of the attractions on the tour.
Via delle Tombe Etrusche;
Tel 05 78/22 44 52;
tours only by arrangement with the Museo Nazionale Etrusco.

La Fattoria

Food like mother makes – or, as here, an Italian *mamma* – in a superb location right on Lago di Chiusi. The best time to eat here is in summer, on the terrace by the lake.
Via Lago di Chiusi 48;
Tel 05 78/214 07.
www.la-fattoria.it

La Solita Zuppa

This *osteria* on the edge of the Old Town sets great store by fresh, regional ingredients, and the menu is determined by what is available in the local markets. True to the restaurant's name, soups are a strong suit on the menu. The excellently cooked food is served in an 18th-century dining room.
Via Porsenna 2;
Tel 05 78/210 06.
www.lasolitazuppa.it

Hotel Letizia

The rooms here are simple, but very clean. The simplicity is more than compensated for by good service which tries to meet the guests' every need. Plant enthusiasts will enjoy a tour of the garden surrounding the hotel, where the plants and trees are clearly identified with labels.
Via Roma 26;
Tel 05 75/59 90 20.
www.hotel-letizia.net

Pienza town hall.

Massa Marittima

(See p. 188.)

Museo di Storia delle Miniere
The collection in this museum situated in the Palazzo delle Armi documents the history of the town with special emphasis on mining in the region. There are also tours of a 700-m (2,300-foot) mine gallery on the Via Corridani.
Piazza Matteotti;
Tel 05 66/90 22 89;
Apr–Oct Tues–Sun 15.00–17.30, advance booking required in winter.

Lago dell'Accesa
The volcanic lake at La Pesta, about 6 km (4 miles) from Massa Marittima, is a tempting place to stop for a swim, although both access and space are limited.

Osteria da Tronca
A restaurant situated near the cathedral square serving typical Maremma dishes such as *boccone di prete*, a sort of veal ragout.
Vicolo Porte 5;
Tel 05 66/90 19 91;
dinner only, closed Mon.

Vecchio Borgo
House specialties include hearty meat dishes; everything is prepared over the open fire in the main hall.
Via Parenti 12;
Tel 05 66/90 39 50;
closed Sun evening and all day Mon.

Grosseto

(See p. 190.)

Hotel Maremma
A three-star hotel with its own car park right in the middle of the pedestrianized zone. Most of the rooms are air-conditioned.
Via F. Paolucci de Calboli 11;
Tel 05 64/222 93.
www.hotelmaremma.it

Museo Archeologico e d'Arte della Maremma
This museum has a collection of prehistoric, Etruscan, and Roman finds from towns in the area (such as Roselle and Vetulonia). The adjoining Pinacoteca has several beautiful panels by artists of the Sienese school, such as the graceful *Madonna delle Ciliege* by Sassetta, from the 16th century.
Piazza Baccarini 3;
May–Sept Tues–Sun 10.00–13.00, 17.00–20.00, Oct–Apr 10.00–13.00, 16.00–19.00.

Il Pelagone
From a few vantage points on this 18-hole championship golf course just north of Grosseto, you can see the sea. The course is quite long, and some of the holes negotiate tricky water hazards. There is also a golfing academy and practice center, if you need to polish up your swing before tackling a round.
Tel 05 66/82 04 71;
open every day, booking recommended.
www.golfclubtoscana.com

Bottega del Seggiolaio
The famous rocking chairs beloved of the *butteri* (the Maremma cowboys) are made here, as are other wicker chairs and armchairs.
Via Chiasso degli Zuavi 5a.

La Buca di San Lorenzo
An elegant, almost futuristic gourmet restaurant located in a cellar under the castle wall. Creative dishes are conjured up from local ingredients and in summer you can eat outside on the cathedral square.
Viale Manetti 1;
Tel 05 64/2 51 42;
closed Sun.

Canto del Gallo
This is a good place in which to find simple but reasonably priced food, with dishes such as *cinghiale alle Saturnia cacciatora* (wild boar with hunter's sauce) on the menu. There are also traditional soups and homemade pasta.
Via Mazzini 29;
Tel 05 64/41 45 89;
dinner only, closed Sun.

Pitigliano

(See p. 194.)

The town
This little town has been nicknamed *Piccola Gerusalemme* ("Little Jerusalem") because of the number of Jews who found refuge here in the 16th and 17th centuries from persecution by the Catholic church. The narrow streets of the Jewish quarter and the nicely renovated 16th-century synagogue are among Pitigliano's highlights, along with the Etruscan exhibits in the Diocesan Museum (in the Palazzo Orsini). Also worth a visit are the 16th-century church of Santa Maria and the beautiful baroque façade of the medieval cathedral.
Piazza Garibaldi 1;
Tel 05 64/61 63 22.
www.comune.pitigliano.gr.it

Sovana

Tourist information
Part of the *comune* of Sorano, Sovana clearly experienced two golden ages: the Etruscan period and the Middle Ages. The Tomba Ildebranda (3rd–4th century BC) is the only Etruscan temple grave in a good state of preservation, while medieval highlights include the Rocca Aldebrandesca, an 11th-century castle, impressive frescoes in the church of Santa Maria Maggiore (11th century), and the Palazzo Pretorio, which now houses the archaeological museum and its treasures.
Tel 05 64/61 40 74.
www.sovana.info

The hot healing springs of Saturnia.

From left: A narrow street in Capalbio; Piazza Garibaldi and the cathedral at Massa Marittima; buildings clustered on a tufa plateau: the houses of Pitigliano; hiking trails in the Parco Regionale della Maremma.

GROSSETO AND THE SOUTH

The insider tips listed here refer to the sights described in the Highlights chapter (pp. 184–205).

Sorano

Tourist information

The medieval town of Sorano is built on a hill of tufa rock. The houses are built in a series of terraces that rise up the hillside. Sorano's origins date back to Etruscan times and it was fortified in the 16th century; there is also a 14th-century castle.
Tel 05 64/63 30 99.
www.comune.sorano.gr.it

Castiglione della Pescaia

Tourist information

The small town of Castiglione della Pescaia dates back to the Etruscan period, although the city walls were not built until it was under Pisan rule (10th–13th centuries). There is an upper and lower town, a small marina, and a long stretch of beach, making the town popular with tourists.
Piazza Garibaldi 6;
Tel 05 64/93 36 78.
www.castiglionepescaia.it

Osteria nel Buco

This traditional old restaurant at the top end of town serves tasty, homemade pizzas. A live band will sometimes be there to serenade you.
Via del Recinto 11;
Tel 05 64/93 44 60;
closed Mon in winter.

Pierbacco

Situated right on the promenade. A table on the terrace at Pierbacco in summer, just as the sun is going down, is magical. Regional fish and seafood dishes are served.
Piazza della Repubblica 24;
Tel 05 64/93 35 22;
closed Mon in winter.
www.pierbacco.it

Hotel L'Approdo

A pleasant hotel with a roof terrace, situated right next to the marina. Most of the modern rooms have their own balcony with a view out over the water.
Via Ponte Giorgini 29;
Tel 05 64/93 34 66.
www.hotellapprodo.com

Parco Regionale della Maremma

(See p. 198.)

Hiking

This nature park bordering the coast south-west of Grosseto slopes down to the Tyrrhenian Sea. Various hiking trails leading through the woods here will take you past meadows where the light-gray longhorn Maremma cattle graze.
Visitor Center in Alberese;
Via del Bersagliere 7/9;
Tel 05 64/40 70 98.
www.parco-maremma.it

Talamone

Tourist information

Located high above the sea, this fishing village was a significant settlement in the Etruscan period. During the Renaissance, it was ruled by the town of Siena, whose troops built the castle and fortifications. Talamone is now a suburb of Orbetello.
Via Cala di Forno 2;
Tel 05 64/88 72 28.
www.prolocotalamone.info

La Buca

Located right beside the old city walls, this restaurant specializes in fish and is a good place to try tasty dishes that incorporate the catch of the day (*mare mosso*).
Via Porta Garibaldi 1–3;
Tel 05 64/88 70 67;
Jul–Aug daily, Sept–Jun Tues–Sun.

Porto Ercole and Porto Santo Stefano

Tourist information Monte Argentario

The *comune* of Monte Argentario comprises both Porto Ercole and Porto Santo Stefano; there are 16th- to 18th-century Spanish fortifications to be seen in both towns. Porto Santo Stefano, founded by the Romans, is principally a seaside resort, and Porto Ercole, presumed to have been established by the Phoenicians, has a flourishing leisure marina and several beaches. The church of Sant' Erasmo in the Old Town is dedicated to the town's patron saint, and there is an annual procession of boats in his honor on 2 July.
Via Sant'Andrea 10;
Tel 05 64/81 23 33.
www.tuttoorbetello.com

Orbetello

Tourist information

Situated on the Orbetello lagoon, various peoples and cultures have left their mark on the town. A wall dating back to the Etruscan period, but reinforced by the Spanish in the 16th century, still surrounds the Old Town. The most striking of Orbetello's buildings are also of Spanish origin and are to be found at the Porta Nova, which is also known as the Porta Medinaceli. The little church of Santa Maria ad Portam has beautiful Romanesque frescoes and Orbetello's long beaches attract many visitors.
Piazza della Repubblica 1;
Tel 05 64/86 04 47.
www.tuttoorbetello.com

I Pescatori

The dishes on the menu here are tasty and reasonably priced. Located in a factory loft, there is a good view of the Orbetello lagoon from the veranda of this trattoria.
Via Leopardi 9;
Tel 05 64/86 06 11;
Jun–Sept daily, Oct–May Thurs–Sun dinner only.

Capalbio Scalo

Riserva Naturale Lago di Burano

A coastal salt-water lake near the Latium border and an overwintering place for many birds from northern climes. Guided tours available in the fall and spring.
Tel 05 64/89 88 29.

Parco Nazionale dell'Arcipelago Toscano

Hiking, tours

The Tuscan islands of Capraia, Elba, Pianosa, Montecristo, Giglio, and Giannutri are part of the largest area of marine protection in Europe, covering an area of approximately 600 sq km (234 sq mi) – the Mediterranean monk seal is just one of the creatures to have found a home here. The smaller islands are closed to the public. Various mineral-hunting excursions (for tourmaline, hæmatite, pyrite, aquamarine) can be booked on Elba.
Via Guerazzi 1;
Portoferraio;
Tel 05 65/91 94 11.
www.parco-nazionale-arcipelago-toscano.it

TUSCANY EXPLORER

MAJOR CITIES

For many, Tuscany conjures up images of cypress trees, rolling hills, and the warm Tyrrhenian Sea, along with ancient towns and cities, full of history and heritage. The old city republics tried to outdo each other, constructing increasingly beautiful buildings. Over the centuries, the narrow streets and squares of these towns were filled with beautiful churches, palaces, and building complexes, all containing exquisite artistic treasures. But aside from history and art, many Tuscan towns have plenty for dedicated shoppers, from stylish stores to markets, while the Tuscan cuisine and wine served in the region's many restaurants make the trip worthwhile on their own.

The sights

❶ Duomo Santa Maria del Fiore and its *campanile*
This basilica is Florence's cathedral. Its magnificent dome, erected by Brunelleschi during the Renaissance, is the pride of the city. The *campanile* was designed by Giotto. The varying shades of the marble cladding that characterize both buildings are typical of Tuscany. The interior of the cathedral has impressive cupola frescoes by Giorgio Vasari, painted equestrian monuments to two mercenary leaders by Paolo Uccello and Andrea del Castagno, and a depiction of Dante (see p. 48).

❷ Baptistry
One of the oldest buildings in the city, the baptistry is famed for its doors: known as the "gates of paradise", the Gothic south door was created by Andrea Pisano, and the north door was designed by Lorenzo Ghiberti in 1401 – the great Michelangelo considered the lifelike figures decorating the door as worthy of adorning the gates of heaven. The mosaic on the cupola in the interior should also not be missed. (see p. 54).

❸ Cathedral museum
The cathedral workshop museum has items from the cathedral's history as well as the priceless statues from the baptistry, cathedral, and *campanile*, which have been removed and are now kept here for conservation reasons. These include the original reliefs from the baptistry "Gates of Paradise", sculptures from the Singing Gallery by Donatello and Luca della Robbia, Donatello's *Magdalena* and Michelangelo's *Pietà*, a late work.

❹ Ospedale degli Innocenti
Don't miss Luca della Robbia's famous *tondi*, terracotta roundels of babes in arms, in Brunelleschi's foundling hospital. Giambologna's equestrian statue of Grand Duke Ferdinand I (late 16th century) is to be found on the Piazza Santissima Annunziata.

❺ Galleria dell'Accademia
The original of Michelangelo's *David* has been housed here in the gallery of the Academy of Art since 1873. Michelangelo crafted his masterpiece from a piece of marble which had been abandoned as unusable. The collection also houses unfinished Michelangelo sculptures depicting four slaves and St Matthew, intended for the tomb of Pope Julius II, the *Palestrina Pietà*, and paintings from the 13th to the 16th century (see p. 72).

❻ San Marco
An old Dominican monastery with a museum dedicated to Fra Beato Angelico, who lived and worked here. There is an exhibition of his works which includes the *Last Judgement* and the *Madonna of the Linen Weavers*, and a portrait of the turbulent priest Savonarola by Fra Bartolomeo. Adjoining the museum is the old monastery library and the former monks' cells, which are decorated with frescoes by Fra Angelico.

❼ Palazzo Medici-Riccardi
The Medici family seat is an early Renaissance palace that surrounds a pretty inner courtyard. Don't miss the palace chapel with Benozzo Gozzoli's *Procession of the Magi* and Luca Giordano's baroque long gallery.

❽ San Lorenzo
Donations by the Medici family turned this Brunelleschi church into a jewel of art history. Unassuming from the outside, the interior is beautiful with early Renaissance features, including two bronze pulpits by Donatello, an *Annunciation* by Fra Filippo Lippi, and Brunelleschi's Old Sacristy. Beyond the cloisters, the anteroom of the Biblioteca Laurenziana was decorated by Michelangelo. The baroque Chapel of the Princes and Michelangelo's New Sacristy are accessed from outside the church. Michelangelo also designed the tombs of Giuliano and Lorenzo de' Medici (see p. 78).

❾ Santa Maria Novella and the Spanish Chapel
This 13th-century Dominican monastery church is a great example of Italian Gothic, but also houses Masaccio's fresco of the *Holy Trinity*, with the first recorded use of central perspective, and chapel decorations by Ghirlandaio and Filippino Lippi. In the 14th century, Andrea da Firenze decorated the Spanish Chapel to the left of the church with a magnificent cycle of frescoes (see p. 76).

❿ Palazzo Strozzi
Considered the finest Renaissance building in Florence, construction of this beautifully proportioned building was begun in 1489 for Filippo Strozzi the Elder, an opponent of Cosimo de' Medici.

Eating and drinking

❶ Caffè Gilli
The various cafés on the Piazza della Repubblica have been its focal point for years. The Gilli was founded in 1733 and both locals and tourists stop by for a cappuccino or an aperitif. Much of the interior is still reminiscent of the *belle époque* and in summer the terrace is a great place to relax and watch the people strolling past.

From left: The cathedral is now a symbol of the city; the Palazzo Strozzi's courtyard; Santa Maria Novella's façade incorporates many kinds of marble; the Ponte Vecchio.

FLORENCE

Most city tours begin near the cathedral. Florence's attractions include museums, churches, and many fine works of art – you can even look around a monk's cell. If you tire of the town's cultural sights, there are plenty of elegant boutiques to explore.

Piazza d. Repubblica 36–39r; Tel 055/21 38 96; Wed–Fri 7.30–22.00, Sat–Mon 7.30–24.00.

2 Enoteca Pinchiorri

With two Michelin stars to its name, and a wine cellar holding over 80,000 bottles, you would be right in expecting this restaurant to be on the pricey side. Gourmets can indulge their palates in the exquisite surroundings of a beautiful Renaissance palace. Excellent service. Appropriate dress is expected.
Via Ghibellina 87; Tel 055/24 27 77; closed Sun, Mon and Wed lunchtime.
www.enotecapinchiorri.com

3 Da Nerbone

If you really want to experience the real Florence, hunt down this simple stall located near the bustling Mercato Centrale. You may need to eat standing up, unless you are lucky enough to grab one of the few seats. To order, you buy a ticket first, then place your order at the counter and hand in the ticket. Try a *panino* with *lampredotto*: veal offal, cooked in well-seasoned stock. You won't want to miss out on a glass of the house wine, either. Very good value.
Mercato Centrale di San Lorenzo, entrance on Via del Ariento;
Tel 055/21 99 49;
Mon–Sat 07.00–14.00.

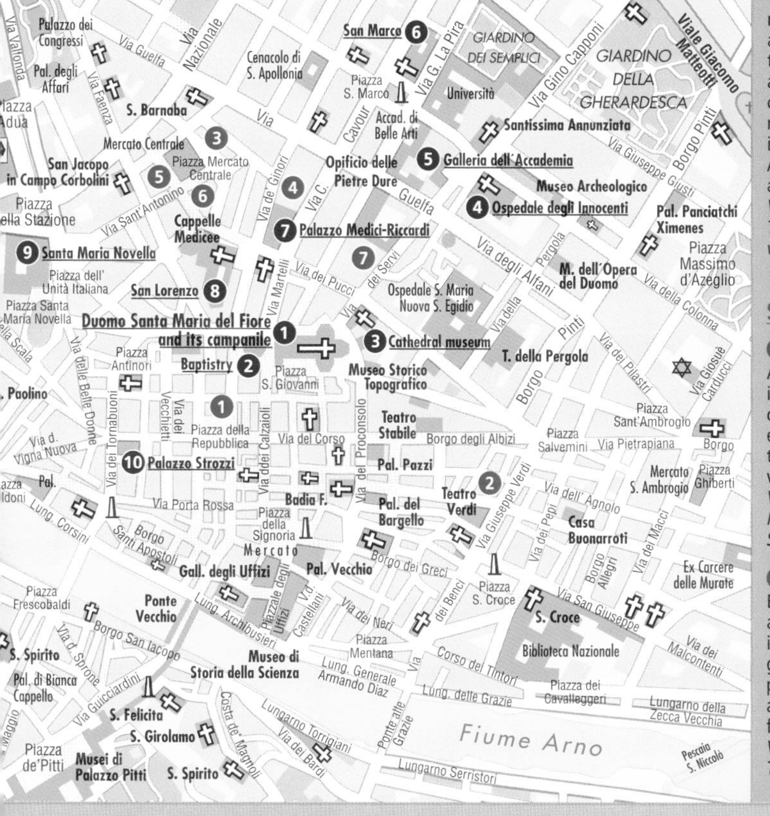

Accommodation

4 Casci

A good family-run two-star hotel just a stone's throw from the cathedral and San Marco. The service is friendly and the rooms are clean; good breakfast buffet. The building dates back to the late Middle Ages.
Via Cavour 13;
Tel 055/21 16 86.
www.hotelcasci.com

5 Azzi

This pensione has only 12 rooms and is frequented by artists and actors as well as tourists. The Azzi is comfortably appointed and has a well-chosen library, a pleasant terrace, a wine cellar, and a Turkish bath. Book well in advance. Arrive by train and you are almost on the doorstep.
Via Faenza 56;
Tel 055/21 38 06.
www.hotelazzi.com

Shopping

6 Mercato Centrale

A food market full of tempting fresh produce for everyone – vegetarians and meat eaters alike: fish and meat on the ground floor, fruit and vegetables on the first.
Via dell'Ariento;
Mon–Fri 7.00–14.00,
Sat 16.00–20.00.

7 Bartolini

Espresso machines (both new and classic models), pans, frying pans, knives, porcelain, glass, and smart designer products. This shop stocks just about everything you need for the kitchen.
Via dei Servi 30r;
Tel 055/21 18 95.

The sights

11 Piazza della Signoria

Passing the elegant stores on the Via de' Calzaiuoli and the sculptural masterpieces (including some by Donatello and Ghiberti) at Orsanmichele, you approach the heart of the city. The piazza, the old political focal point of the republic, is decorated with numerous statues, some of which have a distinctly political edge – Donatello's representation of David and Judith's heroic deeds is symbolic of the courage of the local citizens. Grand Duke Cosimo I is celebrated in the figure of the heroic *Perseus* in the Loggia dei Lanzi, while the face of Neptune on the *Fountain of Neptune* is Cosimo's likeness, and he is represented also in the bronze equestrian statue in the square (see p. 58).

12 Palazzo Vecchio

This well-fortified 14th-century *palazzo* once housed the city regiment. It became the seat of the Grand Dukes under Cosimo I and was remodeled as a magnificent palace. Don't miss the Hall of the Five Hundred, Francesco I's study, and the magnificent reception rooms (see p. 60).

13 Uffizi

Begun by Giorgio Vasari in 1559, the Uffizi was originally used by the city's magistrates (*uffizi* means offices); it now houses one of the world's greatest art galleries, with an exhibition of works from the Gothic period through to the baroque, with works by artists from Giotto and Ducio to Botticelli, Leonardo, Titian, Dürer, Caravaggio, and Rubens.

14 Santa Croce

Despite the Franciscan order's vow of poverty, the Florentines conspired to turn their spacious Gothic "prayer hall" into one of the city's most richly appointed churches. There are works here by Renaissance sculptors such as Giotto and Donatello, as well as the tombs of Ghiberti and Michelangelo, not to mention those of the composers Cherubini and Rossini, the writer and statesman Machiavelli, and the humanist Leonardo Bruni. There are also monuments to Galileo and Dante. Visit Brunelleschi's masterpiece, the Pazzi Chapel to the right of the church, and the museum, with its pride and joy, Cimabue's *Crucifix*, which was badly damaged in the floods of 1966 (see p. 82).

15 Ponte Vecchio

There have been shops on Florence's oldest bridge since the 13th century, but since 1593 only the "better" kind of artisans or tradesmen, such as goldsmiths and art dealers, have been allowed to trade here. By all means indulge in a little window shopping, but don't miss the view of the city and the elegant Ponte Santa Trinità upriver. A secret passage from the Palazzo Vecchio to the Palazzo Pitti is built into the Ponte Vecchio (see p. 66).

16 Palazzo Pitti

This old *palazzo* belonging to the Pitti family was sold to the Medici in 1550. It was enlarged and extended as the main residence of the Grand Dukes of Tuscany, and today its great halls and the Galleria Palatina once again display major paintings by Raphael and Titian, among others. There are also collections of classical paintings, clothing, horse-drawn carriages, and a silver museum (see p. 68).

17 Boboli Gardens

Laid out by the Medici, the gardens have been open to the public since 1766. The combined effect of the park's statues, grottoes, fountains, avenues of cypresses, and natural vantage points ensure it ranks as one of the most beautiful gardens in the Italian style ever created.

18 Santo Spirito

Brunelleschi did not live to see the completion of his second great church after San Lorenzo, but the design of this well-proportioned building is supremely well balanced. It was built on the site of an old Augustinian monastery of which only the refectory remains (now a museum). The fragments of a depiction of the Last Supper and a Crucifixion on the right front wall have been attributed to Andrea Orcagna.

19 Santa Maria del Carmine

One of the most famous early Renaissance fresco cycles by Masolino and Masaccio is to be found in the Brancacci Chapel in this church. Masaccio's *Explusion from the Garden of Eden* is more dramatic and realistic than Masolino's *Fall* (see p. 70).

20 San Miniato al Monte

Situated on one of the highest points in the city, construction on this Romanesque church began in the 11th century. The fresco cycle in the sacristy depicting the life of St Benedict was painted by Spinello Aretino (see p. 86).

Eating and drinking

8 Cambi

One of the oldest *trattorie* in Florence, serving homemade pasta and a selection of regional dishes, including the house specialty: tripe. Sit in the pleasantly air-conditioned vaulted dining room or outdoors on the terrace during the summer.
Via Sant'Onofrio 1r; Tel 055/21 71 34; closed Sun.

From left: Florence has beautiful Renaissance and baroque creations everywhere: the piazza and church of Santo Spirito; the Boboli Gardens; San Miniato al Monte; the Il Cibreo restaurant.

FLORENCE

From the magnificent Piazza della Signoria and the Ponte Vecchio, one of the most famous bridges in the world, to exquisite artistic treasures housed in beautiful medieval buildings such as the Uffizi and the Palazzo Pitti, Florence cannot fail to live up to expectations.

9 Rivoire

The Caffè Rivoire has an enviable location on the Piazza della Signoria and is the café of choice for the Florentine smart set. This comes at a price, as you might imagine, but treat yourself to a cup of the delicious hot chocolate here anyway – it has been a specialty of the café since it opened in 1872.
Piazza della Signoria;
Tel 055/21 44 12;
Tues–Sun 8.00–24.00.

10 Vivoli

Those in the know all agree: if you haven't eaten ice cream made by the Vivoli family, you haven't really "done" Florence. Some insiders even claim that the best ice cream in Italy is served here, so join the queue – it can sometimes be quite a long wait, but the ice cream will make up for everything!
Via Isola delle Stinche 7r;
Tel 055/29 23 34; Tues–Sat 8.00–1.00, Sun 9.30–1.00.

11 Il Pizzaiuolo

Florentine students and well-informed tourists know that the pizza here really is excellent. The prices are reasonable, but the restaurant is tiny so it's best to book.
Via de' Macci 113r;
Tel 055/24 11 71;
Mon–Sat until 24.00.

12 Il Cibreo

Situated right next to the Sant'Ambrogio market, Fabio Picchi runs a number of establishments: a famed gourmet restaurant, a café, the *Teatro del Sale*, and this recommended *trattoria* serving typical Tuscan cuisine. There can be occasional delays in getting a table, but be patient and you will be rewarded with a fine meal.
Via de' Macci 122r;
Tel 055/234 11 00;
closed Sun and Mon.
www.cibreo.com

13 Il Latini

Situated in an outhouse of the Palazzo Rucellai that was once a stable, nowadays you can enjoy authentic Florentine cooking here, served at long tables beneath hams hanging from the ceiling, accompanied by a glass or two of delicious wine.
Via dei Palchetti 6r;
Tel 055/21 09 16;
closed Mon.

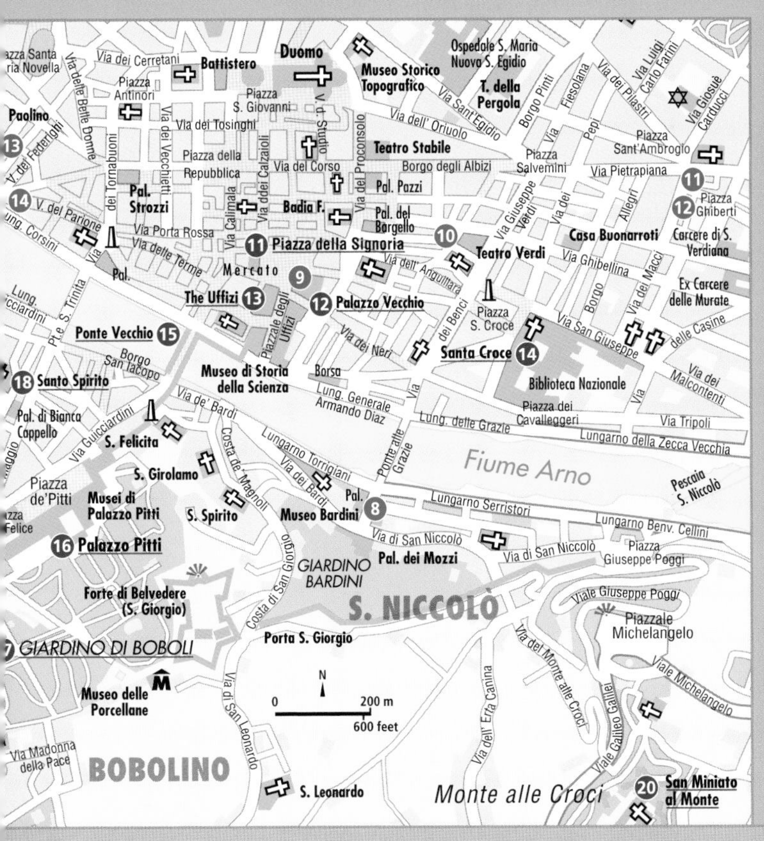

Accommodation

14 Beacci Tornabuoni

The guest rooms of this family-run hotel are situated on the upper floors of a tastefully appointed townhouse and are furnished with antiques. Breakfast is served on the roof terrace so you can take in the incomparable atmosphere of Florence with your morning coffee.
Via dei Tornabuoni 3;
Tel 055/21 26 45.
www.tornabuonihotels.com

15 Boboli

A no frills hotel, and quite reasonable for Florence. Some of the rooms look out over the Boboli Gardens, guaranteeing a magnificent view.
Via Romana 63;
Tel 055/229 86 45.
www.hotelboboli.com

The sights

1 Duomo Santa Maria Assunta
Siena's cathedral was built in the 12th and 13th centuries and is decorated with alternating marble stripes in typical Tuscan style. The Sienese added a choir in the 14th century and began further construction work, which was never completed (the Duomo Nuovo). The richly decorated Gothic façade is as beautiful as the magnificent floor within. Other treasures include a pulpit by Nicola Pisano, sculptures by Donatello and Bernini, and frescoes by Pinturicchio (see p. 160).

2 Museo dell'Opera Metropolitana
The museum is located in the unfinished Duomo Nuovo and contains the original sculptures from the cathedral's façade, many sacred items in gold and silver, works by Pietro Lorenzetti and Simone Martini, and Duccio's *Maestà*, a masterpiece of the Sienese school (see p. 162).

3 Baptistry
The baptistry, built under the eastern bays of the choir, is richly decorated with frescoes. The greatest Tuscan sculptors of the early Renaissance, Lorenzo Ghiberti, Donatello, and Jacopo della Quercia, all co-operated to create the font, which is decorated with depictions of John the Baptist and the prophets (see p. 162).

4 Ospedale di Santa Maria della Scala (Museo Archeologico)
An archeological museum of local Etruscan finds and works from the Roman period, housed in a complex of buildings that once formed a hospital – one of the oldest in Europe. Some of the rooms in which the exhibits are displayed are decorated with fine partially preserved frescoes (see p. 164).

5 Il Campo
The heart of the city, the piazza is surrounded by beautiful *palazzi* in the red-brown brick which is so typical of Siena. A magnet for tourists from all over the world, it is also the site of the *palio*, the famous horse race in which ten bareback riders race horses around the edge of the Piazza. Jacopo della Quercia's *Fonte Gaia*, the old municipal fountain, is also situated here (see p. 166).

6 Palazzo Pubblico
The old – and current – town hall sets the tone: after completion of this Gothic building with its small canopied chapel facing the square, a city statute decreed that all other *palazzi* built on the square had to adapt their façades to match it, creating the consistent and harmonious appearance that still pleases the eye today. There are excellent views of the town and surrounding countryside from the top of the tower; known as the Torre del Mangia, its 505 steps make it the second-highest tower of its kind in Italy. There are world-famous frescoes in the major rooms in the palace's interior, for example Simone Martini's *Maestà* and his *Guidoriccio at the Siege of Montemassi*, and a cycle of frescoes by Ambrogio Lorenzetti (see p. 166).

7 Pinacoteca Nazionale
This gallery located in the Palazzo Buonsignori offers a comprehensive overview of elegant Sienese painting from the 12th to the 16th century, with major works by Guido da Siena, Duccio, and the Lorenzetti brothers.

8 Sant'Agostino
The frescoes by Ambrogio Lorenzetti and Matteo di Giovanni in the Cappella Piccolomini have survived, although this Augustinian church was remodeled in the baroque period. There is also a *Crucifixion* by Perugino, Raphael's teacher, on the second altar on the right.

9 Casa di Santa Caterina
A complex of oratories was built to contain the crowds of pilgrims visiting the house where Catherine of Siena was born (1347–1380). Cycles of frescoes depict scenes from the life of the patron saint of Siena and of Italy.

10 San Domenico
This magnificent Gothic church is closely associated with St Catherine and holds her head in a reliquary. In a chapel near the west end of the church is the only authentic contemporary depiction of St Catherine, by Andrea Vanni, and there are frescoes by Il Sodoma in the Chapel of St Catherine. The church building was founded in the 12th century by the Dominicans as part of their friary.

11 San Francesco
A Gothic Franciscan church situated on a hillside, with magnificent frescoes by Pietro and Ambrogio Lorenzetti in its two choir chapels.

Eating and drinking

1 La Torre
A small but popular *trattoria* near the Campo serving tempting Tuscan cuisine at reasonable prices. Enjoy homemade pasta and *vitello arrosto* (roast veal) in the simple dining rooms. Book in advance or arrive early.
Via Salicotto 7–9;
Tel 05 77/28 75 48 17;
Fri–Wed 12.00–15.00, 19.00–22.00; closed Aug–1 Sept.

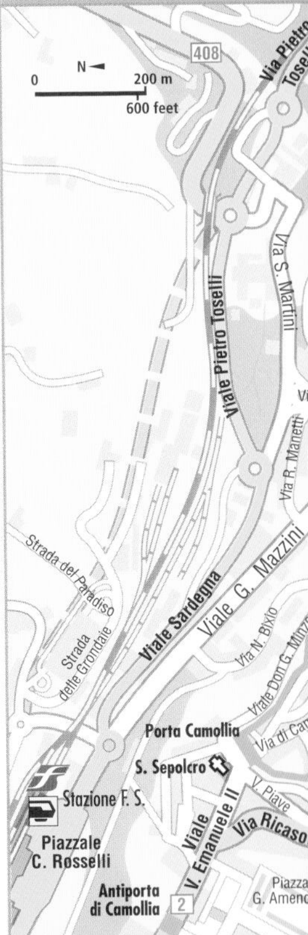

From left: Immaculate reflection: the cathedral of Santa Maria Assunta; the Campo and the Palazzo Pubblico; San Francesco, a Gothic jewel; a salon in the Palazzo Ravizza.

SIENA

Spread over three hills, Siena is yet another jewel in the Tuscan crown: the Campo, one of the most beautiful town squares in the world, picturesque streets, and beautiful churches, it's no wonder the historic center has been designated a UNESCO World Heritage Site.

2 Grotta Di Santa Caterina Da Bagoga

In a quiet side street, away from the very busy Piazza del Campo, this restaurant is run by a former rider in the *palio.* Authentic cuisine both from Siena and from the rest of Tuscany, including *pici* (thick spaghetti) with *ragù, ribollita* (stew), and various meat dishes (such as turkey prepared according to an 18th-century recipe). There is also a selection of excellent wines.
Via Galluzza 26;
Tel 05 77/28 22 08; closed Sun evenings and all day Mon.

3 La Taverna del Capitano

A *trattoria* near the cathedral serving traditional Sienese dishes. Enjoy *pappardelle* with rabbit *ragù, pici* with tomatoes, or various meat-based main courses in a relaxed atmosphere. Game dishes regularly feature on the menu during the hunting season. The homemade desserts are also a temptation.
Via del Capitano 6/8;
Tel 05 77/28 80 94;
closed Tues.

4 Osteria Le Logge

This fine restaurant located directly behind the Torre del Mangia is noted for its down-to-earth Tuscan cooking, and Gianni Brunelli's skills are famed throughout Siena. Locals and tourists alike come here. Try the roast pork with creamed lentils. An excellent wine list.
Via del Porrione 33;
Tel 05 77/480 13; closed Sun.

Accommodation

5 Albergo Chiusarelli

A pleasant three-star hotel in a neo-classical villa built in the 1870s but restored in 2004. A total of 48 comfortable rooms (many with views of the Old Town) are decorated in the same style. The hotel has a restaurant, a terrace, a small garden, and parking.
Viale Curtatone 15;
Tel 05 77/28 05 62;
www.chiusarelli.com

6 Palazzo Ravizza

This charming hotel, situated behind the walls of a Renaissance palace, is an oasis of peace among the narrow streets of the old town. The small lobby with its window seats is comfortably furnished and the garden has a wonderful view of the gentle hills surrounding Siena. There is also a restaurant and parking. The hotel served as an Allied base in World War II, and Helen Frick, JFK, Evelyn Waugh, and Aldous Huxley have all stayed here.
Piano dei Mantellini 34;
Tel 05 77/28 04 62;
www.palazzoravizza.it

Shopping

7 Antica Pizzicheria

This delicatessen, located in the Palazzo della Chigiana, serves delicious homemade local specialties at very reasonable prices.
Via di Città 93–95;
Tel 05 77/28 91 64;
Mon–Fri 8.00–20.00.

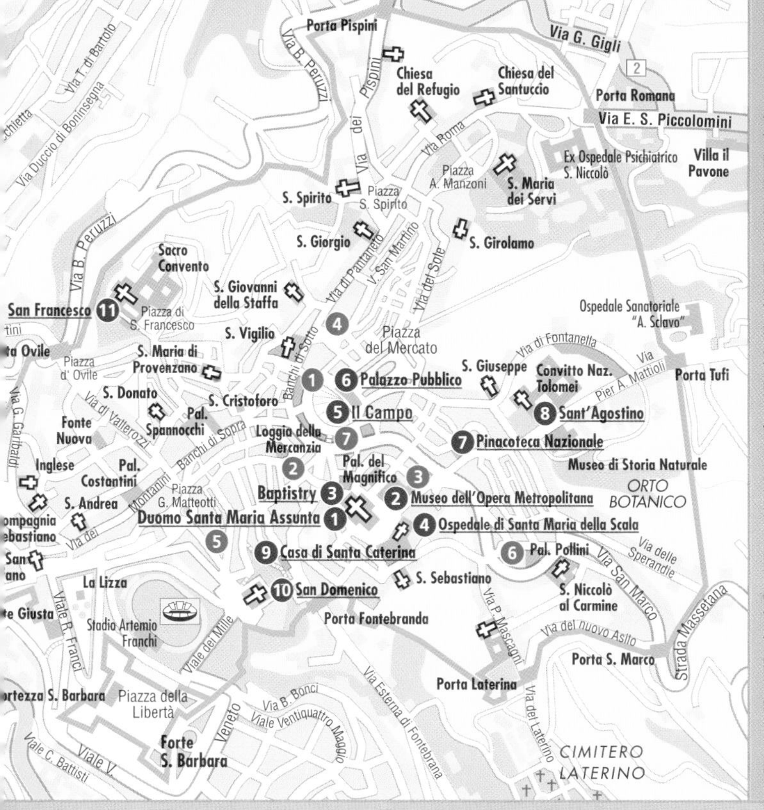

The sights

1 Duomo Santa Maria Assunta
The city financed the construction of its cathedral with booty from a victory over the Saracens in 1063; the result was a spectacular achievement of Romanesque architecture, with five naves and a dome. The façade is composed of colonnades inlaid with marble. The Romanesque bronze Porta di San Ranieri depicts scenes from the life of the Virgin. Giovanni Pisano's pulpit, the mosaic in the apse, and the dome covered in frescoes are of particular note in the interior. The cathedral also contains the bones of St Ranieri and Holy Roman Emperor Henry VII is also buried here (see p. 108).

2 The Leaning Tower
This 55-m (183-ft) bell tower is a Pisan icon and one of Italy's greatest tourist attractions. Built on loose, sandy soil, the *campanile* started leaning even as it was being constructed (from 1173). The final deviation from the vertical amounted to 4.5 m (14 ft). The tower was closed for a considerable number of years while essential building work was carried out to counteract the lean, but it has finally been stabilized and is once again open to the public, for a price (see p. 112).

3 Baptistry
Begun during the Romanesque period, the circular baptistry was completed in a Gothic style, with pointed arches and an impressive cupola, which is topped with a statue of John the Baptist. Nicola Pisano designed the marble pulpit in the interior of the building (see p. 110). He was the father of Giovanni who designed the pulpit in the cathedral.

4 Camposanto
This walled cemetery is also part of the cathedral complex. The inner colonnade is lined with ancient sarcophagi and many funerary relics. The fame of the Camposanto over the centuries has, however, largely rested on its 14th and 15th-century frescoes, especially the monumental *Triumph of Death*. The majority of the frescoes were badly damaged in World War II and are now lost. As the remaining frescoes were being removed for restoration, numerous *sinopie* (preliminary cartoons in ochre paint) were revealed and these are now displayed in the Museo delle Sinopie. The old Jewish cemetery is adjacent to the Camposanto, but beyond the city walls (see p. 116).

5 Piazza dei Cavalieri
The political hub of the city was once a Roman forum and in the Middle Ages the administrative buildings were located here. It was rebuilt in 1550 by Giorgio Vasari at the command of Grand Duke Cosimo I. The newly formed Knights of St Stephen (a military order to combat Ottoman Turks and pirates in the Mediterranean) found a base in the Palazzo dei Cavalieri (whose *sgraffiti* decorations repay closer inspection) and a chapel in the church of Santo Stefano, which is decorated with booty from the sea victory over the Turks at the Battle of Lepanto in 1571. There is also a famous organ here. A statue of Cosimo I now stands on the square and the Scuola Normale Superiore, an elite university, is housed in the *palazzo* (see p. 118).

6 Santa Caterina
A Dominican church built between 1251 and 1310. The bell tower was added during the 14th century. The façade is decorated with 46 busts resembling Roman statuary. There is a fine marble *Annunciation* group from about 1360 in the interior beside the high altar and a fresco of the *Glory of St Thomas Aquinas* (*c.* 1350) on the left wall.

7 Santa Maria della Spina
Cross the river at the Ponte di Mezzo, the oldest bridge over the Arno, pass the old cloth market (Logge di Banchi) and you will reach this church standing right beside the river like a fossilized, filigreed reliquary. It was built in the 14th century along Gothic lines to house a great treasure – a thorn (echoed in the church's name – *spina* means thorn), venerated as a relic of Christ's legendary crown of thorns (see p. 118).

8 San Paolo a Ripa d'Arno
Another church south of the Arno, and worth a visit not least for its beautiful façade, which was modeled on the cathedral. The founding of the church is thought to date back to the 10th century, but it was then modified in the 11th and 12th centuries. It was also modified in the 19th century and again after World War II, when it suffered serious damage. The Sant'Agata Chapel is a free-standing octagonal building dating from the 11th century.

Eating and drinking

1 Ristoro dei Vecchi Macelli
Situated in the historical heart of the city, the home-made green pasta with seafood (*pasta verde con i frutti di mare*) has made this restaurant famous. Locals and tourists alike come here, and it's easy to see why they are so enthusiastic.
Via Volturno 49;
Tel 050/204 24; closed Sun lunchtime and all day Wed.

2 Osteria dei Cavalieri
A small, two-room restaurant in the Old Town, serving a range of freshly prepared Pisan and Tuscan dishes, including tripe *alla pisana*, wild boar, and plenty of fish dishes. The wine list has plenty of local choices.
Via San Frediano 16;
Tel 050/58 08 58;
closed Sat lunchtime and all day Sun.
www.osteriacavalieri.pisa.it

3 La Mescita
A small *osteria* whose menu is much determined by the fresh produce on offer at the nearby Vettovaglie market. Sweet desserts or the good cheese board will round off a wonderful meal.
Via Domenica Cavalca 2;
Tel 050/54 42 94; closed Mon.

4 Antico Caffè dell'Ussero
The café has been indulging its patrons with delicacies since 1794. Be tempted by the *torta con i bischeri*, a cake made with chocolate, sultanas, and pine nuts. The infamous Casanova came here in the 18th century.
Lungarno Pacinotti 27;
Tel 050/58 11 00; closed Sat.

From left: Focal points of Pisan culture and power: the Palazzo dei Cavalieri; the Piazza dei Miracoli with baptistry, cathedral and the Leaning Tower; Tuscan cheeses.

PISA

Once a mighty seafaring republic, this city on the banks of the Arno has seen its maritime importance diminish, but its iconic tower draws thousands of visitors every year. The white Carrara marble buildings on the Campo dei Miracoli attest to its former greatness.

Accommodation

5 Hotel Amalfitana

This very popular hotel, housed in a recently renovated medieval building dating from 1400, is situated only a short walk from the Piazza dei Miracoli. The rooms are air-conditioned and booking in advance is recommended during the high season.
Via Roma 44;
Tel 050/290 00.
www.hotelamalfitana.it

6 Ariston

Situated just around the corner, this three-star hotel has the best view of the Leaning Tower. Comfortable and decorated with plants, the hotel has a terrace where guests can take breakfast – an excellent start to a day's sightseeing in Pisa.
Via Cardinale Pietro Maffi 42; Tel 050/56 18 34.
www.hotelariston.pisa.it

Entertainment

7 Boat trips on the Arno

Take a one-hour boat trip on the River Arno and get to know Pisa from a whole new perspective, just like the merchants, pilgrims, and knights who once followed the river into the town. Maps can be purchased on board. Start from one of the following boarding points: San Paolo a Ripa d'Arno, Roncioni, Piagge, and Renaioli. The *Tour Natura e Bocca d'Arno* will take you to the San Rossore nature park and the mouth of the Arno.
Il Navicello;
Tel 050/54 01 62;
1 Jul–31 Aug.
www.ilnavicello.it

The sights

1 The city walls
The city walls, some 4 km (2.5 miles) long with 12 bastions and six gates, are the largest fortifications of their kind to be preserved in Europe. Lined with plane trees and oaks, the walls have now become a pedestrian promenade and are a popular place to take an evening stroll, having served for centuries to guarantee the independence of a city whose chosen motto is *Libertas* – "freedom" (see p. 31).

2 Duomo San Martino
The San Martino cathedral has a beautiful Romanesque façade and an impressive portico. Other highlights include an equestrian statue of St Martin on the inside wall of the façade and works by Tintoretto and Giambologna. Among the many tombs, don't miss that created by Jacopo della Quercia for the young wife of Paolo Guinigi, the most powerful man in the city at the time. The most precious relic in the church is the *Volto Santo*, or "Holy Face". Legend has it that this figure of the crucified Christ was carved after Jesus' death by St Nicodemus, whose hand was guided by an angel. The work was miraculously transported to Lucca in the 8th century and is said to have worked further wonders there. To this day the relic is carried round the city in a procession held annually on 13 September. The cathedral museum is located in the former bishop's palace, which exhibits the cathedral's treasures and various historic sculptures (see p. 32).

3 Santa Maria Forisportam
The church of St Mary was built, as the name suggests, outside the Roman city walls around 1200 and later extended. Here too, there is a façade with arcades and galleries, a feature typical of Pisa and Lucca. Two altarpieces by Guercino adorn the interior.

4 Palazzo dei Guinigi
Every visitor to Lucca should climb the mighty tower of the Guinigi family's *palazzo*, not for the curiosity of the oak trees planted on the top, but for the magnificent view.

5 Piazza del Mercato
The square still retains the oval shape of the Roman amphitheater which once occupied this site. It was destroyed during a time of tribal migration, and the houses built on its foundations have a mixture of classical and medieval features (see p. 30). The only market still held here takes place in December, but concerts are sometimes held in the square in the summer.

6 San Frediano
Legend has it that there was a church on this site as early as the 6th century. The current building is Romanesque, with a few later alterations and additions. The façade mosaic of the *Ascension of Christ* dates back to the 13th century. The highlight of the interior is the Romanesque font. The second chapel on the left houses Amico Aspertini's representation of the story of the *Volto Santo* (Holy Face).

7 Palazzo Pfanner
Set in beautiful grounds dating back to the 18th century, this *palazzo* has formal rooms decorated with frescoes and fittings of a similar age. There is also an exhibition of surgical instruments collected by Dr Pietro Pfanner.

8 San Michele in Foro
This was the site of the forum during the Roman period, and the church here dates back to the 12th century, although this was preceded by an earlier building. The façade, with its *loggie* and depictions of wild animals and hunters, is topped with a statue of the Archangel Michael. A painted crucifix from around 1200 and a painting of four saints by Filippino Lippi are the most significant works of art to see inside (see p. 31).

9 Casa di Puccini
Giacomo Puccini was born in 1858 in his parents' house in Lucca, which is now open to the public. Here you can gaze upon portraits, opera costume designs, one of the maestro's own pianos, and many other mementos, although you may get closer to the real man at the Museo Villa Puccini in Torre del Lago.

10 Palazzo Ducale
Once called the Palazzo della Signoria, the Palazzo Ducale was begun in 1578 by Bartolomeo Ammanati but completed only in 1730. The modern façade dates back to the Napoleonic era, when the interior was also altered. The statue that stands in front of the *palazzo* is of Elisa Baciocchi, Napoleon's sister, who lived here from 1805 to 1815, first as the redoubtable Princess of Piombino and then from 1809 as the Grand Duchess of Tuscany.

Eating and drinking

1 Da Giulio in Pelleria
A popular and airy *trattoria* with an authentic feel that attracts as many locals as it does tourists and students. The friendly staff will explain the menu and talk about the hearty Lucchese cuisine that is served here. Try the tasty homemade *zuppa di pane con verdure* (bread soup with vegetables), which is a real specialty here.

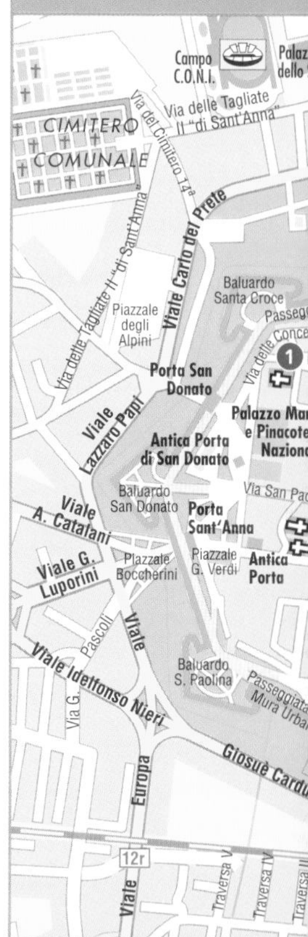

From left: Built over an amphitheater: the oval Piazza del Mercato; San Michele; the Puccini monument in front of the Casa di Puccini; the foyer of the Hotel Universo.

LUCCA

Once a Roman city, Lucca has retained its Roman layout and the medieval streets of its wonderful Old Town. Romanesque churches, beautiful squares, and smart stores make this old cloth merchants' city a great place in which to stay.

Via delle Conce 45; Tel 05 83/559 48; closed Sun.

2 Osteria Baralla

This friendly *trattoria*, located near the Piazza dell'Anfiteatro, has been welcoming guests with delicious dishes such as *agnello nostrale arrosto* (roast lamb) and *polpette di Baralla* (homemade meatballs) since 1860. The tempting desserts are also homemade, and the wine list is extensive.

Via Anfiteatro 5; Tel 05 83/44 02 40; closed Sun. www.osteriabaralla.it

3 Antico Caffè di Simo

This most entrancing *belle époque* café in Lucca has nostalgically elegant rooms, which are still beautifully furnished with the original fixtures and fittings.
Via Fillungo 58; Tel 05 83/49 62 34; closed Mon. www.caffedisimo.it

4 Trattoria Da Leo

This popular *trattoria*, which has been in business for over 50 years, is never short of customers. Locals and tourists alike sit back and enjoy old-fashioned hospitality and simple, rustic Tuscan dishes such as *ribollita*, *zuppa di farro*, *pici al ragù toscano*, and *ravioli porcini* in a relaxed, family atmosphere.
Via Tegrini 1; Tel 05 83/49 22 36. www.trattoriadaleo.it

Accommodation

5 Piccolo Hotel Puccini

Situated just round the corner from the Piazza San Michele, this romantic old hotel is right in the heart of Lucca. Traditionally decorated, with a smart interior and comfortable rooms; the hotel bar has a view of the narrow street. The hotel is named after the great Lucchese composer Giacomo Puccini, who was born near the hotel.
Via di Poggio 9; Tel 05 83/554 21. www.hotelpuccini.com

6 Hotel Universo

A historic *palazzo* with a central location on the bustling Piazza del Giglio. The *palazzo* was built some time in the 16th century and became a hotel in 1857. All 56 rooms are decorated in the classical style; some of the rooms have marble baths and offer a view of the piazza or the tree-lined Piazza Napoleone.
Piazza del Giglio 1; Tel 05 83/49 36 78. www.universolucca.com

Shopping

7 La Cacioteca

A wonderful delicatessen selling fresh produce and food from the region, such as sheep's cheese, hams, and olive oil.
Via Fillungo 242; Tel 05 83/49 63 46.

8 Cariola

A small household goods store on the piazza selling artisan ceramics from the Tuscan area at fairly reasonable prices.
Piazza San Michele 10; Tel 05 83/476 77.

The sights

❶ The town wall and towers

When you enter the town through the imposing Porta San Giovanni, an old pilgrim's route will take you past *palazzi* into the central part of town. The 15 towers that remain of the 72 that were here at one time are indications of San Gimignano's former wealth, but they are more than mere symbols of prosperity; a succession of internecine feuds caused the local nobility to construct the towers as places of refuge. Well-preserved sections of wall provide proof of the town's readiness to defend itself against attack from further afield. The principal aggressor was the neighboring town of Volterra. There is a well dating back to 1273 in the picturesque Piazza della Cisterna in the middle of town, and during the summer months this magical setting becomes the backdrop for opera performances.

❷ Collegiata Santa Maria Assunta

Founded in the 12th century, this church was altered in the 15th century and although it is known as a "cathedral", it was never an episcopal seat. Enter via the flight of steps outside and admire the frescoes within. The oldest, in the nave, are from *circa* 1350 and depict scenes from the life of Christ, arranged in three rows on the right. Barna di Siena is credited with their creation and is also said to have died in a fall from the scaffolding as he was painting them. The frescoes on the left-hand side, the work of Bartolo di Fredi, are slightly more modern and show scenes from the Old Testament. There is a depiction of the *Last Judgement* on the entrance wall by Taddeo di Bartolo and beneath this is Benozzo Gozzoli's *Martyrdom of St Sebastian*. There is also a group of wooden figures by Jacopo della Quercia depicting the *Annunciation*. Domenico Ghirlandaio decorated the chapel of St Fina, who was born and lived in San Gimignano, with beautiful frescoes depicting the saint's life (see p. 171).

❸ Palazzo del Popolo

Once the *palazzo* of the town's Great Council, the building dates back to the 13th century and has been extended and altered considerably over the years, as can be seen from the varied construction of the walls. There is a pretty *loggia* (with a fresco of the Madonna) and a beautiful courtyard. The Sala Dante in the museum on the first floor is a reminder that the poet came here as an envoy from Florence to negotiate a treaty in 1300. Only a few years later, Lippo Memmi was to decorate the Council Chamber and other rooms with a *Maestà*, an image of the enthroned Madonna, and a picture of the town's patron saint, San Gimignano. In the gallery on the second floor there is an early crucifix by Coppo di Marcovaldo, a picture of the Madonna by Pinturicchio, and other works by Gozzoli and Filippino Lippi. The Torre Grossa, the 54-m (177-foot) *palazzo* tower, is open to the public and commands stunning views of the town and of the hills surrounding it.

❹ Palazzo del Podestà

The mayor's *palazzo* was begun in 1239 and extended in 1337. Its 51-m (167-foot) tower, known as La Rognosa, is one of the oldest in the town. A decree issued at the time forbade the construction of privately owned buildings that exceeded the height of the tower.

❺ Sant'Agostino

This 13th-century church, the second-largest in San Gimignano, is located in the north-west of the town. Like the Collegiata, it is also richly decorated with major frescoes and sculptures. Benozzo Gozzoli's depiction of angels removing arrows from the body of St Sebastian is to be found beside the pulpit and the *Coronation of the Virgin* on the high altar (1483) is Piero Pollaiuolo's masterpiece. The walls of the main choir chapel are also decorated with frescoes by Benozzo Gozzoli; these depict scenes from the life of St Augustine, from his days as a student to his death and burial. The nave of the church is also worth seeing.

❻ Porta delle Fonti

If you would like to see where the townswomen – or their maids – drew their water and washed their linen in times gone by, head for the Fonti Medievali, the public well and washhouses by the Porta delle Fonti, to see the arcades and enormous basins. Parts of the well complex date as far back as the 12th century. The round-arched arcades are Romanesque and the pointed Gothic arches are from the 13th century, while the wider arches are 14th century.

Eating and drinking

❶ Gelateria di Piazza

If you have a sweet tooth, head straight for the ice cream experts at Sergio Dondoli's ice cream emporium, where they count many celebrities among their clients. People have been known to drive here specially for a delicious end to a main meal taken at home. The assortment of flavors is overwhelming – try the chocolate creations!
Piazza della Cisterna 4;
Tel. 05 77/94 22 44.

❷ Ristorante La Griglia

Try the Tuscan cuisine dished up under the vaulted roof of this restaurant located in the medieval tower of the Palazzo Pesciolini – they specialize in game dishes and there is, of course, homemade pasta.
Via San Matteo 34/36.

❸ Le Vecchie Mura

Tasty pizza and pasta dishes are served here in the old stables by the city wall. The panoramic terrace has a wonderful view. Try *ribollita*, wild boar in Vernaccia wine, Florentine beefsteak, and white beans.
Via Piandornella 15;
Tel. 05 77/94 02 70;
From 18.00.
www.vecchiemura.it

❹ Dorando

A small restaurant with a medieval feel: Tuscan cuisine drawing on old Etruscan and Medici-era recipes and a selection of good wines. The interior is hung with works by local artists.
Vicolo dell'Oro 2;
Tel. 05 77/94 18 62;
12.00–14.30, 19.00–21.30.
www.ristorantedorando.it

From left: The medieval towers of San Gimignano can be seen from a distance: Sant'Agostino; the Piazza della Cisterna; the entrance to the hotel L'Antico Pozzo.

SAN GIMIGNANO

This beautiful old town is now a UNESCO World Heritage Site. It is well known for its medieval buildings, in particular its many towers, and the white wine Vernaccia di San Gimignano, which is produced in the vineyards around the town.

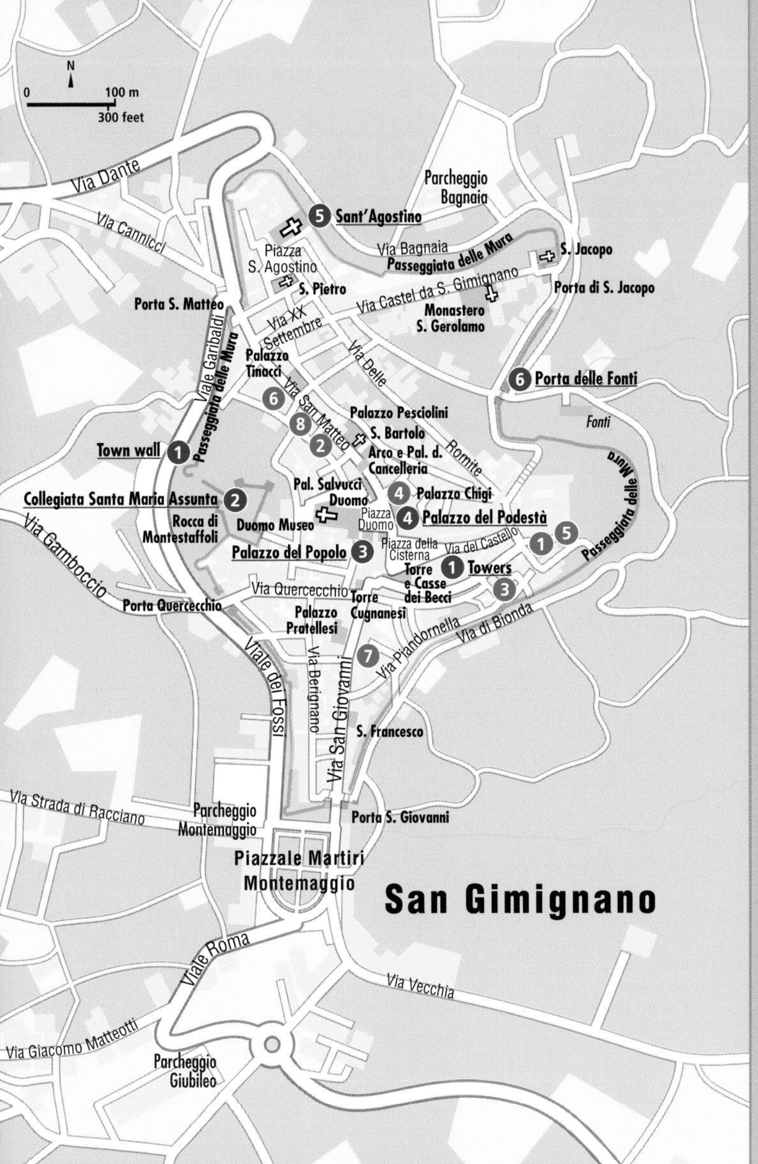

Accommodation

5 Leon Bianco
Centrally located on the Piazza della Cisterna, this 11th-century *palazzo* exudes a friendly charm. The renovated rooms are comfortable and well furnished. Take breakfast in the courtyard.
Piazza della Cisterna 13; Tel. 05 77/94 12 94. www.leonbianco.com

6 L'Antico Pozzo
This renovated building has retained the original charm and style of a 15th-century townhouse. The hotel is named after the medieval well near the hotel reception. Local legend has it that maids who refused their lord and master his *droit de seigneur* were suspended in the well shaft for three days and nights.
Via San Matteo 87; Tel. 05 77/94 20 14. www.anticopozzo.com

Shopping

7 Convento San Francesco
The Azienda Agricola Tollena wine estate has an outlet in the town in a former monastery, where you can buy Vernaccia, Chardonnay, and Sangiovese wines, along with other regional Tuscan products such as olive oil, balsamic vinegar, honey, and preserves.
Via San Giovanni 71. www.tollena.it

8 Bottega d'Arte Povera
Arte povera means "poor art", but the selection of arts and crafts here is anything but and extremely wide: the finest olive wood bowls and plates, wickerwork, and terracotta.
Via San Matteo 83; Tel. 05 77/94 19 51.

TUSCANY EXPLORER

ROAD TRIPS

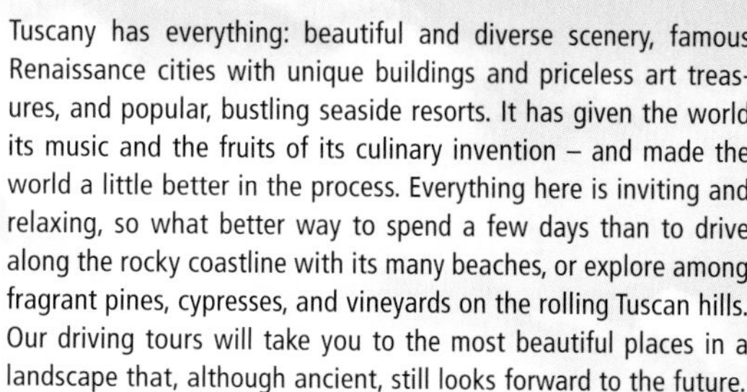

Tuscany has everything: beautiful and diverse scenery, famous Renaissance cities with unique buildings and priceless art treasures, and popular, bustling seaside resorts. It has given the world its music and the fruits of its culinary invention – and made the world a little better in the process. Everything here is inviting and relaxing, so what better way to spend a few days than to drive along the rocky coastline with its many beaches, or explore among fragrant pines, cypresses, and vineyards on the rolling Tuscan hills. Our driving tours will take you to the most beautiful places in a landscape that, although ancient, still looks forward to the future.

Dining out

1 Buca di Sant'Antonio
Rustic dishes such as *coniglio in umido con olive* (braised rabbit with olives) and fresh homemade pasta such as *maccheroni lucchesi* feature on the menu of this restaurant, which is one of the most famous in Lucca. Here, traditional Lucchese recipes are combined with modern cuisine with great skill.
Via della Cervia 3, Lucca; Tel 05 83/558 81. www.bucadisantantonio.com

2 Ristorante Pirana
Dino Giannini and Gian Luca Santini have been running this excellent restaurant for 40 years. The fish and seafood dishes are superb.
Via Valentini Giuseppe 110, Prato; Tel 05 74/257 46. www.ristorantepirana.it

Accommodation

3 Hotel Patria
This simply furnished but comfortable hotel in Pistoia has 28 rooms and is located in a side street right in the middle of town. From the top floor there is a magnificent view of the cathedral.
Via Crispi 8, Pistoia; Tel 05 73/251 87. www.patriahotel.com

4 Villa San Michele
This romantic hotel and its beautiful grounds are located in a 15th-century monastery on a hill with a magnificent view of Florence. A medium-sized hotel with 46 rooms and 25 suites. Tuscan cuisine is served in the restaurants.
Via Doccia 4, Fiesole; Tel 055 567 82 00. www.villasanmichele.com

The sights

1 Massa
Pretty much everything in Massa, the capital of the province of Massa-Carrara, is in some way connected with marble and what can be made out of it (though the results are of varied artistic merit). Situated on a hill, the medieval upper town is dominated by the imposing Castello Malaspina, one of the largest fortresses in Tuscany, dating back to the 11th century. The lower, or "new" town (Massa Nuova), with the Frigido river running through it, was built on the plain in the 16th century and shows the architectural influence of the cathedral of Santi Pietro e Francesco, originally Gothic but later redesigned. The last remodeling was carried out in the 1930s, when a neo-classical façade of Carrara marble was fitted. The focal point of the lower town is the Piazza degli Aranci with its obelisk fountain. The Palazzo Cybo Malaspina, with its magnificent early 18th-century baroque façade, lies on the south side of the square, which is lined with orange trees.

2 Pietrasanta
Pietrasanta lies at the foot of the Apuan Alps in Versilia, as this part of Tuscany is known. This is another Tuscan town that depends on the working of marble; the stone is the mainstay of both the town's economy and its artistic pursuits. Countless sculptors and masons have taken up residence here and countless marble copies of classical statues are produced in their workshops. The charming brick *campanile* of the 13th-century cathedral of San Martino is architecturally interesting, and the town's other highlights include the 16th-century Torre dell' Orologio (clock tower), the 14th-century church of Sant' Agostino, and the 17th-century Palazzo Moroni. The town was named after Guiscardo Pietrasanta, the Lucchese count who founded the town in the 13th century.

3 Lucca
With its *palazzi*, towers, and well-preserved 16th-century walls, Lucca is generally considered one of the most charming cities in Tuscany – a stroll through the atmospheric streets of its historic Old Town is a must for all visitors. The 11th-century cathedral of San Martino is the most important sacred building in Lucca, with a Gothic interior constructed between the 13th and 15th centuries. A series of Romanesque arches and columns line the exterior of San Michele in Foro – it was built on the site of the old Roman forum. Medieval merchants' houses still surround the Piazza San Michele, which has been the town's focal point for centuries. The adjacent Guinigi family villa has an unusual tower with trees growing on it – said to have been planted by the lord of Lucca as a way of making the building look taller to demonstrate his wealth and power; the view of the city's red roofs from the top is unparalleled. Round off your visit with a stroll round the 11 bastions and 4 km (2.5 miles) of city wall, enjoying the superb views of the Serchio valley and beyond. The town's most famous son is the great opera composer Giacomo Puccini, who was born at Corte San Lorenzo 9 (see pp. 30 and 236).

4 Pescia
This small town in the province of Pistoia lies along both banks of the eponymous river and is famous for paper production and cut flowers. The town is strangely divided between the sacred and the profane: religious buildings, such as the 17th-century cathedral and the church of San Francesco, are situated in the right-hand part of town, on the eastern bank, while all the municipal buildings, such as the town hall, are in the western half. *Palazzi* and merchants' houses such as the Palazzo Galeotti and the Palazzo della Podestà are typical of the architecture in the Old Town.

5 Montecatini Terme
Tuscany's largest spa town is also one of the most famous spas in Europe: the warm springs with their soda, sulfates, water regimes, bathtubs, and mud packs provide relief from all kinds of ailments. The spa business was promoted by visits from the Grand Duke, and later Emperor, Leopold II in the late 18th century. The neo-classical Terme Tettuccio are among the town's most beautiful buildings. Apart from the spa treatments, Montecatini offers many other cultural entertainments, including film festivals and fashion shows. There is a funicular railway to take spa visitors to medieval Montecatini Alto, from which there are excellent views of the surrounding hills (see p. 36).

From left: A bridge links the two halves of Pescia; the church of San Michele in Foro is situated on the site of Lucca's old forum; Prato's cathedral has an external pulpit.

FROM MASSA TO FIESOLE

A tour of northern Tuscany leads from the Apuan Alps, via the city walls of Lucca and the spa at Montecatini Terme, to Florence, ending in the Etruscan town of Fiesole. Allow two to three days.

6 Pistoia

A lively town in the Ombrone valley, surrounded by a riot of shrubs and flowers in the local nurseries and allotments. There are plenty of tempting markets here, and the 8th to 9th century church of Sant'Andrea, with its legendary Pisano pulpit (1298), is also worth a visit. The cathedral square, surrounded by medieval buildings such as the bishop's palace, the 13th to 14th century Palazzo Communale, and the 14th-century Palazzo del Podestà, is the heart of the Old Town. The Romanesque cathedral of San Zeno has a 66-m (119-foot) *campanile*. North of the square, the cloistered arcade of the 13th-century Ospedale del Ceppo has an eye-catching majolica frieze (see p. 38).

7 Prato

Prato, Tuscany's third-largest city, is a daring mixture of medieval and modern in terms of architecture. Wool weavers settled in this city of textile factories as early as the Middle Ages, and the historic Old Town is surrounded by a wall. The cathedral, Santo Stefano, whose construction betrays both Pisan and Lucchese influences, lies within the wall; the external pulpit (1434–38) catches the eye immediately. The imposing Castello dell'Imperatore was built by the German emperor Frederick II between 1237 and 1248, and the church of Santa Maria delle Carceri, which was built in the second half of the 15th century, is located opposite (see p. 42).

8 Florence

No other city has influenced the history of western art as much as Florence; the Renaissance was born here, and the cultural palette is as rich today as it ever was. A good way to start your visit is by taking a look at Florence from above – walk up to the Piazzale Michelangelo, 104 m (340 feet) above the Old Town, and enjoy the great views of the picturesque city across both banks of the Arno. Florence is very tourist friendly by nature in that almost all the sights in the Old Town can be reached on foot. Brunelleschi's magnificent octagonal dome on the cathedral of Santa Maria del Fiore (1294–1436) dominates the central part of town, and opposite it lies the 11th to 13th century baptistry of San Giovanni, with its bronze doors designed by Pisano and Ghiberti. The latter's Gates of Paradise in particular display a unique expressiveness. The famed Uffizi Gallery houses one of the greatest art collections in the world and the Ponte Vecchio crosses the Arno nearby; the city's oldest bridge is crowded with jewelers and goldsmiths. The bridge escaped damage during World War II, though it suffered considerably in the devastating flood of 1966. The Via Calzaiuoli leads to the Piazza della Signoria, the most beautiful square in the city (see pp. 48 and 228).

9 Fiesole

Enjoy the beautiful panoramic view of Florence from this 6th-century Etruscan town. Nestling between two hills above the city, it was a refuge from the oppressive heat of summer for Florentine aristocrats in centuries past. The town's charms seduced foreigners too: the American writers Gertrude Stein and Alice B. Toklas spent summers here at the beginning of the 20th century. The Piazza Mino da Fiesole lies at the heart of the town, where you will find the cathedral of San Romolo, which was begun in 1028. Well-preserved Roman finds have been discovered to the north-east of the cathedral (see p. 88).

The sights

1 Carrara

From a distance, the splashes of white dotted about the landscape look like snow: there are excavated quarries everywhere you look. Carrara has been known since Roman times for the unique quality of its fine-grained marble – Michelangelo toured the quarries himself to find the appropriate raw material for his famous statue of *David*. Visit the spectacular quarries, but don't miss the Museo Civico del Marmo: the marble museum is located just outside the town and illustrates quarrying techniques reaching back into antiquity. The imposing marble cladding of the Duomo Sant'Andrea on the Piazza Alberica is also worth seeing, as are the works of art inside. The three-naved basilica was begun in the 11th century and completed in the 14th century (see p. 24).

2 Forte dei Marmi

This urbane resort lies on the Riviera Versiliese in the province of Lucca. Today it is one of the most popular seaside resorts in the region, although it began life simply as a jetty used to load marble and other goods. The town's symbol is the fortress (Il Fortino) on the Piazza Garibaldi; it was built in 1788 and gave the town its name. European nobility, artists, industrialists, and diplomats have frequented the town for more than 100 years, as can be seen from the beautiful parks, the elegant villas, and the summer residences. The town is also noted for its excellent art galleries, including the unusual Museum of Satire and Caricature housed in the old fortress.

3 Viareggio

This town makes its living principally from tourism, though there is some marble carving too. A former fishing village, it was discovered by the European upper classes in the 19th century, as can be witnessed from the numerous "gingerbread house" villas and the art nouveau buildings. The palm-lined promenade of Versilia's major seaside resort boasts miles of fine hotels, pensiones, stores, boutiques, restaurants, and cafés. Viareggio's famous carnival, of which the highlights are the masked balls and the parades of beautifully crafted and animated papier-maché floats, has taken place annually since 1873.

4 Pisa

Pisa is still universally associated with the Leaning Tower (1175) on the Campo dei Miracoli; however, the tower is just part of the extraordinary complex that includes the cathedral (construction work began here in 1063), the cemetery (1278), and the baptistry (built 1152–1284). The whole complex was designated a UNESCO World Heritage Site in 1987. A city of merchants, Pisa's influence in Italy was once second to none – indeed, it was considered to be the "queen of the seas" – but it was eventually ousted from this position by its powerful rivals, Genoa and

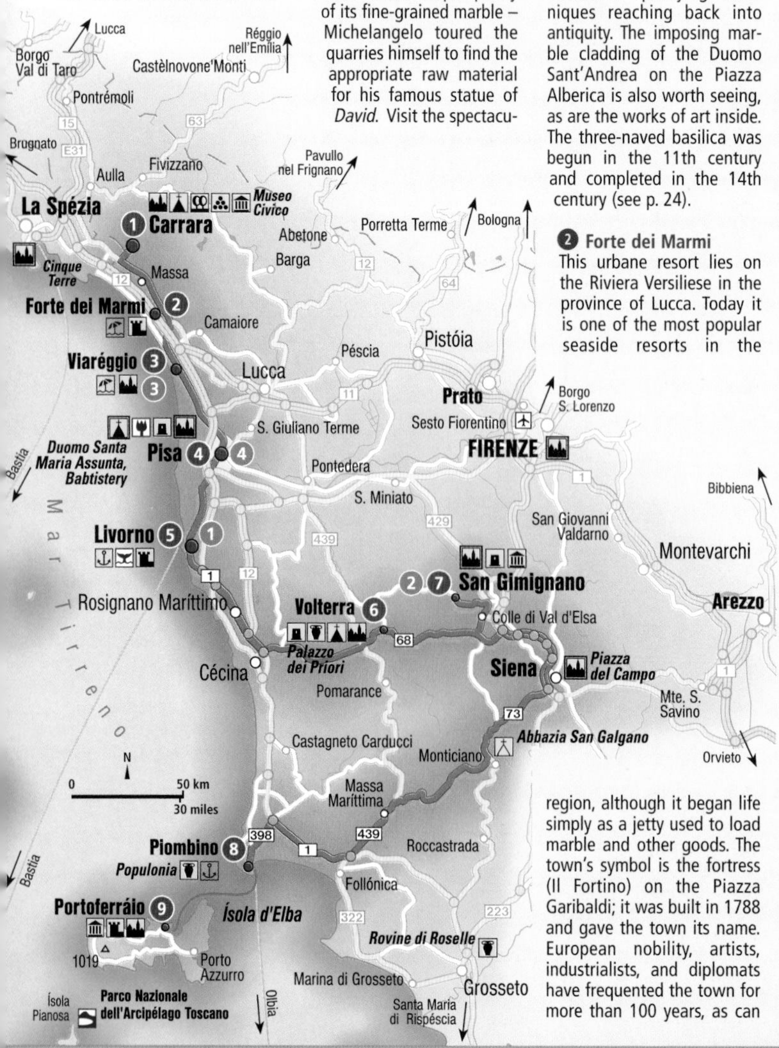

From left: The Torre di Calafuria is located on the Riviera degli Etruschi, south of Livorno; a snack on a farm near Volterra; Portoferraio stands on a rocky peninsula on Elba.

FROM CARRARA TO PORTOFERRAIO

Follow the Tuscan coast south from Carrara, known throughout the world for its marble – with a detour to Volterra and San Gimignano – and continue along the Etruscan Riviera; Portoferraio on the island of Elba is the eventual destination. Allow at least three days for this route.

Dining out

❶ La Chiave Di Fusari Sandro
The house specialties in this restaurant right next to the Fosso Reale, the fortress moat, are good, traditional meat and fish dishes. The menu has plenty of highlights and changes monthly.
Scali delle Cantine 52, Livorno; Tel 05 86/82 98 65; closed Wed.

❷ Le Terrazze
The restaurant of La Cisterna hotel has been housed in this medieval building since 1918. Take in the magical view of the surrounding hills as you enjoy delicious local dishes.
Piazza della Cisterna 23, San Gimignano; Tel 05 77/94 03 28; Wed–Mon 12.30–14.30, 19.30–21.30, closed Wed afternoon. www.hotelcisterna.it

Accommodation

❸ Hotel President
Originally built in 1949, this excellent and comfortable hotel, with a roof-top restaurant and a view of the sea and the Viareggio promenade, has been completely renovated. Many of the rooms have a balcony and are well equipped.
Viale Carducci 5, Viareggio; Tel 05 84/96 27 12. www.hotelpresident.it

❹ Royal Victoria Hotel
Despite the central location of its typically Tuscan-style 19th-century premises (not far from the Piazza dei Miracoli), this small family-run hotel is peaceful and charming. Check out the old visitors' books during your stay and you may well see some names you recognize.
Lungarno Pacinotti 12, Pisa; Tel 050/94 01 11. www.royalvictoria.it

Venice, and its port silted up. Only the city's university, indicative of a deeply rooted tradition of scholarship, has retained its leading place in the country. Visitors can relax in the city's Botanic Gardens, laid out for Prince Cosimo I de' Medici in 1543 (see pp. 106 and 234).

❺ Livorno
It's difficult to believe that Livorno is part of Tuscany, the bustling atmosphere of the city is so different from that of its serene surroundings. This is probably due to its relatively late flourishing: the little fishing port that was originally here was extended by Prince Cosimo I de' Medici in 1571, when Pisa's port was threatening to silt up. The breakwater protecting the quay area was built between 1607 and 1621, and Livorno is now the largest port in Tuscany. The Fortezza Vecchia ("Old Fortress") is situated right on the quayside and the Fortezza Nuova ("New Fortress", 1590) and its moat are to be found in the Old Town, which is confusingly called "Venezia Nuova" (New Venice). The aquarium is worth a visit (see p. 126).

❻ Volterra
The city of Volterra stands on a cliff some 550 m (1,800 feet) above sea level, looking down on a bare and rocky moon-like landscape. The narrow streets and corners of the Old Town, surrounded by a medieval curtain wall, are frequently in shadow. Culture fans should not miss the Etruscan Museum with its wealth of treasures including urns, jewelry, and sculptures such as the bronze *Ombra della sera* (*Shadow of the Evening*). Volterra is also famed for its alabaster industry. The view from the Palazzo dei Priori (1208–57), the oldest preserved town hall in the whole of Tuscany, takes in the surrounding hills and – on a clear day – the sea. Opposite the town hall, the Palazzo del Pretorio stands next to the Torre del Podestà (known locally as the Torre del Porcellino, "little pig's tower", as there is an alabaster pig on one of the ledges). The 12th-century Duomo Santa Maria Assunta shows clear Pisan influences and opposite the cathedral is a 13th-century octagonal baptistry with a green and white striped façade (see p. 122).

❼ San Gimignano
The frequent civil unrest in San Gimignano in the late Middle Ages led rich merchant families to build a total of 72 defensive towers, which stood guard over the otherwise sleepy Piazza della Cisterna in the heart of the Old Town. Of these, only 15 are still standing today, but they give the town its instantly recognizable appearance. In fact, the 14th-century buildings are so well preserved, it is almost like stepping back to the Middle Ages, when San Gimignano was an important trading base; the nearby Via Francigena took pilgrims and merchants from Canterbury to Rome. As the route's importance faded, so did the town's, but this had some positive consequences. No longer of interest to conquering armies, the town has remained so well preserved that the "Manhattan of the Middle Ages" now attracts hordes of tourists every year (see pp. 170 and 238).

❽ Piombino
Catch the ferry to Elba from this industrial port town. The views from the promenade of the old port and across to the island are charming, and the middle of town is an interesting mix of historic buildings and new architecture. There is also a well-preserved town gate and adjoining ramparts. Nearby Populonia, once an Etruscan port, is also worth a visit to see the impressive necropolis of San Cerbone, as well as the huge 15th-century fortress, which was built with stone reclaimed from the Etruscan remains.

❾ Portoferraio/Elba
The island's capital is situated on the north coast and its mighty Renaissance fortifications, which were commissioned in 1548 by Prince Cosimo I de' Medici, should not be missed. The 16th-century Franciscan monastery now houses a conference center and the Pinacoteca Foresiana gallery. The Archeological Museum on the Darsena, the old quayside, has a comprehensive exhibition covering the history of the island from the 8th century BC to the 2nd century AD. The Villa Napoleonica, the deposed emperor's summer residence, is in the valley of San Martino, to the southwest of the town (see p. 132).

The sights

❶ Grosseto

The heart of the Maremma region and the capital of the province of Grosseto lies on the right bank of the Ombrone river. The historic Old Town is surrounded by 16th-century fortifications designed by Baldassarre Lanci, with a curtain wall which is open to the public as a park and walking area. The Romanesque cathedral of San Lorenzo (begun in 1294), with its distinctive red and white striped marble façade, is located near the neo-Gothic Palazzo della Provincia on the Piazza Dante, while the Piazza dell'Indipendenza boasts the 13th-century Gothic church of San Francesco. The Museo Archeologico e d'Arte della Maremma on the Piazza Baccarini has plenty of local Etruscan finds (see p. 190).

❷ Vetulonia

This small town, noted for its Etruscan ruins and necropoleis, is located in the Bruna valley. It enjoyed its heyday as the former Etruscan port of Vetluna in the 7th and 6th centuries BC – the remains of dwellings and the old city walls from the period can be found just outside the town. The impressive necropoleis contain stone circle graves buried beneath mountains of earth (tumuli), including the Tomba della Pietrera and the Tomba di Belvedere. Vetulonia's importance declined in the Roman age.

❸ Massa Marittima

Around 26 km (16 miles) from the sea, Massa Marittima lies on the edge of the Maremma, an extensive area of marshland which was only reclaimed during the last century. There is a panoramic view of the red roofs of the Old Town and the surrounding area from the top of town, particularly from the Torre del Candeliere. Evidence of the town's importance as an episcopal seat in the 9th century can be witnessed today in its various impressive medieval buildings, including the imposing cathedral of San Cerbone. Surrounded by ancient buildings, the Piazza Garibaldi forms the heart of the older part of town; the

From left: The typical red-brown tones of Siena's houses; the imposing cathedral of San Cerbone at Massa Marittima; the round chapel of San Biagio near Montepulciano.

FROM GROSSETO TO CHIUSI

This tour heads northward from southern Tuscany before veering east into the heart of the region. The route passes through captivating scenery on its way to historic towns such as Siena and wine regions such as Montalcino and Montepulciano. Allow two to three days for the trip.

Logge del Comune, Palazzo Comunale, Palazzo Pretorio, and the cathedral combine to create the picturesque medieval skyline (see p. 188).

4 San Galgano

The impressive remains of the Abbazia San Galgano are situated some 35 km (22 miles) from Siena. Once the most powerful monastery in the area, this Cistercian abbey was abandoned in 1652. There are claims that the Arthurian legend of the "sword in the stone" originated here.

5 Siena

A worthy rival to Florence in terms of cultural heritage, the so-called "City of Gothic" is spread out across three hills in the heart of Tuscany. Its focal point, ringed by Gothic *palazzi*, is the Piazza del Campo, the most beautiful town square in Italy, where the legendary *palio* is held. Visit the Duomo Santa Maria Assunta (the cathedral, begun in the 12th century) and don't miss the Palazzo Pubblico (1288–1309), a Gothic mixture of brickwork and travertine marble. There is also the slender Torre del Mangia, (102 m/335 feet), one of the most ambitious towers built during the Italian Middle Ages (see pp. 160 and 232).

6 Asciano

The defensive walls of this small medieval town located in the upper Ombrone valley are still largely intact. Visit the Romanesque Collegiata Sant'Agata church (11th–14th centuries) in the middle of town and explore the Etruscan Museum housed in San Bernardino church, which displays all kinds of local finds from the necropolis at Poggiopinci and the tumulus at Molenello.

7 Buonconvento

Buonconvento lies at the confluence of the Arbia and the Ombrone. The Old Town is surrounded by an angular wall built between 1371 and 1383. The well-preserved buildings that it encircles primarily date back to the 14th century. Visit the Museum of Sacred Art, which has numerous works by the Gothic-inspired painters of the Sienese school.

8 Montalcino

Brunello di Montalcino, one of Italy's greatest wines, has made this village situated on a hill above the Ombrone and Asso valleys world-famous. Begun in the second half of the 14th century, the fortress of La Rocca has become the village's symbol; the heart of village life is the Piazza del Popolo with its ring of beautiful buildings dating from the 14th century (see p. 176).

9 Pienza

This almost perfect Renaissance town lies on a hill near the border with Umbria. Pienza was planned by one man working alone and built within three years, starting in 1459. Pope Pius II commissioned the architect Bernardo Rossellino to rebuild his birthplace Corsignano as a model town. He certainly achieved his brief, as can be seen from the Palazzo Piccolomini, the cathedral, the Palazzo Comunale, and the cardinal's palace (see p. 182).

10 Montepulciano

A magical town set in a picturesque location on a hillside overlooking the Orcia and Chianti valleys, Montepulciano has lost none of its unique Renaissance charm. Wine bars and subterranean wine cellars offer tempting opportunities to sample the famous Vino Nobile di Montepulciano at every turn, while a stroll through the medieval town will take you past magnificent Renaissance *palazzi* such as the Palazzo Comunale designed by Michelozzo, a little like a mini version of the Palazzo Vecchio in Florence; there is a fantastic view from the tower. Visit the wine cellar off the 16th-century Palazzo Contucci, and the baroque cathedral on the Piazza Grande with its richly decorated Gothic triptych. The Palazzo del Capitano del Popolo betrays the influences of the local style of Gothic, which first developed in Siena (see p. 174).

11 Chiusi

This sleepy little village is located on one of the many tufa plateaus in southern Tuscany. As elsewhere in the region, the cathedral and its square form the focal point: the Duomo San Secondiano has origins dating as far back as the 6th century, but its current form was begun in the 13th century and completed in the 19th. The series of tunnels known as the Labirinto Porsenna (labryinth) extend beneath the cathedral museum, and the Museo Nazionale Etrusco and the many Etruscan tombs are a must for fans of classical art and culture.

Dining out

1 Bracali

A family restaurant with an elegant feel and an imaginative menu; Francesco Bracali artfully conjures up creative variations on traditional Maremma cuisine. An excellent wine list.
Via di Perolla 2, Località Ghirlanda, Massa Marittima; Tel 05 66/90 23 18.

2 Taverna dei Barbi

They will just as happily serve down-to-earth fare (such as crostini, Montalcini bean soup, and homemade pasta with wild boar *ragù*) as the more famous Brunello wines in this rustic taverna. The sausage and cheeses are homemade.
Località Podernovi, Montalcino; Tel 05 77/84 12 00.

Accommodation

3 Hotel Certosa di Maggiano

An exclusive hotel housed in an early 14th-century Carthusian monastery in an idyllic location in the countryside. The rooms are very elegantly furnished.
Strada di Certosa 82, Siena; Tel 05 77/28 81 80. www.certosadimaggiano.com

4 Hotel Albergo Il Marzocco

The oldest hotel in town resembles a *palazzo*: the rooms have many original 18th-century furnishings, and some have a terrace or a private balcony.
Piazza Savonarola 18, Montepulciano; Tel 05 78/75 72 62. www.albergoilmarzocco.it

March

Scoppio del Carro

Florence. Watch out for one of the more unusual folk celebrations in the form of the "exploding cart" on the square in front of the cathedral on Easter Sunday. A cart full of fireworks is hauled in procession to the square, where it is connected to the high altar with a wire. A mechanical dove with a fuse in its beak is similarly stuffed with fireworks. At exactly midday the dove is lit, and shoots down the wire like a rocket. The lit fuse in its beak sets off the fireworks in the cart, which then also ignites; a successful display (lasting around 20 minutes) is supposed to presage a good year for Florence. The origins of the ceremony date back to the time of the Crusades when troops laid siege to the city of Jerusalem in the name of Christianity.
Tel 055/233 20;
Easter Sunday. www.firenze.turismo.toscana.it

May

Balestro del Girifalco

Massa Marittima. This tournament involving crossbows takes place between the *terzieri*, the three historic districts of the town, twice a year. Each district sends eight bowmen to the competition, which is held among the medieval buildings on the Piazza Garibaldi. The crowds first enjoy a procession of some 150 participants dressed in 15th-century costume, with the flag-waving *sbandieratori* as its high point. The competitors then shoot at a stylized wooden falcon from a distance of 36 m (120 feet) and the first to pierce the falcon's heart is the winner. The winning bowman receives a gold arrow and the winning district a *palio*, a painted silk cloth.
Tel 05 66/90 47 56;
first Sun after 20 May and second Sun in Aug.
www.massamarittima.info

Giostra dell'Archidado

Cortona. Toward the end of May, Cortona steps back in time to the 14th century, when the champion crossbowmen of each district of the town compete in a competition. Dressed in medieval costume, they shoot at targets with crossbows for the so-called *dado*, a trophy in the form of a cube with sides of 15 cm (6 inches). The Giostra dell'Archidado is in fact the climax of a festival commemorating the 1397 marriage of Francesco Casali, Lord of Cortona, and Antonia Salimbeni of Siena. The festival is held before the shooting competition and includes a procession of townsfolk in costume as well as music and dancing.
Tel 05 75/63 03 52;
end of May.
www.comune.cortona.ar.it

Maggio Musicale Fiorentino

Florence. Thought to be the biggest of its kind in Italy, and ranking alongside Bayreuth and Salzburg as one of the oldest and most important in Europe, this classical music festival features performances from both the Florence municipal orchestra and international music stars in either the Teatro Comunale (*c.* 2,000 seats) or the Teatro Piccolo (*c.* 600 seats). Maria Callas once performed at the festival. A must for fans of opera, symphonies, chamber music, and ballet.
Tel 055/277 93 50; May–Jun.
www.maggiofiorentino.com

Merca del Bestiame

Alberese. The stars of this three-day festival rodeo on the Campo Sportivo are yearling Maremma calves and foals, and the *butteri*, mounted cowherds who are also known as "Maremma Cowboys"; the *butteri* are required to rope, throw, and brand several hundred of the disapproving and frightened calves.
Tel 05 64/221 11; 1–3 May.
www.parco-maremma.it

June

Calcio in Costume

Florence. Roared on by spectators, two opposing teams in motley Renaissance garb face one another in this historic "football" tournament – *calcio* means variously kick/football/soccer. In fact, the game is more akin to a mixture of rugby and wrestling, as pretty much any tactics are allowed to propel the ball into the net. Each team of 27 players is from one of the four oldest districts of Florence. The semifinals are played at the beginning of June and the final takes place on the Piazza Santa Croce on 30 June. Each match lasts an exhausting – for the participants – hour. The origins of the game date back to 1530 and the Siege of Florence, when the citizens wished to show defiance for the besieging Imperial and Spanish armies. The festival begins with a procession in historic dress through the Old Town and the winning district celebrates extensively into the evening.
Tel 055/29 08 32; Jun.
www.firenzeturismo.it

Estate Fiesolana

Fiesole. Every summer, this music and drama festival fills the colossal Roman amphitheater with life – it is one of the oldest open-air festivals in Italy, held in a unique setting that offers excellent acoustics. The partially rebuilt ancient rows of seats provide 3,000 places for spectators to watch performances ranging from the classics via folk and jazz to ballet and theater productions, with artists from all over the world. Additional cultural events have also recently been staged during the festival in two nearby private villas.
Tel 055/59 87 20; Jun–Sept.
www.comune.fiesole.fi.it

Giostra del Saracino

Arezzo. For two Sundays, one in June and one in September, the Piazza Grande in Arezzo is transformed into an arena for medieval tournaments. Crowds gather to witness an exciting riding competition, which is not entirely free from danger. With its origins in the Middle Ages when Christian troops attempted to drive the Moors from North Africa out of Europe, a "Saracen" provides the target – a wooden puppet with a shield in one hand and rope with a spiked ball on the end in the other, mounted on a rotating pole. Lance in hand, eight champions from Arezzo's various districts gallop up and attempt to hit the shield without getting caught by the spiked ball.

Celebrations: Tuscan festivities are full of bright life and pageantry. From left: Florence, Scoppio del Carro; Cortona, Giostra dell'Archidado; Pisa, Gioco del Ponte; Florence, Calcio in Costume – football with a difference.

FESTIVAL CALENDAR

The towns and villages of Tuscany are known for their historic pageantry, tournaments, and music festivals: visitors flock to the *palio* in Siena and open-air performances of Puccini operas in Torre del Lago, but the *sagre* – folk festivals, celebrations of patron saints, and feast days – are also extremely popular.

Points are collected during several passes and the winner is awarded a golden lance. The tournament is preceded by a procession of people and horsemen in medieval costume, a traditional blessing, and a recital.
Tel 05 75/23 95 23; third Sun in Jun and first Sun in Sept.
www.apt.arezzo.it

Gioco del Ponte
Pisa. After parading through the town dressed in bright Renaissance costumes, two teams face one another on the Ponte di Mezzo. The purpose of the contest is to push the seven-ton wooden cart placed between them over the opposing team's touchline. The competing teams are traditionally drawn from north (*tramontana*) and south (*mezzogiorno*) of the Arno and the contest, held on the oldest bridge in the city, is documented as far back as the 16th century.
Tel 050/92 97 77;
last Sun in Jun.
www.pisaturismo.it

Luminara e Regatta di San Ranieri
Pisa. An evening in June sees the *palazzi* and other buildings on the banks of the Arno illuminated by some 70,000 candles and torches lit in honor of San Ranieri, Pisa's patron saint. Lights floating in the Arno enhance the supremely romantic atmosphere. The next day features a rowing regatta between four brightly painted boats representing the four oldest districts of the city. The costumed rowers have to race toward a boat anchored in the middle of the river. The first cox to leap aboard the boat, climb its 10-m (33-foot) mast, and grab the *paliotto* (the boat's pennant) is the winner.
Tel 050/92 97 77; 16–17 Jun.
www.pisaturismo.it

July

Palio
Siena. Siena's legendary horse race is held twice a year. Riders from the 17 *contrade* (municipal districts) compete on the Piazza del Campo to win a likeness of the Madonna printed on the silk banner that gave the race its name (Lat. *pallium* = "cloth"). Riding bareback, the jockeys risk life and limb to force their mounts to the fore during three breakneck laps of the Piazza. The Campo is turned into a bustling arena of 58,000 spectators for the *palio*, and the spectacle begins with the Corteo Storico, a costumed procession with flag-waving standard-bearers, lancers, pages, riders, and a triumphal wagon bearing the victory trophy. The procession lasts for hours, while the race itself is usually over in less than two minutes.
Tel 05 77/28 05 51; 2 Jul and 16 Aug. www.terresiena.it

Puccini-Festival
Torre del Lago. Several weeks every year are dedicated to a festival commemorating the Italian composer Giacomo Puccini. The large open-air theater by the lake resounds to the immortal opera arias from the hand of the great maestro, who spent the latter half of his life in the villa only a stone's throw from the stage. Internationally famous artists and orchestras routinely perform here.
Tel 05 84/35 05 67;
Jul–Aug.
www.puccinifestival.it

Pistoia Blues Festival
Pistoia. In July, the Piazza del Duomo is taken over by fans of the blues, while the town stages one of Italy's best-known blues and rock festivals. Local and internationally famous artists serve up musical treats during the three-day open-air festival.
Jul.
www.pistoiablues.com

August

Bravio delle Botti
Montepulciano. One of the stranger of the Tuscan festivals, this bizarre contest sees the eight municipal districts compete in rolling 80-kg (180-lb) wine barrels up the steep streets leading to the Piazza Grande. The feat is accomplished by two *spingitori* ("pushers") and the winning team is the one that covers the distance in the shortest time. The victors are awarded the *bravio* (Lat. *bravium* = "cloth"), a banner decorated with a likeness of San Giovanni Decollato, the town's patron saint. A two-hour procession with more than 300 participants in bright and festive historic costumes precedes the race.
Tel 05 78/75 73 41;
last Sun in Aug.
www.prolocomontepulchiano.it

September

Luminaria di Santa Croce
Lucca. The residents of the Old Town place a candle in every window and at 21.00 a procession winds its way through the atmospherically torchlit streets. The *Volto Santo* (the "Holy Face", a wooden crucifix supposedly carved from cedarwood by St Nicodemus with the aid of angels, and which subsequently arrived in Lucca in equally miraculous fashion) is carried wrapped in brocade.
Tel 05 83/91 99 31; 13 Sept.
www.luccaturismo.it

Sagra dell'Uva
Greve in Chianti. The most important fair celebrating Chianti wine is held in the Chianti region's capital and lasts a week. The new Chianti Classico is introduced, and there is a procession, folk dancing, various performances, and other events based on the theme of wine.
Tel 055/854 62 87;
second week in Sept.
www.commune.greve-in-chianti.fi.it

October

Sagra del Tordo
Montalcino. The "Festival of the Thrush" begins in the main square with a performance by dancers in historic dress, followed by an equally elaborate and extravagant procession. There is an archery competition between the local districts (*quartieri*) in the afternoon, which is followed by a feast lasting late into the night, with the participants sitting on long benches. The Sagra del Tordo is supposed to herald the start of the autumn thrush-hunting season, but these days feast-goers tend to eat quail or chicken.
Tel 05 77/84 93 31;
last Sun in Oct.
www.prolocomontalcino.it

The gently rolling hills of central Tuscany (below, the Val d'Orcia), from where there are superb views – as far as the mountains in the north and to the Tyrrhenian Sea in the west.

KEY

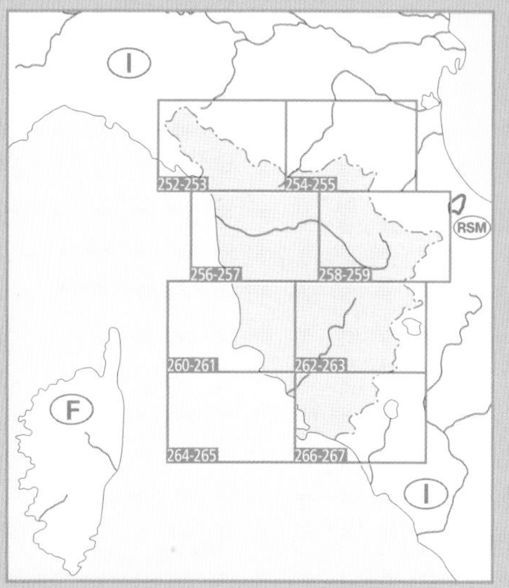

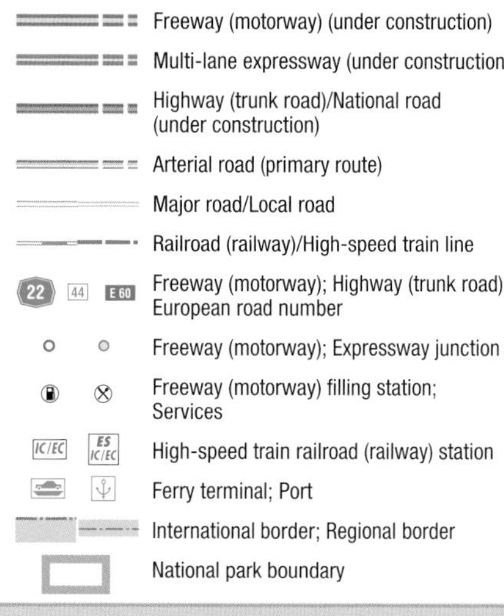

ATLAS

The maps in the Atlas section give detailed practical information to help make your visit more enjoyable. Clear symbols indicate the position of buildings and monuments of note, facilities and services, public buildings, the transport network, and built-up areas and green spaces (see the key to them maps below).

Diving (subaqua)
Amusement park
Viewpoint
Hiking area

Scenic car route
Scenic railroad route
Domestic airport

UNESCO World Heritage Site
Roman remains
Etruscan culture
Christian culture site
Ruined church
Roman Catholic Church
Gothic church
Renaissance church
Christian monastery
Cultivated landscape
Historic town/city area

Canoeing/Rafting
Mountain refuge/Alp. pasture
Racetrack
Camping area
Ski area

Shipping route
Tourist route
International airport

Castle/Fortress/Defenses
Ruined castle
Palace/Castle
Notable lighthouse
Notable bridge
Notable tower
Notable building
Open-air museum
War site/Battlefield
Theater
Vineyard

ATLAS: THE APUAN ALPS, VERSILIA, GARFAGNANA

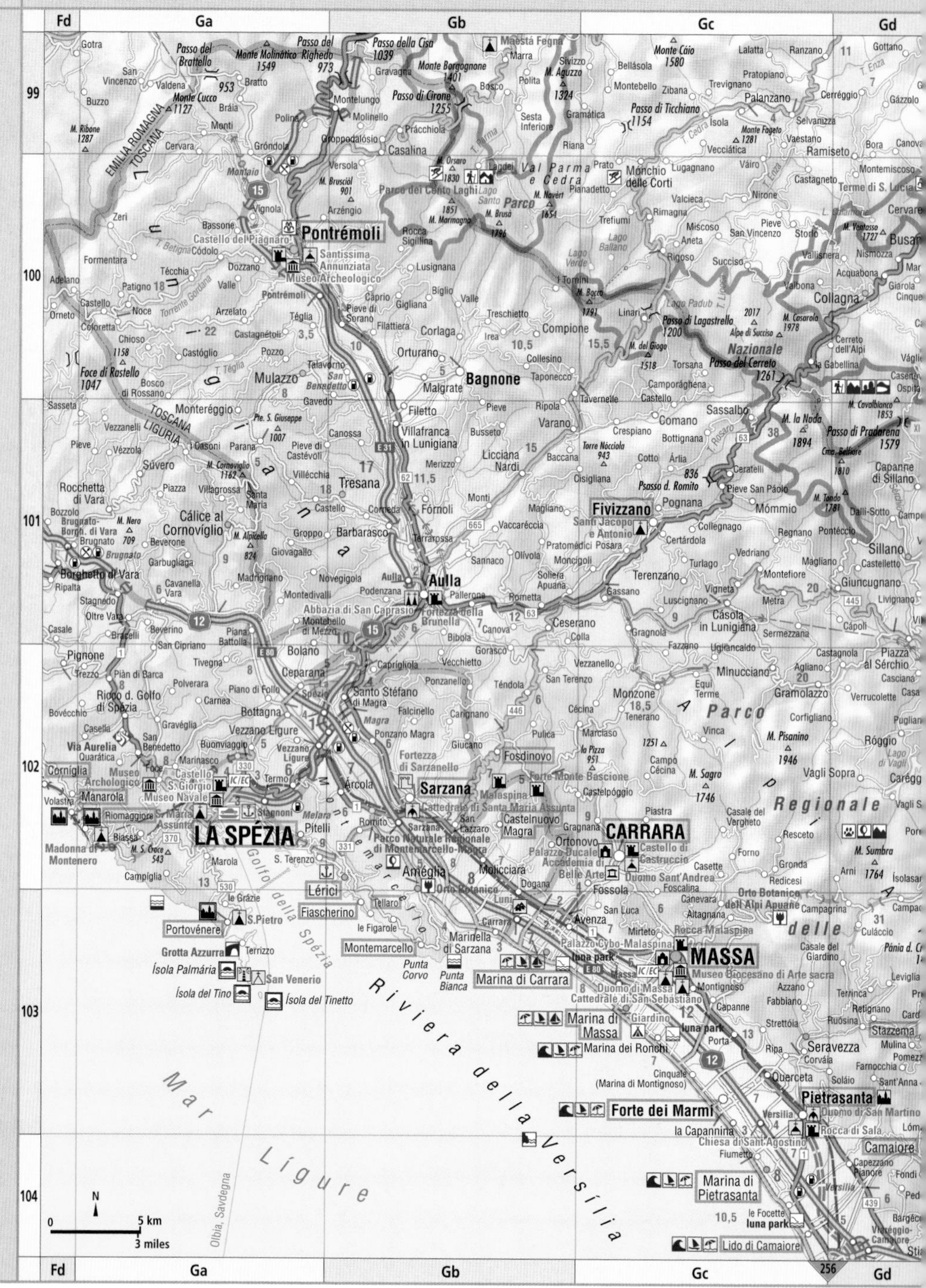

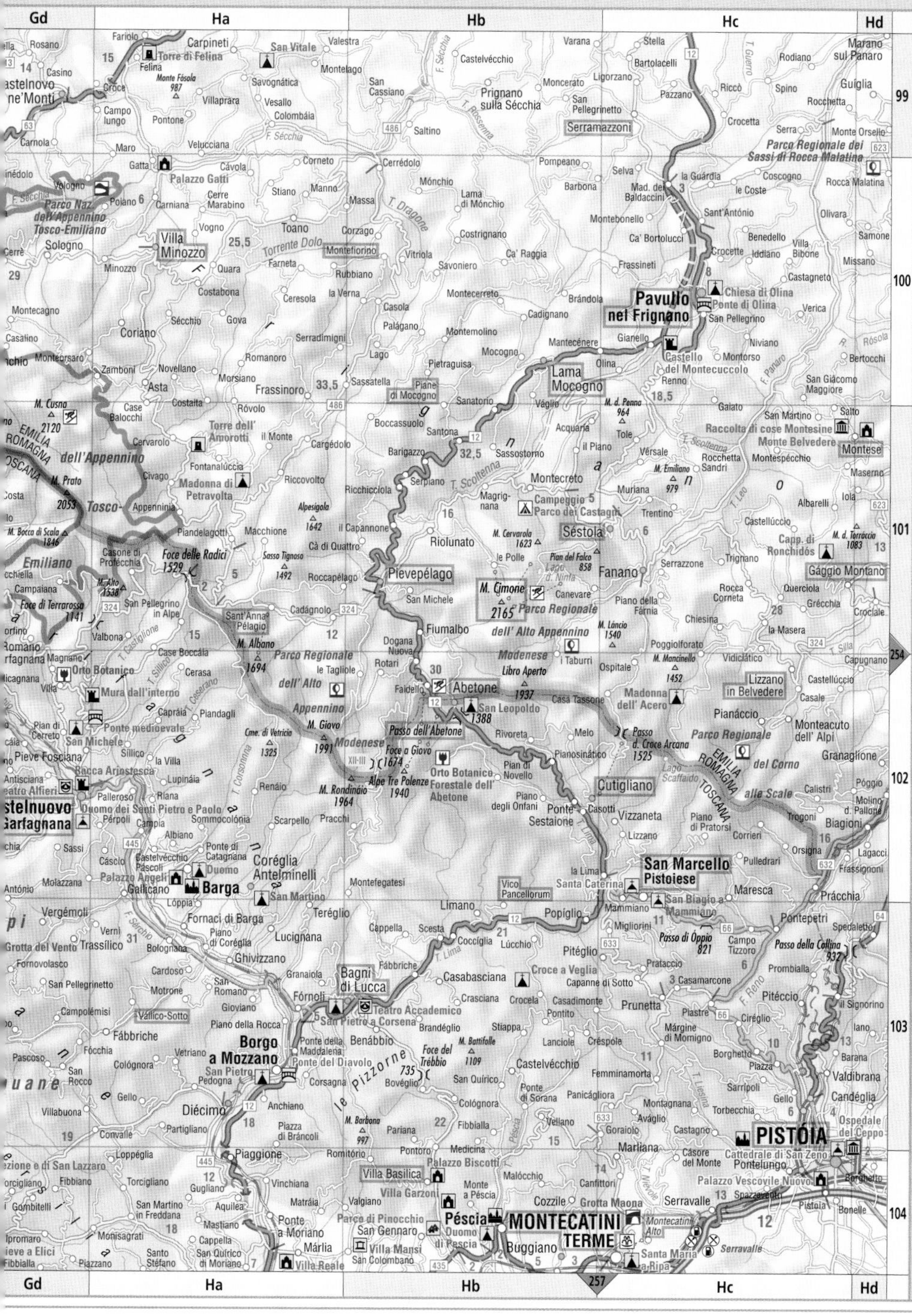

Gd | Ha | Hb | Hc | Hd

99

100

101

254

102

103

104

257

Gd | Ha | Hb | Hc | Hd

ATLAS: THE BORDER WITH EMILIA ROMAGNA

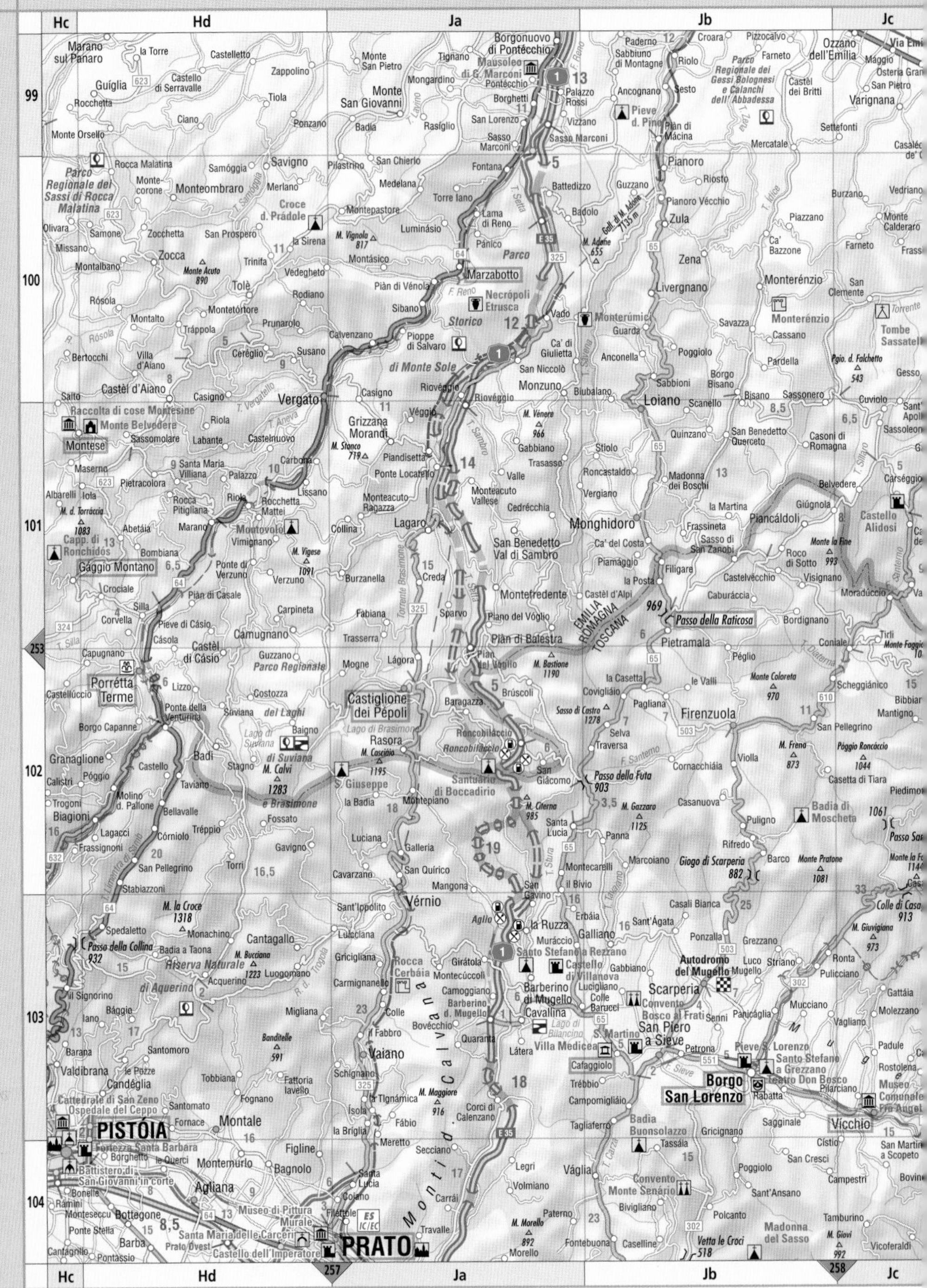

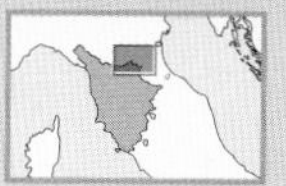

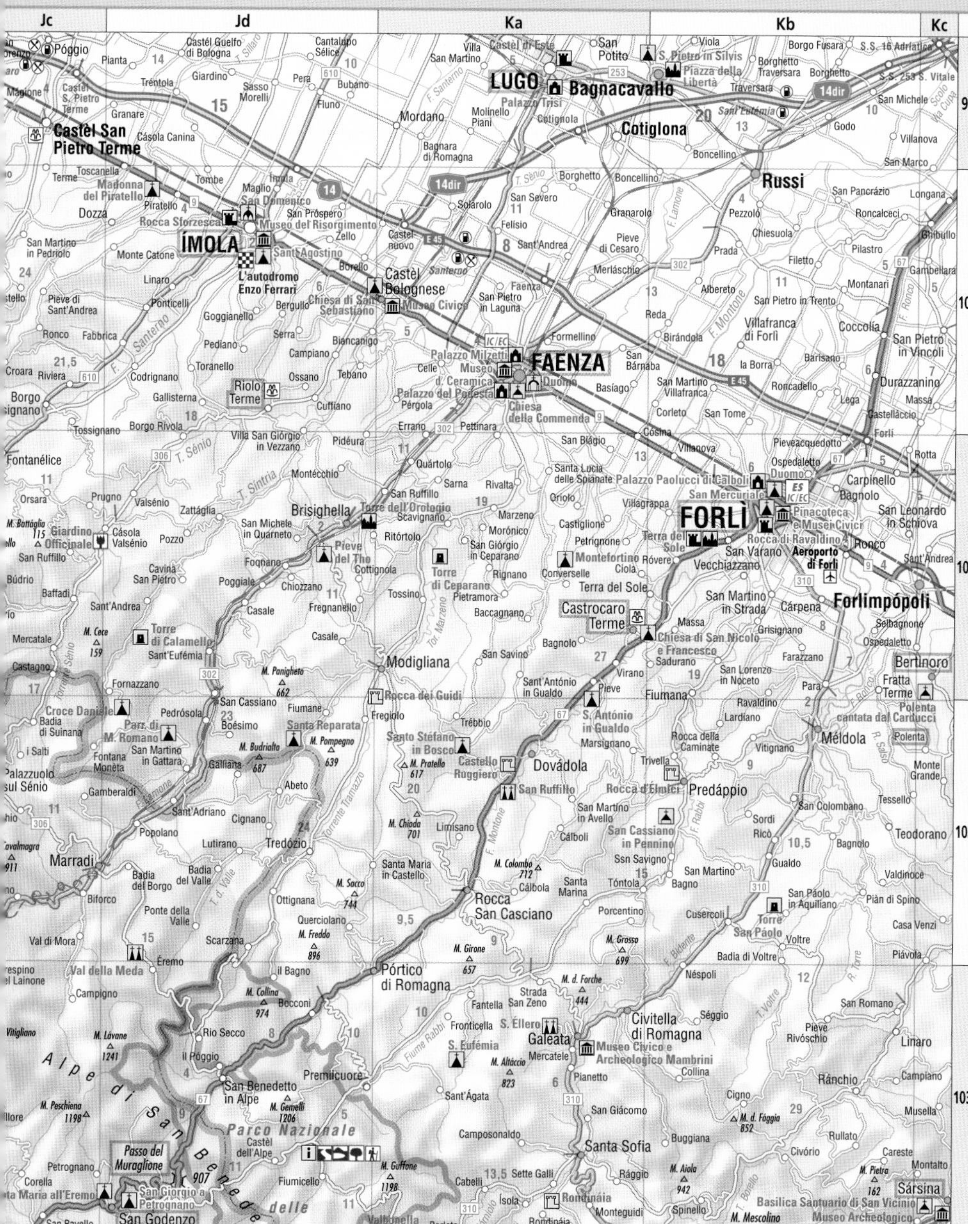

Jc	Jd	Ka	Kb	Kc

Póggio · Pianta · Castèl Guelfo di Bologna · Cantalupo Sélice · Villa San Martino · Castèl di Este · San Potito · S. Pietro in Silvis · Viola · Borgo Fusara · S.S. 16 Adriatica · Trèntola · Giardino · Sasso Morelli · Pera · Bubano · LUGO · Bagnacavallo · Palazzo Trisi · Piazza della Libertà · Borghetto Traversara · Traversara · S.S. 253 S. Vitale · San Michele · Magione · Castel S. Pietro Terme · Granare · Fluno · Mordano · Molinello Piani · Cotignola · Cotiglona · Sant'Eufémia · Godo · Villanova · 99

Castèl San Pietro Terme · Cásola Canina · Bagnara di Romagna · Boncellino · Russi · San Marco · Terme · Toscanella · Madonna del Piratello · Tombe · Maglio · Ímola · San Doménico · Borghetto · San Severo · Granarolo · San Pancrázio · Longana · Piratello · Dozza · Rocca Sforzesca · San Prospero · Museo del Risorgimento · Solarolo · Felisio · Pezzolo · Roncalceci · ÍMOLA · Sant'Agostino · Zello · Castel nuovo · Sant'Andrea · Pieve di Cesaro · Chiesuola · Ghibullo · San Martino in Pedriolo · Monte Catone · L'autodromo Enzo Ferrari · Borello · Castèl Bolognese · Santerno · Merláschio · Prada · Pilastro · Filetto · Gambellara · Linaro · Chiesa di San Sebastiano · Museo Civico · Faenza · San Pietro in Laguna · Alberto · San Pietro in Trento · Montanari · Pieve di Sant'Andrea · Ponticelli · Bergullo · Goggianello · Reda · Villafranca di Forlì · Coccolia · 100

Ronco · Fabbrica · Serra · Pediano · Biancanigo · Formellino · Birándola · San Pietro in Vincoli · Croara · Riviera · Codrignano · Toranello · Campiano · Palazzo Milzetti · Museo d. Ceramica · FAENZA · Duomo · San Bárnaba · la Borra · Barisano · Durazzanino · Borgo Tossignano · Gallisterna · Riolo Terme · Ossano · Tebano · Celle · Palazzo del Podestà · Pérgola · Chiesa della Commenda · Basiágo · San Martino Villafranca · Roncadello · Lega · Massa · Tossignano · Borgo Rivola · Cuffiano · Errano · Pettinara · Corleto · San Tome · Castellàccio · Forlì · Fontanélice · Villa San Giórgio in Vezzano · Pidéura · Quártolo · San Blágio · Cosina · Villanova · Pieveacquedotto · Ospedaletto · Rotta · Montécchio · Sarna · Rivalta · Santa Lucia delle Spianate · Palazzo Paolucci di Calboli · Duomo · Carpinello · Bagnolo · Orsara · Prugno · Valsénio · San Ruffillo · Oriolo · Villagrappa · San Mercuriale · Zattáglia · Brisighella · Torre dell'Orologio · Scavignano · Marzeno · Castiglione · FORLÌ · Pinacoteca e Musei Civici · San Leonardo in Schiova · M. Battáglia 115 · Giardino Officinale · Cásola Valsénio · San Michele in Quarneto · Pozzo · Ritórtolo · Morónico · San Giórgio in Ceparano · Petrignone · Terra del Sole · Rocca di Ravaldino · Ronco · San Ruffillo · Foqnano · Pieve del Tho · Cottignola · Torre di Ceparano · Rignano · Montefortino · Róvere · San Varano · Aeroporto di Forlì · Sant'Andrea · 101

Búdrio · Baffadi · Caviná · San Pietro · Poggiale · Chiozzano · Tossino · Pietramora · Converselle · Ciola · Terra del Sole · Vecchiazzano · San Martino in Strada · Cárpena · Forlimpópoli · Sant'Andrea · Casale · Fregnanello · Baccagnano · Castrocaro Terme · Massa · Grisignano · Selbagnone · Mercatale · M. Cece 159 · Torre di Calamello · Casale · Bagnolo · Chiesa di San Nicolò e Francesco · Ospedaletto · Castagno · Sant'Eufémia · Modigliana · San Savino · Sadurano · Farazzano · Bertinoro · Fornazzano · M. Panigheto 662 · Sant'Antonio in Gualdo · Virano · San Lorenzo in Noceto · Fratta Terme · Croce Daniele · Badia di Suinana · San Cassiano · Fiumane · Rocca dei Guidi · Pieve · Fiumana · Ravaldino · Polenta · cantata dal Carducci · Pedrósola · Boésimo · Santa Reparata · Fregiolo · Trébbio · S. Antonio in Gualdo · Lardiano · Parr. di M. Romano · M. Pompegno 639 · Santo Stéfano in Bosco · Marsignano · Rocca della Caminate · Vitignano · Méldola · Polenta · I Salti · Fontana Monéta · San Martino in Gattara · M. Budrialto 687 · M. Pratello 617 · Castello Ruggiero · Dovádola · Trivella · Monte Grande · Palazzuolo sul Sénio · Gamberaldi · Galliana · Abeto · San Ruffillo · Rocca d'Elmici · Predáppio · Tessello · Sant'Adriano · Cignano · San Martino in Avello · San Colombano · Popolano · Lutirano · Tredózio · M. Chioda 701 · Limisano · Cálboli · San Cassiano in Pennino · Sordi · Ricò · Teodorano · 102

Marradi · Badia del Borgo · Badia del Valle · Santa Maria in Castello · M. Colombo 712 · Ssn Savigno · Tóntola · San Martino · Bagno · Gualdo · Valdinoce · Biforco · Ponte della Valle · M. Sacco 744 · Cálbola · Santa Marina · San Pàolo in Aquilliano · Piàn di Spino · Val di Mora · Ottignana · Querciolano · Rocca San Casciano · Porcentino · Cusercoli · Torre San Pàolo · Casa Venzi · M. Freddo 896 · Voltre · Scarzana · M. Girone 657 · M. Grosso 699 · Badia di Voltre · Piávola · Éremo · Val della Meda · il Bagno · Pórtico di Romagna · M. d. Forche 444 · Néspoli · Campigno · M. Collina 974 · Bocconi · Strada San Zeno · Fantella · San Romano · Vitigliano · Rio Secco · Fronticella · S. Éllero · Galeata · Civitella di Romagna · Séggio · Pieve Rivóschio · Linaro · M. Lávane 1241 · Alpe di San Benedetto · il Poggio · S. Eufémia · Mercatale · Museo Civico e Archeologico Mambrini · Collina · M. Altáccio 823 · Premilcuore · Pianetto · Ránchio · Campiano · M. Peschiena 1198 · San Benedetto in Alpe · M. Gemelli 1206 · Sant'Ágata · Cigno · M. d. Fóggia 852 · Musella · 103

Parco Nazionale delle Foreste Casentinesi, Monte Falterona-Campigna · San Giácomo · Camposonaldo · Castèl dell'Alpe · Santa Sofía · Buggiana · Rullato · Passo del Muraglione 907 · Petrognano · M. Guffone 1198 · Sette Galli · Rággio · M. Aiola 942 · Civório · Careste · Montalto · Corella · Fiumicello · Cabelli · M. Pietra 162 · Sársina · Santa Maria all'Eremo · San Giórgio a Petrognano · Ísola · Rondináia · Monteguidi · Spinello · Basilica Santuario di San Vicinio · Museo Archeologico · San Godenzo · Valbonella · Berleta · Rondináia · M. Mescolino 969 · Valbiano · Turrito · San Bavello · Ficciana · M. Ritoio 1199 · Cámiolo · Póggio alla Lastra · San Silvestro · Vessa · Saiaccio · Quarto · Tivo · Carbonile · M. Campáccio 1018 · Casale · Lago di Quarto · Badia Agnano · il Castagno d'Andrea · Ridrácoli · M. Marino 1066 · Colle del Carnáio 776 · Montegranelli · Selvapiana · il Palazzo · Monte Falterona · Campigna · S. Pàolo in Alpe · Strabatenza · Lago di Ridrácoli · Rio Salso · San Pàolo · Castello · Acquapartita · Rincine · Londa · 1654 · Passo la Calla 1296 · San Piero in Bagno · Castello di Carzano · Passo dell' Insica 822 · 0 · 5 km · 3 miles · N · 104

Jc	Jd	Ka	Kb	Kc

259

ATLAS: FROM PISA TO VOLTERRA, FROM LIVORNO TO FLORENCE

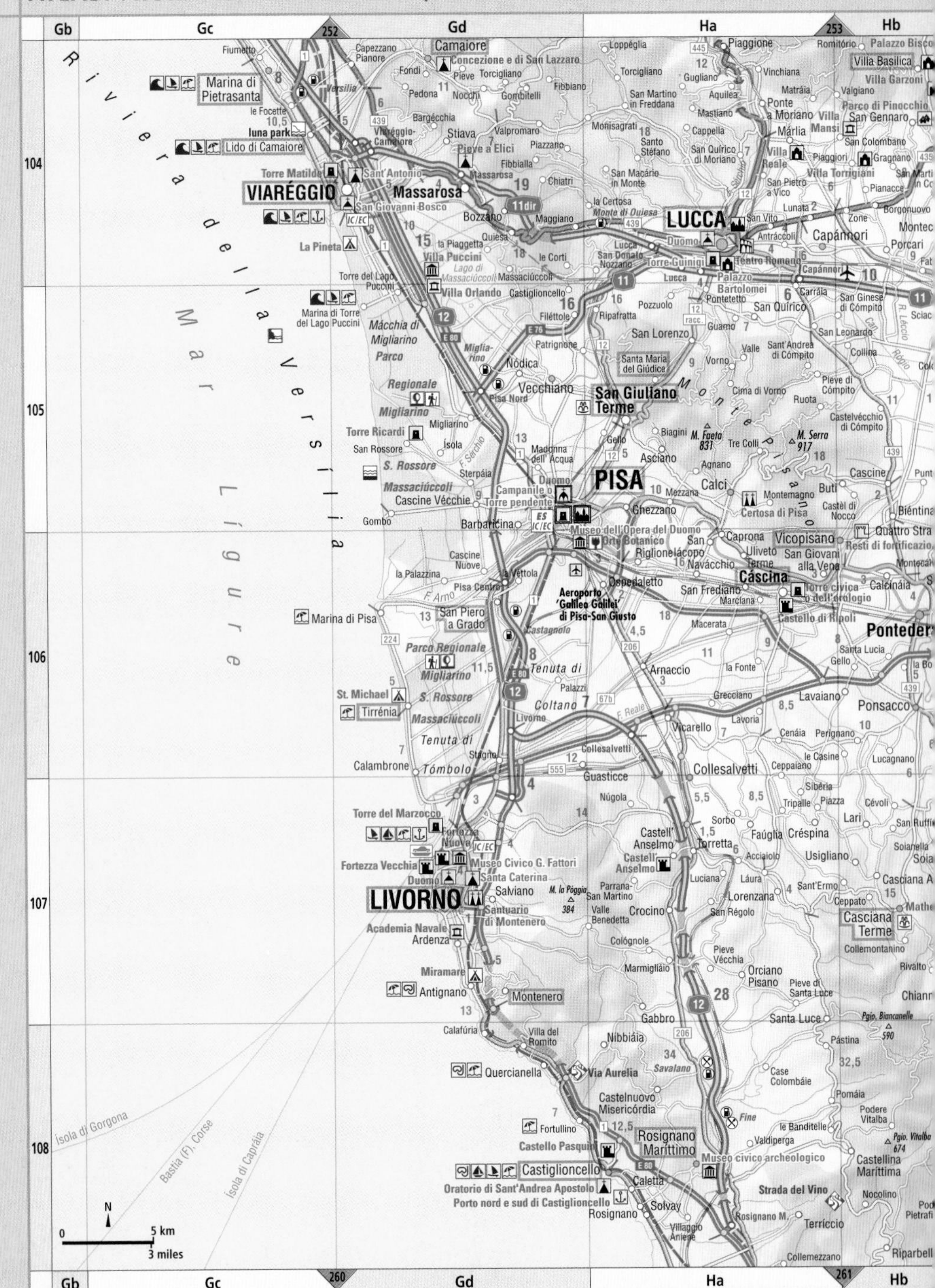

Hb
Hc
Hd
Ja
Jb
253
254
258
261
262
104
105
106
107
108
PISTÓIA
PRATO
FIRENZE
MONTECATINI TERME
Monsummano Terme
Sesto Fiorentino
Campi Bisénzio
Signa
Lastra
Empoli
Fucécchio
San Miniato
Quaratta
Póggio a Caiano
Vinci
Cerreto Guidi
Montelupo Fiorentino
Scandicci
Impruneta
San Casciano in Val di Pesa
Castelfiorentino
Certaldo
Poggibonsi
San Gimignano
Colle di Val d'Elsa
Monteriggioni
Volterra
Barberino Val d'Elsa
Tavarnelle
Montespértoli
Santa Croce sull' Arno
Castelfranco di Sotto
Montópoli in Val d'Arno
Gambassi Terme
Montaione
Lajático
Péccioli
Palazzo Vescovile Nuovo
Fortezza Santa Barbara
Battistero di San Giovanni in corte
Museo di Pittura Murale
Santa Maria delle Carceri
Castello dell'Imperatore
Palazzo Pretorio
Villa Póggio a Caiano
Museo Ideale Leonardo da Vinci
Collegiata di S. Andrea
Certosa del Galluzzo
Palazzo Vecchio
Galleria degli Uffizi
Palazzo Pitti
Santa Croce
Santa Maria Novella
Padule di Fucecchio
Santuario di Santa Verdiana
Collegiata dei Santi Lorenzo e Leonardo
Rovine Castelvécchio
Abbadia Isola
Badia dei Santi Salvatore e Cirino
Palazzo dei Priori
Museo etrusco Guarnacci
Torre di Montemiccioli
Strada del Vino
Saline di Volterra
Montecatini Val di Cécina
E 35
E 76
1
11

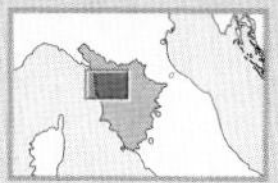

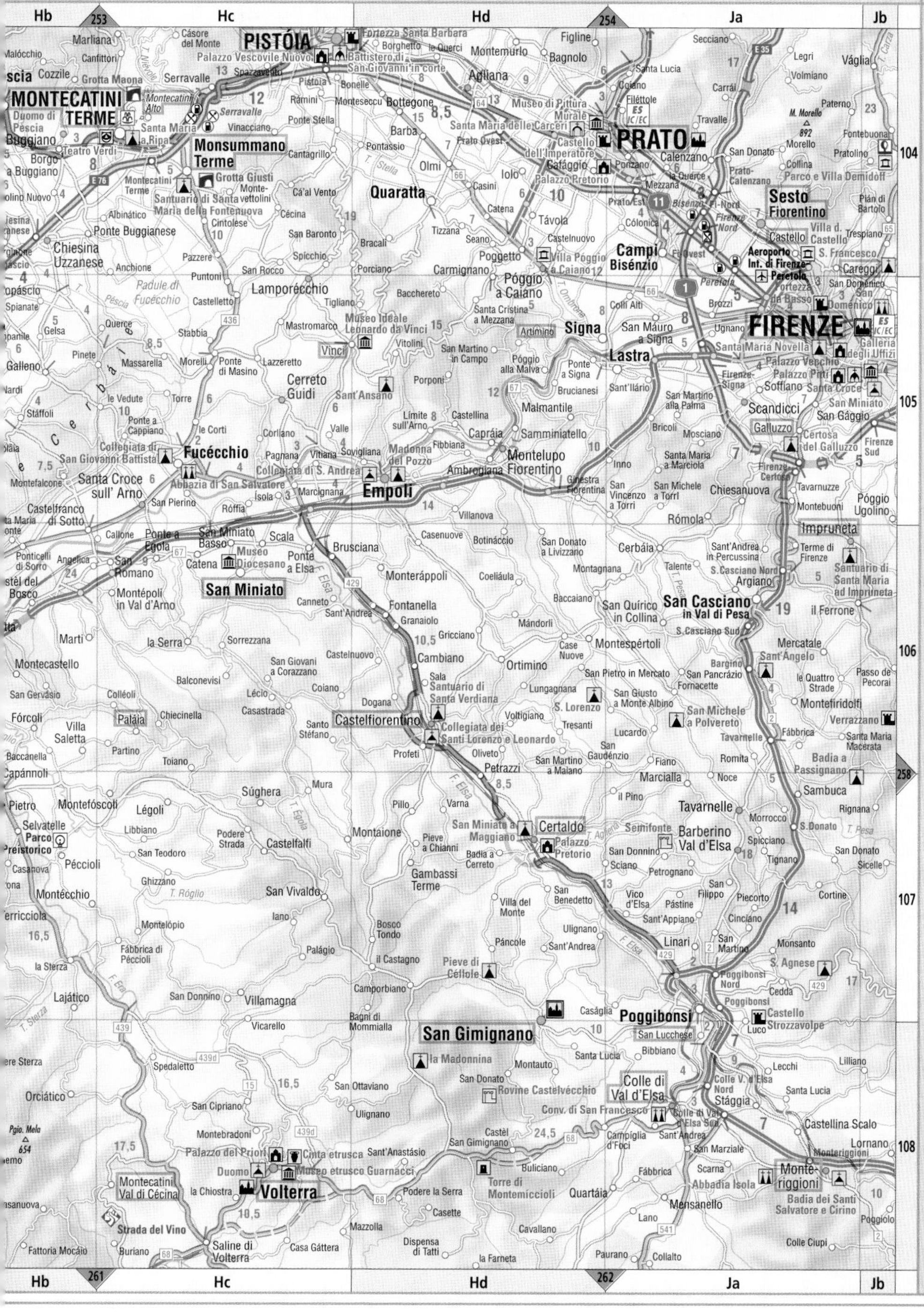

ATLAS: CHIANTI AND PRATOMAGNO

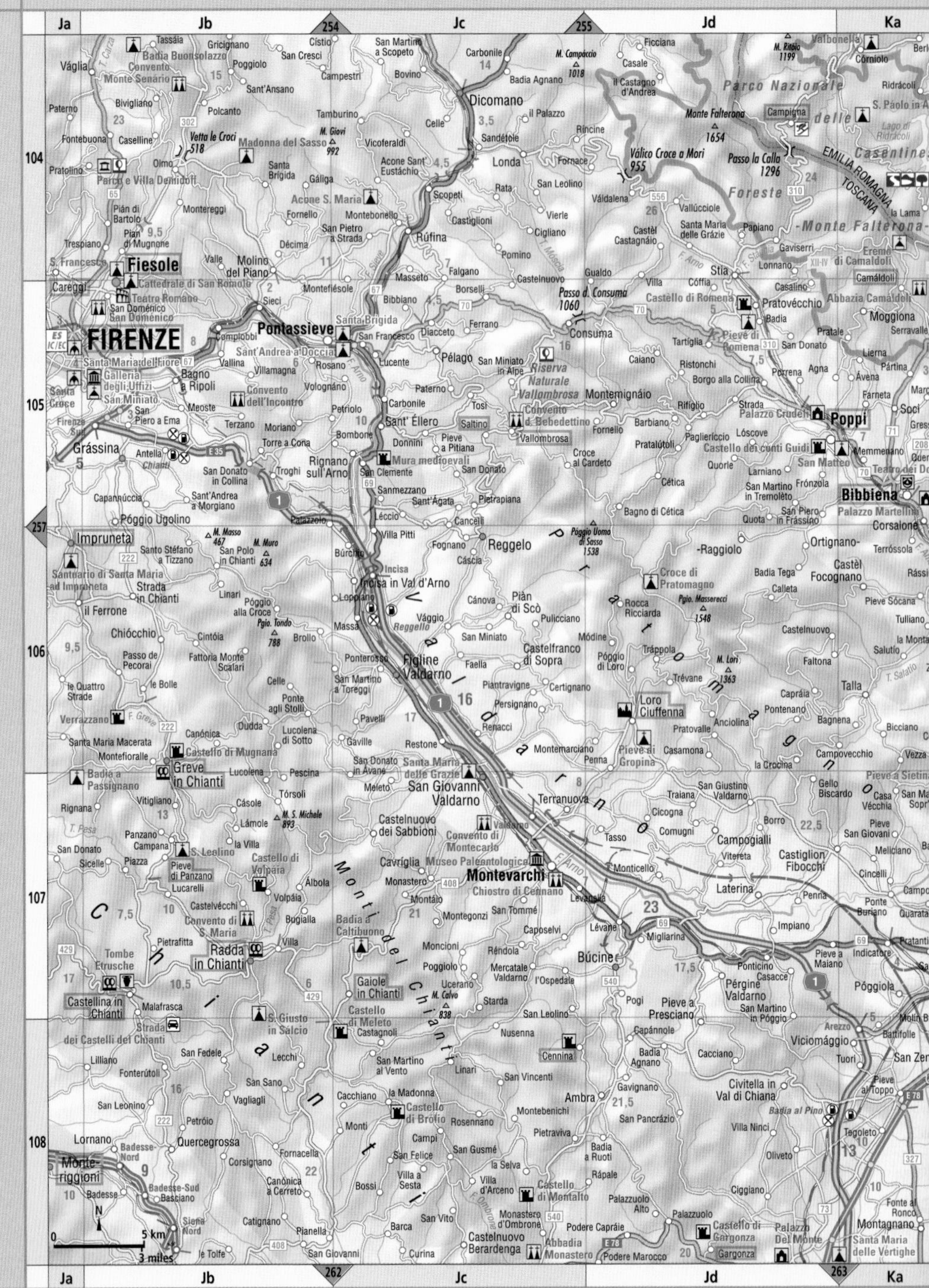

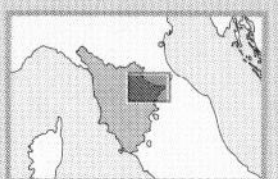

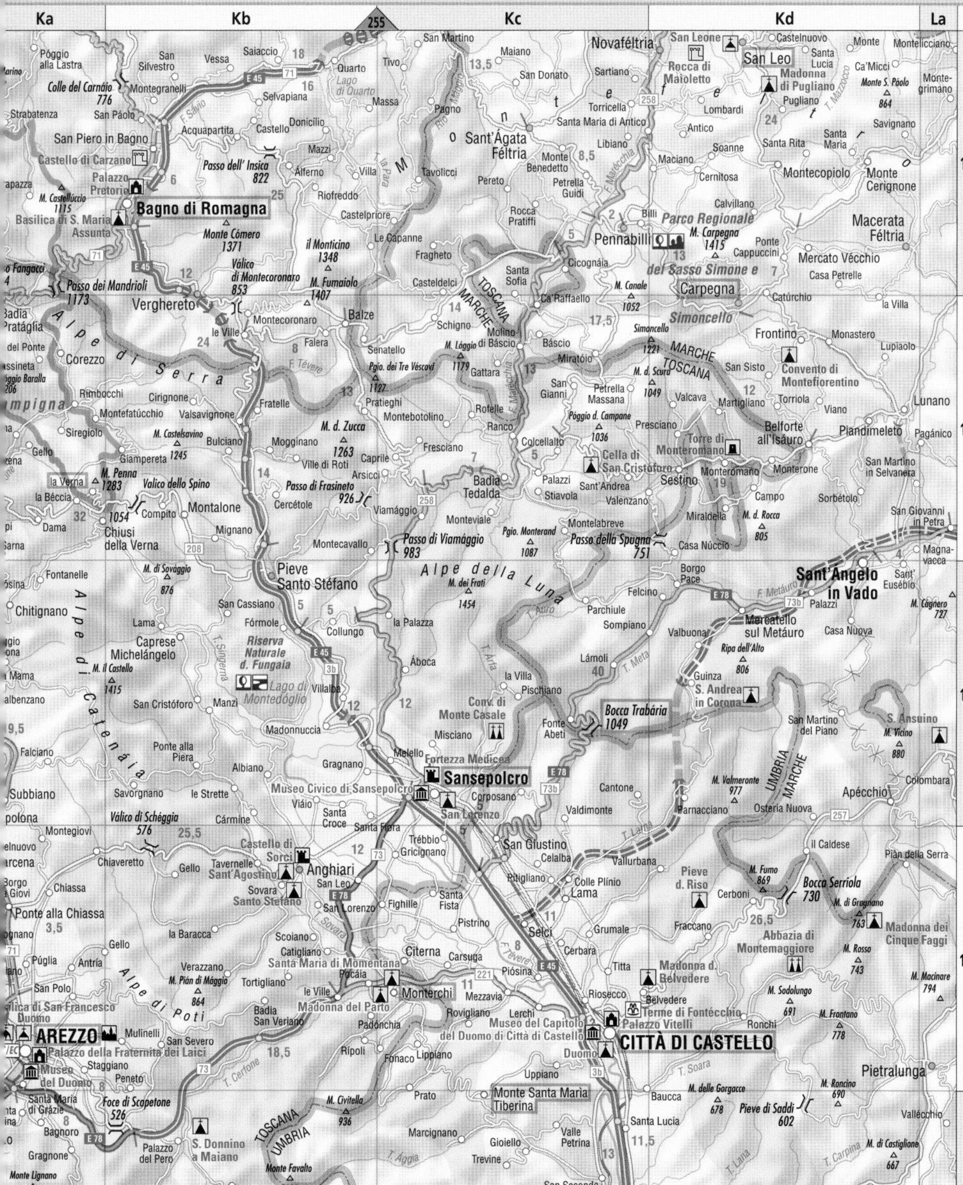

Ka
Kb
Kc
Kd
La
255
263
104
105
106
107
108
Póggio alla Lastra
San Silvestro
Vessa
Saiaccio
Colle del Carnáio 776
Montegranelli
Strabatenza
San Páolo
San Piero in Bagno
Castello di Carzano
Palazzo Pretorio
Bagno di Romagna
Basilica di S. Maria Assunta
M. Castellúccio 1115
Passo dei Mandrioli 1173
Verghereto
Badia Pratáglia
Corezzo
Alpe di Serra
Rimbocchi
Montefatúcchio
Siregiolo
Gello
la Verna
M. Penna 1283
la Bêccia
Dama
Chiusi della Verna
Valico dello Spino
Montalone
Mignano
Compito
Fontanelle
Chitignano
Alpe di Catenáia
Caprese Michelángelo
M. il Castello 1415
San Cristóforo
Manzi
Falciano
Subbiano
Montegiovi
Chiaveretto
Chiassa
Ponte alla Chiassa
Gello
Púglia
Antria
San Polo
Alpe di Poti
Basilica di San Francesco
Duomo
AREZZO
Palazzo della Fraternita dei Laici
Museo del Duomo
Staggiano
Peneto
Foce di Scapetone 526
Santa Maria di Grázie
Bagnoro
Gragnone
Monte Lignano 838
Pieve di Rigutino
Rigutino
Vitiano
Mammi
Pieve di San Giuliano
Castiglion Fiorentino
Misericórdia
Cantalena
Quarto
Lago di Quarto
Selvapiana
Acquapartita
Castello
Donicílio
Passo dell' Insica 822
Mazzi
Alferno
Riofreddo
Monte Cómero 1371
il Monticino 1348
Válico di Montecoronaro 853
M. Fumaiolo 1407
Montecoronaro
le Ville
Falera
Fratelle
Cirignone
Valsavignone
M. Castelsavino 1245
Giampereta
Bulciano
Mogginano
Ville di Roti
M. d. Zucca 1263
Passo di Frasineto 926
Cercétole
Montecavallo
Pieve Santo Stéfano
San Cassiano
Lama
Fórmole
Collungo
Riserva Naturale d. Fungaia
Lago di Montedóglio
Villalba
Madonnuccia
Ponte alla Piera
Albiano
Savorgnano
le Strette
Válico di Schéggia 576
Cármine
Castello di Sorci
Tavernelle
Sant'Agostino
Sovara
Santo Stefano
Anghiari
San Leo
San Lorenzo
la Baracca
Scoiano
Catigliano
Verazzano
M. Pián di Mággio 864
Tortigliano
Santa Maria di Momentana
Pocáia
le Ville
Monterchi
Madonna del Parto
Badia San Veriano
Mulinelli
San Severo
Padónchia
Ripoli
Fonaco
Lippiano
M. Civitella 936
TOSCANA
UMBRIA
Palazzo del Pero
S. Donnino a Maiano
Monte Favalto 1082
Sant'Ágata del Terrine
Monte Corneta 742
Santa Maria Rassinata
Volterrano
Ánsina
Polvano
Collesecco
Pieve di Chio
Poggioni
Ruffignano
S. Pietro a Dame
Petrelle
San Martino
Tivo
Massa
Pagno
Villa
Tavolicci
Castelpriore
Le Capanne
Fragheto
Casteldelci
Balze
Senatello
Pgio. dei Tre Véscovi 1127
Pratieghi
Montebotolino
Schigno
M. Lóggio 1179
Gattara
Molino di Báscio
Rofelle
Ranco
Fresciano
Caprile
Arsicci
Badia Tedalda
Viamággio
Monteviale
Passo di Viamággio 983
Alpe della Luna
M. dei Frati 1454
la Palazza
Áboca
Conv. di Monte Casale
Misciano
Melello
Fortezza Medicea
Gragnano
Sansepolcro
Museo Civico di Sansepolcro
Viáio
Santa Croce
Santa Fiora
Trébbio
Gricignano
Citerna
Carsuga
Piósina
Mezzavia
Rovigliano
Lerchi
Museo del Capitolo del Duomo di Città di Castello
Uppiano
Prato
Monte Santa María Tiberina
Marcignano
Gioiello
Trevine
Valle Petrina
Ronti
Morra
Petróia
Roccagnano
Lugnano
Calzolaro
San Vincenzo
l'Olmo
San Pietro a Monte
Maiano
San Donato
Sant'Ágata Féltria
Pereto
Monte Benedetto
Petrella Guidi
Rocca Pratiffi
Santa Sofia
Ca'Raffaello
Cicognáia
Báscio
Miratóio
San Gianni
Petrella Massana
Póggio d. Campane 1036
Colcellalto
Cella di San Cristoforo
Palazzi
Sant'Andrea
Stiavola
Pgio. Monterand 1087
Montelabreve
Passo della Spugna 751
Parchiule
Sompiano
Felcino
Lámoli
la Villa
Pischiano
Fonte Abeti
Bocca Trabária 1049
Cantone
Valdimonte
Corposano
San Lorenzo
San Giustino
Celalba
Pitigliano
Colle Plínio
Lama
Selci
Grumale
Cerbara
Titta
Madonna d. Belvedere
Riosecco
Belvedere
Terme di Fontécchio
Palazzo Vitelli
CITTÀ DI CASTELLO
Duomo
Baucca
Santa Lucia
San Secondo
Fabbrecce
Trestina
Ranchi
Montecastelli
Niccone
Novaféltria
San Leone
Rocca di Maioletto
Sartiano
Torricella
Santa Maria di Antico
Libiano
Maciano
Billi
Pennabilli
Parco Regionale del Sasso Simone e Simoncello
M. Carpegna 1415
M. Canale 1052
Carpegna
Simoncello 1221
MARCHE
TOSCANA
M. d. Scura 1049
Presciano
Torre di Monteromano
Sestino
Valenzano
Casa Núccio
Borgo Pace
Valbuona
Mercatello sul Metáuro
Ripa dell'Alto 806
Guinza
S. Andrea in Corona
M. Valmeronte 977
Parnacciano
Vallurbana
Pieve d. Riso
Cerboni
Fraccano
Abbazia di Montemaggiore
M. Sodolungo 691
Ronchi
M. delle Gorgacce 678
Pieve di Saddi 602
Promano
Montone
San Leo
Castelnuovo
Santa Lucia
Madonna di Pugliano
Pugliano
Lombardi
Antico
Soanne
Santa Rita
Santa Maria
Montecopiolo
Cernitosa
Calvillano
Ponte Cappuccini
Casa Petrelle
Catúrchio
Frontino
Convento di Montefiorentino
San Sisto
Martigliano
Torriola
Valcava
Monteromano
Monterone
Campo
Miraldella
M. d. Rocca 805
Belforte all'Isáuro
Sorbétolo
Sant'Angelo in Vado
Palazzi
Casa Nuova
San Martino del Piano
UMBRIA
MARCHE
Osteria Nuova
il Caldese
M. Fumo 869
Bocca Serriola 730
M. di Gragnano 763
Madonna dei Cinque Faggi
M. Rosso 743
M. Frontano 778
M. Roncino 690
Pietralunga
Corlo
S. Benedetto Vécchio
Santa Maria di Sette
Civitella Ranieri
Monte
Montelicciano
Ca'Micci
Monte S. Páolo 864
Montegrimano
Savignano
Monte Cerignone
Macerata Féltria
Mercato Vécchio
la Villa
Monastero
Lupiaolo
Lunano
Viano
Piandimeleto
Pagánico
San Martino in Selvanera
San Giovanni in Petra
Magnavacca
Sant' Eusébio
M. Cágnero 727
S. Ansuino
M. Vicino 880
Colombara
Apécchio
Piàn della Serra
M. Macinare 794
Vallécchio
M. di Castiglione 667
M. Civitello 735
Cárpini
Campo-reggiano

Ga
Gb
Gc
Gd
256
264
108
109
110
111
112
113
Torre Nuova
255
P. Gorgona
Punta Cala Scirocco
Parco Nazionale dell'Arcipélago Toscano
Ísola di Gorgona
Livorno
Castello Pasquini
Castiglioncello
Oratorio di Sant'Andrea Apostolo
Porto nord e sud di Castiglioncello
La Riviera degli Etruschi
Mar Tirreno
Olbia, Sardegna
Parco Nazionale dell'Arcipélago Toscano
Ísola di Capráia
Punta della Téia
Monte Castello
445
Punta della Manza
Capráia Ísola
Castello San Giórgio
Monte Pontica
426
Santo Stefáno
Punta della Civitata
Cala del Ceppo
Punta del Trattoio
Cala il Moreto
Punta del Zenóbito
Ísola d'Elba
Cala Mandriola
Cala dell Inferno
Sole e Mare
Bastia, Corse (F)
N
0
5 km
3 miles

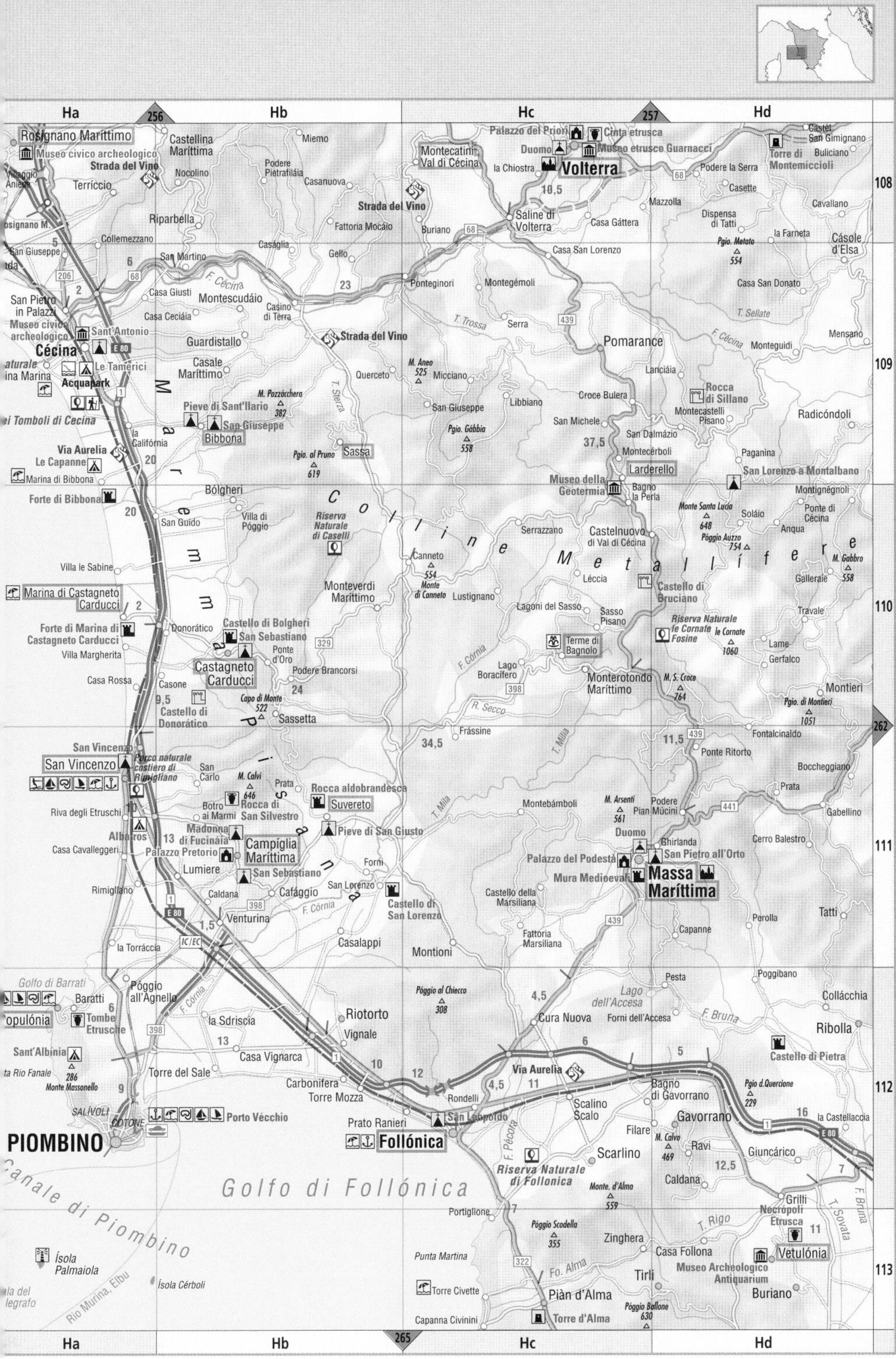

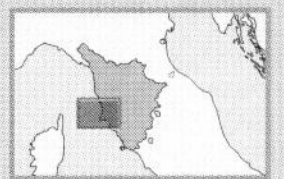

Ha | 256 | Hb | Hc | 257 | Hd

108

Rosignano Maríttimo
Museo civico archeologico
Strada del Vino
Villaggio Aniene
Terríccio
Castellina Maríttima
Nocolino
Miemo
Podere Pietrafiláia
Casanuova
Montecatini Val di Cécina
Strada del Vino
Palazzo dei Priori
Cinta etrusca
Duomo
Museo etrusco Guarnacci
la Chiostra
Volterra
18,5
Castel San Gimignano
Torre di Montemíccioli
Buliciano
Podere la Serra
Casette
Mazzolla
Cavallano
Riparbella
Collemezzano
Fattoria Mocáio
Buriano
68
Saline di Volterra
Casa Gáttera
Dispensa di Tatti
la Farneta
Cásole d'Elsa
Pgio. Metato 554
San Giuseppe
Caságlia
San Martino
Gello
Casa San Lorenzo
6
206
68
2
F. Cécina
23
Ponteginori
Montegémoli
Casa San Donato
San Pietro in Palazzi
Casa Giusti
Montescudáio
Casino di Terra
T. Sellate
Museo civico archeologico
Sant'Antonio
Casa Ceciáia
T. Trossa
Serra
439
Cécina
E 80
Guardistallo
Strada del Vino
Pomarance
F. Cécina
Monteguidi
Mensano

109

Casale Maríttimo
Le Tamerici
Querceto
M. Aneo 525
Micciano
Lanciáia
Cécina Marina
Acquapark
T. Sterza
Rocca di Sillano
Croce Bulera
Libbiano
M. Pozzácchera 382
Pieve di Sant'Ilario
San Giuseppe
Montecastelli Pisano
Radicóndoli
Tomboli di Cecina
la Califórnia
San Giuseppe
Bibbona
San Michele
San Dalmázio
Pgio. Gábbia 558
37,5
Via Aurelia
20
Pgio. al Pruno 619
Sassa
Montecérboli
Paganina
Le Capanne
Larderello
San Lorenzo a Montalbano
Marina di Bibbona
Museo della Geotermia
Bagno la Perla
Montignégnoli
Forte di Bibbona
Bólgheri
Monte Santa Lucia 648
Soláio
Ponte di Cécina
20
San Guido
Villa di Póggio
Riserva Naturale di Caselli
Colline Metallífere
Serrazzano
Castelnuovo di Val di Cécina
Póggio Auzzo 754
Anqua
Villa le Sabine
Canneto 554
Monte di Canneto
M. Gabbro 558
Léccia
Galleraie

110

Marina di Castagneto Carducci
2
Monteverdi Maríttimo
Lustignano
Castello di Bruciano
Forte di Marina di Castagneto Carducci
Donorático
Castello di Bolgheri
San Sebastiano
Lagoni del Sasso
Sasso Pisano
Riserva Naturale le Cornate Fosine
le Cornate 1060
Travale
Villa Margherita
Maremma Pisana
Ponte d'Oro
329
Terme di Bagnolo
Lame
Gerfalco
Casa Rossa
Castagneto Carducci
Podere Brancorsi
F. Córnia
Lago Boracifero
Monterotondo Maríttimo
M. S. Croce 764
Montieri
Casone
9,5
24
398
Pgio. di Montieri 1051
Castello di Donorático
Capo di Monte 522
Sassetta
R. Secco
262
Fontalcinaldo
San Vincenzo
Parco naturale costiero di Rimigliano
Frássine
34,5
T. Milia
11,5
439
Ponte Ritorto
San Vincenzo
San Carlo
Boccheggiano
M. Calvi 646
Prata
Rocca aldobrandesca
Suvereto
Prata

111

Riva degli Etruschi
10
Botro ai Marmi
Rocca di San Silvestro
T. Milia
Montebámboli
M. Arsenti 561
Podere Pian Múcini
441
Gabellino
Albatros
13
Madonna di Fucináia
Pieve di San Giusto
Duomo
Casa Cavalleggeri
Palazzo Pretorio
Campíglia Maríttima
Ghirlanda
San Pietro all'Orto
Cerro Balestro
Lumiere
San Sebastiano
Forni
Palazzo del Podestà
Massa Maríttima
Mura Medioevali
Rimigliano
Caldana
Cafággio
San Lorenzo
Castello della Marsiliana
398
F. Córnia
Castello di San Lorenzo
1
E 80
Venturina
1,5
439
Perolla
Tatti
Casalappi
Fattoria Marsiliana
Capanne
IC/EC
la Torráccia
Montioni
Poggibano
Golfo di Barrati
Póggio all'Agnello
Pesta
Baratti
6
F. Córnia
Póggio al Chiecco 308
4,5
Lago dell'Accesa
Collácchia
Populónia
Tombe Etrusche
la Sdriscia
Riotorto
Cura Nuova
Forni dell'Accesa
F. Bruna
Ribolla
398
Vignale
13
Sant'Albinia
6
5
Castello di Pietra
Rio Fanale 286
Monte Massonello
Casa Vignarca
1
Torre del Sale
10
12
Via Aurelia
9
Carbonifera
4,5
11
Bagno di Gavorrano
Pgio d. Quercione 229

112

Torre Mozza
Rondelli
Scalino Scalo
SALÍVOLI
COTONE
Porto Vécchio
Prato Ranieri
San Leopoldo
Filare
Gavorrano
16
la Castellaccia
1
E 80
PIOMBINO
Follónica
F. Pécora
M. Calvo 469
Ravi
Riserva Naturale di Follonica
Scarlino
Giuncárico
Canale di Piombino
Golfo di Follónica
12,5
Caldana
7
Monte. d'Alma 559
Portiglione
7
Grilli
Necrópoli Etrusca
F. Bruna
T. Sovata
T. Rigo
11
Póggio Scodella 355
Zinghera
Ísola Palmaiola
Punta Martina
322
Fo. Alma
Casa Follona
Vetulónia
Museo Archeologico Antiquarium
Ísola Cérboli
Rio Murina, Elbu
Torre Civette
Tirli
Buriano

113

Piàn d'Alma
Póggio Ballone 630
Capanna Civinini
Torre d'Alma

Ha | Hb | 265 | Hc | Hd

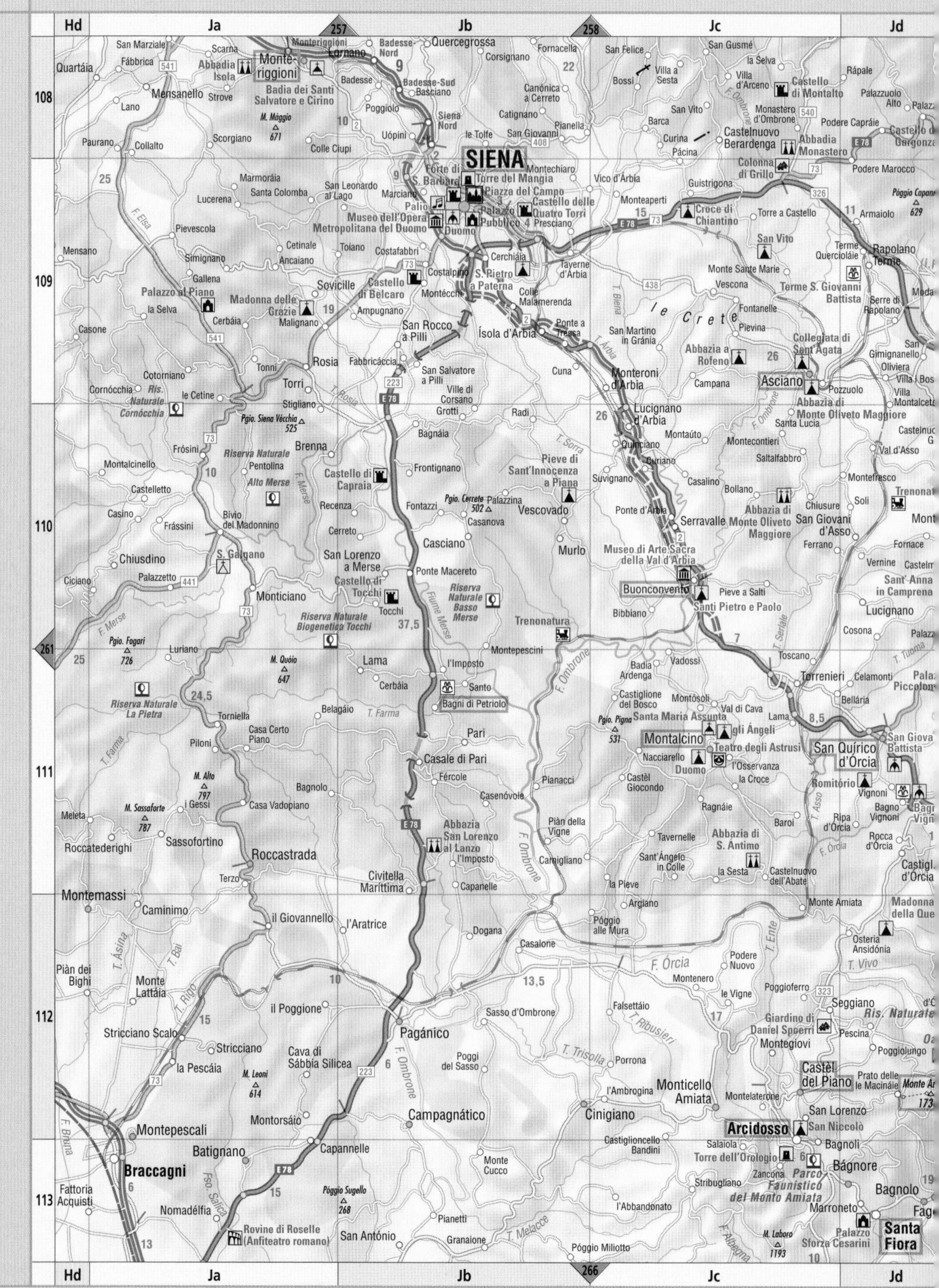

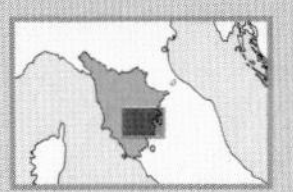

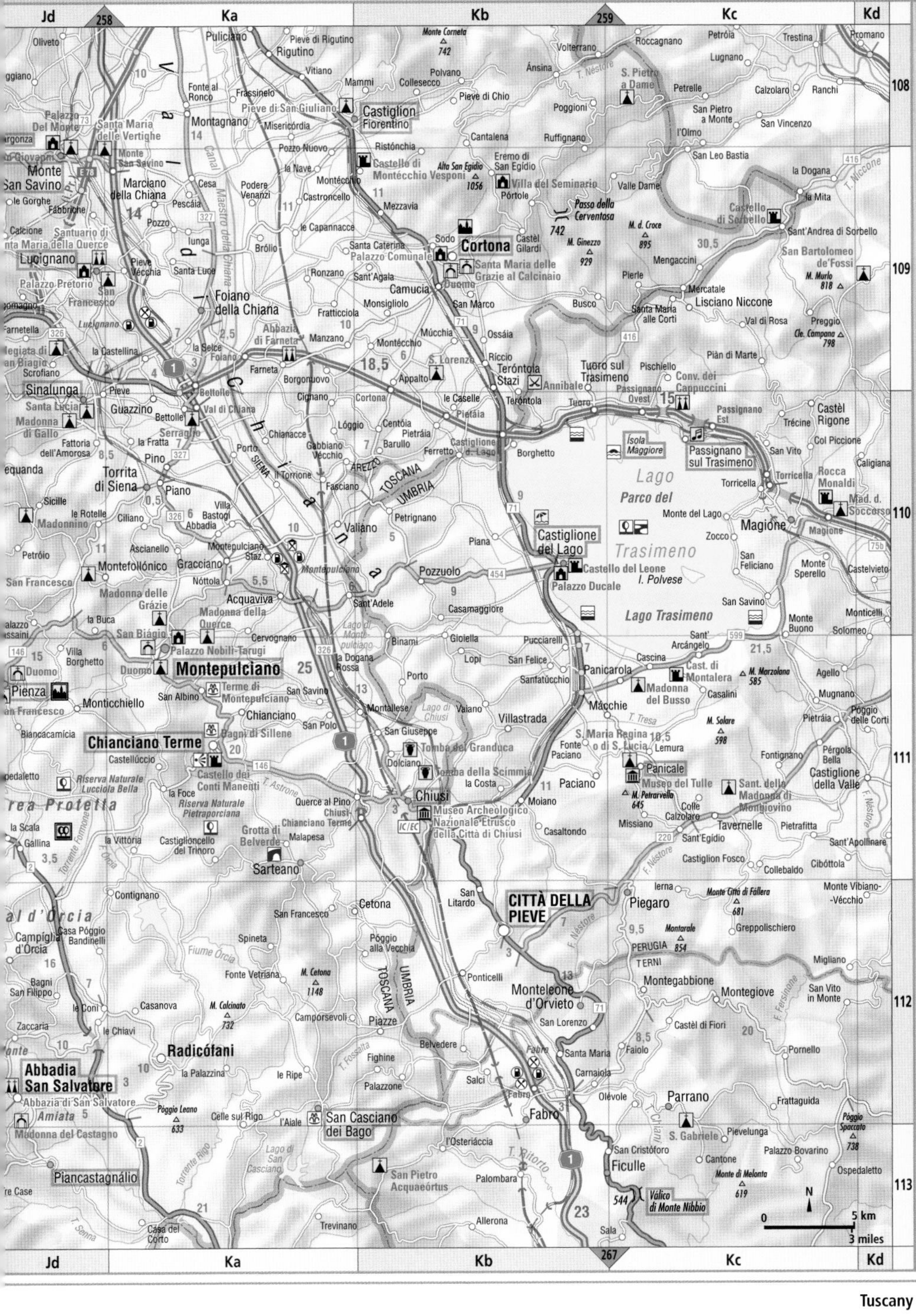

Jd
258
Ka
Kb
259
Kc
Kd
108
109
110
111
112
113
Oliveto
Puliciano
Pieve di Rigutino
Rigutino
Monte Cornetа
742
Volterrano
Roccagnano
Petróia
Trestina
Promano
Lugnano
Vitiano
Mammi
Polvano
Ánsina
T. Nèstore
S. Pietro a Dame
Petrelle
Calzolaro
Ranchi
Fonte al Ronco
Frassineto
Collesecco
Pieve di Chio
Poggioni
San Pietro a Monte
San Vincenzo
Palazzo Del Monte
Santa Maria delle Vertighe
Montagnano
Pieve di San Giuliano
Misericórdia
Castiglion Fiorentino
Cantalena
Ruffignano
l'Olmo
Monte San Savino
Pozzo Nuovo
Ristónchia
San Leo Bastia
Marciano della Chiana
Cesa
Podere Venanzi
la Nave
Castello di Montécchio Vesponi
Alta San Egidio
1056
Eremo di San Egidio
Villa del Seminario
Pórtole
Valle Dame
la Dogana
la Mita
le Gorghe
Fábbriche
Pescáia
Castroncello
Montécchio
Mezzavia
Passo della Cerventosa
742
Castello di Sorbello
Calcione
Santuario di Santa Maria della Querce
Pozzo
Iunga
le Capannacce
Sodo
Cortona
Castèl Gilardi
M. d. Croce
895
Sant'Andrea di Sorbello
Lucignano
Brólio
Santa Caterina
Palazzo Comunale
M. Ginezzo
929
30,5
Mengaccini
San Bartolomeo de' Fossi
Palazzo Prétorio
San Francesco
Pieve Vécchia
Santa Luce
Ronzano
Sant'Agata
Santa Maria delle Grazie al Calcinaio
Duomo
Pierle
M. Murlo
818
Foiano della Chiana
Camucia
Monsigliolo
San Marco
Busco
Mercatale
Lisciano Niccone
Fratticciola
Santa Maria alle Corti
Val di Rosa
Preggio
Farnetella
Lucignano
Abbazia di Farneta
Manzano
Múcchia
Ossáia
Cle. Campana
798
Collegiata di San Biagio
la Castellina
la Selce
Foiano
Montécchio
Ríccio
Piàn di Marte
Scrofiano
Farneta
Borgonuovo
18,5
S. Lorenzo
Appalto
Teróntola
Stazi
Annibale
Tuoro sul Trasimeno
Pischiello
Conv. dei Cappuccini
Sinalunga
Pieve
Bettolle
Passignano Ovest
Santa Lucia
Guazzino
Cignano
Cortona
le Caselle
Pietáia
Terόntola
Tuoro
15
Passignano Est
Castèl Rigone
Madonna di Gallo
Bettolle
Val di Chiana
Lóggio
Centóia
Pietráia
Trécine
Fattoria dell'Amorosa
la Fratta
Serraglio
Chianacce
Gabbiano Vécchio
Barullo
Castiglione d. Lago
Ferretto
Borghetto
Isola Maggiore
Col Piccione
Pino
Porto
Passignano sul Trasimeno
San Vito
Caligiana
Torrita di Siena
Il Torrione
Arezzo
Toscana
Umbria
Lago
Torricella
Rocca Monaldi
Piano
Fasciano
Parco del
Monte del Lago
Mad. d. Soccorso
Sicille
le Rotelle
Ciliano
Villa Bastogi
Abbadia
Petrignano
Magione
Madonnino
Valiano
Castiglione del Lago
Trasimeno
Zocco
Magione
Petróio
Ascianello
Montepulciano Staz.
Piana
San Feliciano
Monte Sperello
Castelvieto
Montefollónico
Gracciano
Montepulciano
Pozzuolo
Castello del Leone
I. Polvese
San Francesco
Nóttola
5,5
Palazzo Ducale
Madonna delle Grázie
Acquaviva
Sant'Adele
Casamaggiore
San Savino
Monticelli
Madonna della Querce
Lago Trasimeno
Monte Buono
Solomeo
la Buca
San Biágio
Cervognano
Lago di Montepulciano
Binami
Gioiella
Pucciarelli
Sant' Arcángelo
21,5
Villa Borghetto
Palazzo Nobili-Tarugi
la Dogana Rossa
Lopi
San Felice
Cascina
Duomo
Montepulciano
25
Porto
Sanfatùcchio
Panicarola
Cast. di Montalera
M. Marzolana
585
Agello
Pienza
Monticchiello
San Albino
Terme di Montepulciano
San Savino
Madonna del Busso
Casalini
Mugnano
San Francesco
Chianciano
Montallese
Lago di Chiusi
Vaiano
Mácchie
Poggio delle Corti
San Polo
Villastrada
T. Tresa
M. Solare
598
Pietráia
Biancacamícia
San Giuseppe
S. Maria Regina o di S. Lucia
10,5
Lemura
Chianciano Terme
Bagni di Sillene
Tomba del Granduca
Fonte Paciano
Pérgola Bella
Castellúccio
Dolciano
Fontignano
Castello dei Conti Manenti
Tomba della Scimmia
Panicale
Castiglione della Valle
Riserva Naturale Lucciola Bella
la Costa
Paciano
Museo del Tulle
Sant. della Madonna di Mongiovino
la Foce
T. Astrone
Chiusi
M. Petrarvella
645
Riserva Naturale Pietraporciana
Quercia al Pino
Chiusi Chianciano Terme
Moiano
Colle
Calzolaro
Tavernelle
Pietrafitta
Museo Archeologico Nazionale Etrusco della Città di Chiusi
Missiano
la Scala
Gallina
la Vittória
Castiglioncello del Trinoro
Grotta di Belverde
Malapesa
Casaltondo
Sant'Egidio
Sant'Apollinare
3,5
Sarteano
Castiglion Fosco
Cibóttola
Collebaldo
Contignano
San Litardo
Città della Pieve
Ierna
Monte Città di Fállera
681
Monte Vibiano-Vécchio
Cetona
Piegaro
San Francesco
Campiglia d'Orcia
Casa Póggio Bandinelli
Póggio alla Vecchia
9,5
Montarale
854
Greppolischiero
Spineta
Fiume Orcia
Perugia
Terni
Migliano
Bagni San Filippo
Fonte Vetriana
M. Cetona
1148
Ponticelli
Montegabbione
Monteleone d'Orvieto
Montegiove
San Vito in Monte
le Coni
Casanova
M. Calcinato
732
Camporsevoli
Piazze
San Lorenzo
Zaccaria
le Chiavi
Castèl di Fiori
8,5
20
Radicófani
Belvedere
Santa Maria
Faiolo
Pornello
Abbadia San Salvatore
la Palazzina
le Ripe
Fighine
Fabro
Carnaiola
Abbazia di San Salvatore
Amiata
Palazzone
Salci
Olèvole
Parrano
Frattaguida
Póggio Leano
633
Celle sul Rigo
l'Aiale
San Casciano dei Bagni
Fabro
S. Gabriele
Pievelunga
Póggio Spaccato
738
Madonna del Castagno
Lago di San Casciano
l'Osteriáccia
San Cristóforo
Palazzo Bovarino
Ficulle
Cantone
San Pietro Acquaeórtus
Monte di Melonta
619
Ospedaletto
Piancastagnálio
Palombara
Válico di Monte Nibbio
544
Case
21
Trevinano
Allerona
23
0
5 km
3 miles
N
Casa del Corto
Sala
Jd
Ka
Kb
267
Kc
Kd

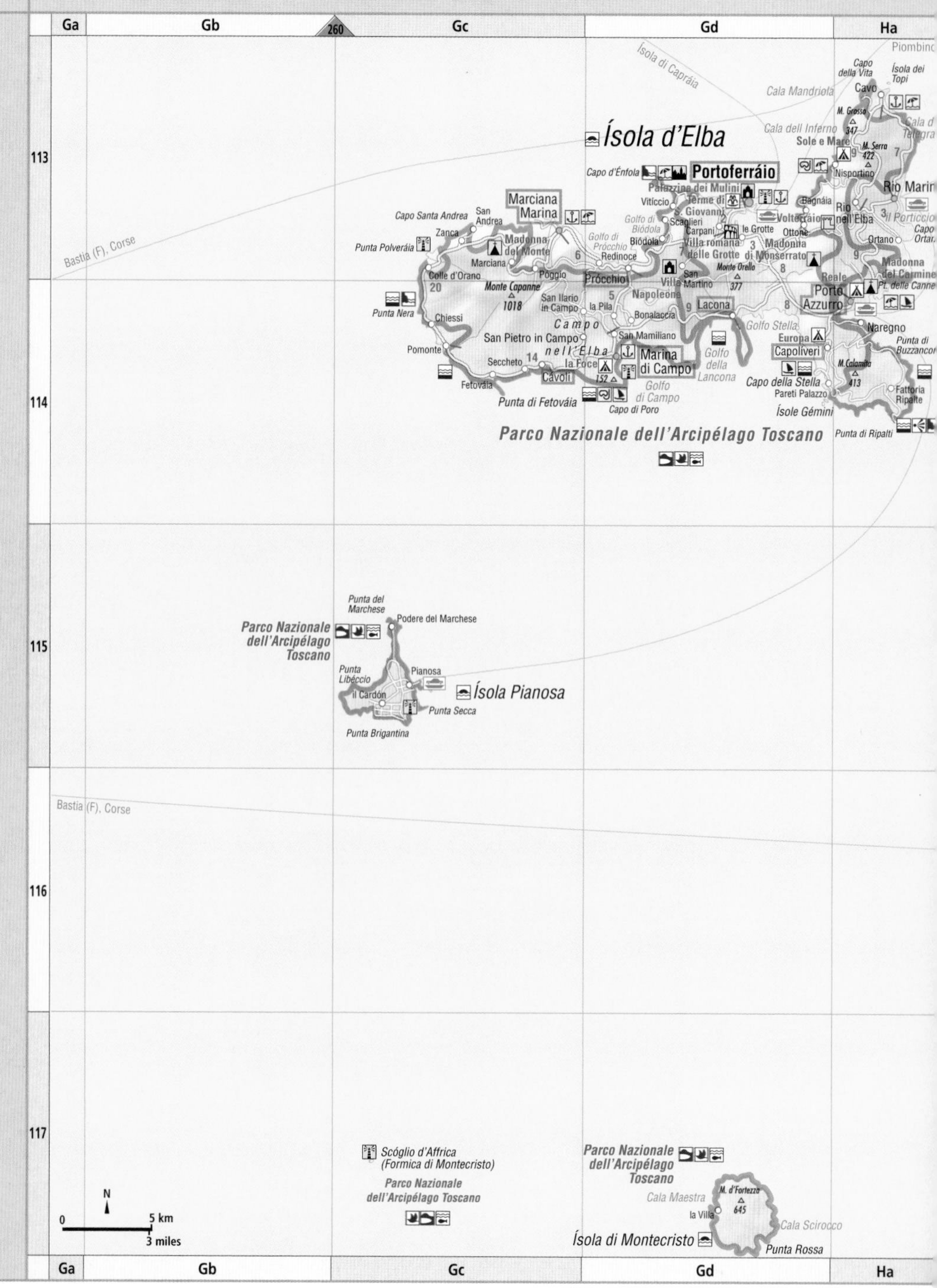
Ga
Gb
260
Gc
Gd
Ha
113
114
115
116
117
Ísola d'Elba
Portoferráio
Marciana Marina
Capo d'Énfola
Capo Santa Andrea
San Andrea
Zanca
Punta Polveráia
Madonna del Monte
Marciana
Poggio
Colle d'Orano
Monte Capanne
1018
San Ilario in Campo
Prócchio
Punta Nera
Chiessi
Pomonte
Seccheto
Fetováia
Punta di Fetováia
Cávoli
San Pietro in Campo
Campo nell'Elba
la Foce
Marina di Campo
Golfo di Campo
Capo di Poro
La Pila
Napoleone
Bonalaccia
San Mamiliano
Lacona
Golfo della Lancona
Golfo Stella
Capo della Stella
Capoliveri
Europa
Porto Azzurro
Naregno
Punta di Buzzancor
Fattoria Ripalte
Pareti Palazzo
Ísole Gémini
Punta di Ripalti
Parco Nazionale dell'Arcipélago Toscano
Rio Marina
Rio nell'Elba
Ortano
Nisportino
Cavo
Capo della Vita
Ísola dei Topi
Cala Mandriola
Cala dell Inferno
Sole e Mare
M. Grosso
M. Serra
Piombino
Ísola di Capráia
Bastia (F), Corse
Viticcio
Scaglieri
Biódola
Golfo di Biódola
Golfo di Prócchio
Redinoce
Terme di S. Giovanni
Palazzina dei Mulini
Carpani
le Grotte
Villa romana delle Grotte
Madonna di Monserrato
Monte Orello
377
Villa San Martino
Bagnáia
Ottone
Volterráio
Reale
Madonna del Carmine
Pt. delle Canne
M. Calamita
413
Ísola Pianosa
Punta del Marchese
Podere del Marchese
Punta Libéccio
Pianosa
il Cardón
Punta Secca
Punta Brigantina
Scóglio d'Affrica (Formica di Montecristo)
Ísola di Montecristo
Cala Maestra
la Villa
M. d'Fortezza
645
Cala Scirocco
Punta Rossa
N
0
5 km
3 miles

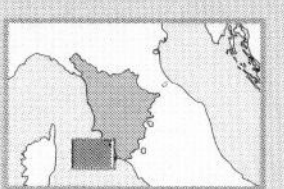

Ha | Hb | 261 | Hc | Hd | Ja

Canale di Piombino
Piombino
la
maiola
Ísola Cérboli
Portiglione
Póggio Scodella 355
Zinghera
T. Rigo
Necrópoli Etrusca
T. Sovata
Braccagni
Punta Martina
Casa Follona
Vetulónia
Museo Archeologico Antiquarium
Fattoria Acquisti
Torre Civette
Fo. Alma
Tirli
11
Buriano
Capanna Civinini
Piàn d'Alma
Póggio Ballone 630
T. Ampio
Póggio Bruno 369
Torre d'Alma
322
113
Castello di Punta Ala
12,5
Fosso la Valle
Punta Hidalgo
Punta Ala
Macchiascandona
Torre Hidalgo
Case Badiola
Punta Ala
Póggio Peroni 349
Piàn di Rocca
11,5
Canale Molla
Scóglio dello Sparviero
Báia Verde
Póggio Petriccio 342
Bruna
Badiola
10
Roccamare
Castiglione della Pescáia
Ris. Nat.
le Rocchette
Riva del Sole
Canale Diversivo
Marrucheto
San Giovanni Battista
Casotto dei Pescatori
Diaccia Botrona
9
Pineta del Tombolo
Fosso Tanaro
11
Tenuta Pingrosso
322
Marina di Grosseto
114
Rosmarina
Trappola
Principina a Mare
F. Ombrone
Marina di Alberese
Torre di Collelungo

M a r

115
Formiche di Grosseto
Parco Nazionale dell'Arcipélago Toscano
266
Porto Santo Stéfano
116

T i r r e n o

Porto Santo Stéfano
Ísola del Gíglio
Punta del Fenáio
Gíglio Castello
Punta Faraglione
Gíglio Campese
Gíglio Porto
117
Póggio d. Pagana 498
Cala delle Canelle
Parco Nazionale dell'Arcipélago Toscano
Cala degli Álberi
Punta del Capel Rosso

Ha | Hb | Hc | Hd | Ja

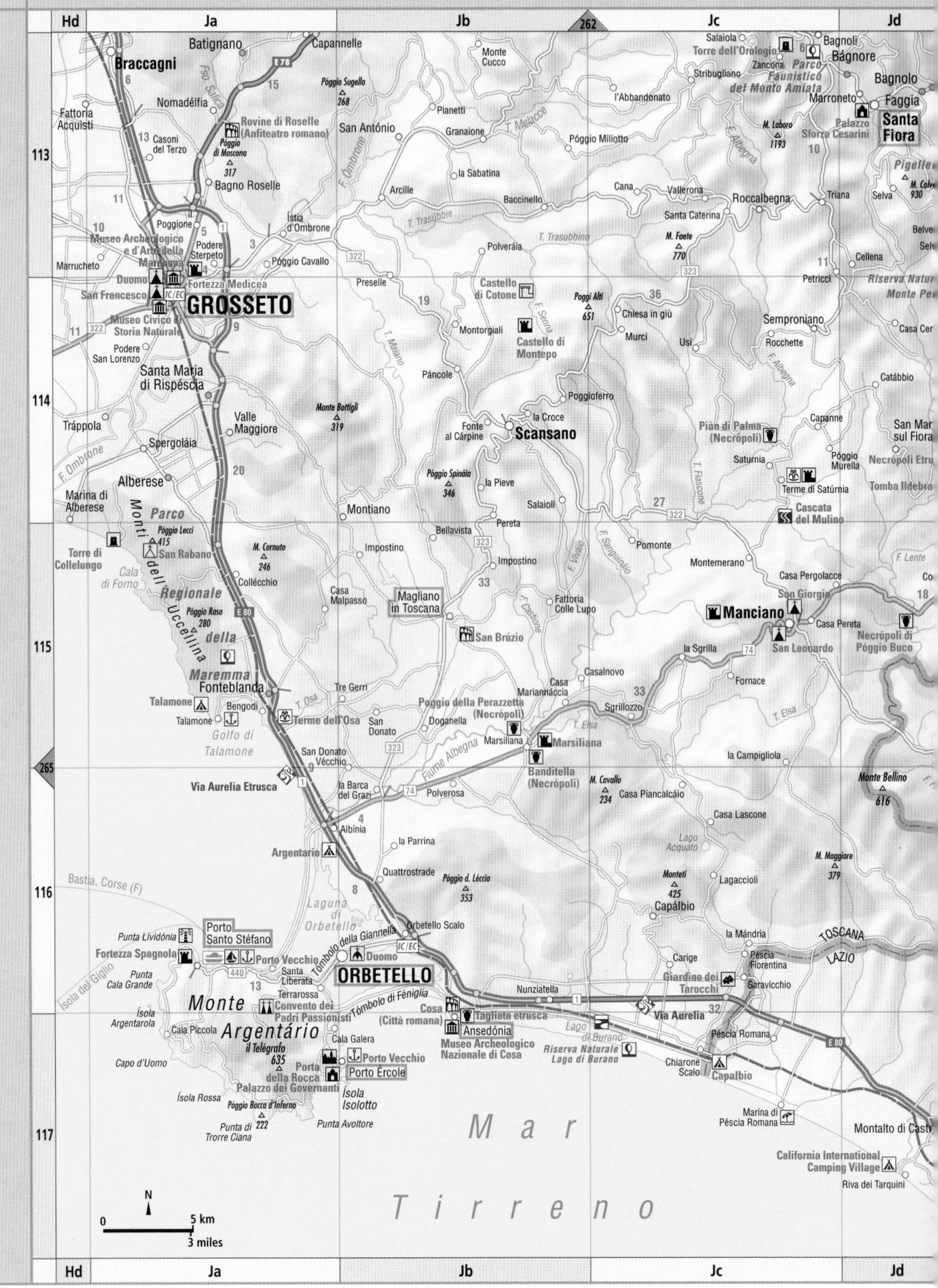
Hd
Ja
Jb
Jc
Jd
262
265
113
114
115
116
117
Batignano
Capannelle
Braccagni
Nomadélfia
Fattoria Acquisti
Rovine di Roselle (Anfiteatro romano)
Póggio di Moscona 317
Casoni del Terzo
Bagno Roselle
Póggio Sugello 268
Monte Cucco
Pianetti
San António
Granaione
Póggio Miliotto
l'Abbandonato
Salaiola
Torre dell'Orologio
Bagnoli
Bagnore
Stribugliano
Zancona
Parco Faunistico del Monte Amiata
Bagnolo
Marroneto
Faggia
Santa Fiora
Palazzo Sforza Cesarini
M. Labbro 1193
la Sabatina
Arcille
Baccinello
Cana
Vallerona
Roccalbegna
Triana
Selva
Santa Caterina
Poggione
Museo Archeologico e d'Arte della Maremma
Podere Sterpeto
Ístia d'Ombrone
Marrucheto
Póggio Cavallo
Polveráia
T. Trasubbino
M. Faete 770
Cellena
Petricci
Duomo
Fortezza Medicea
San Francesco
GROSSETO
Museo Civico di Storia Naturale
Preselle
Castello di Cotone
Poggi Alti 651
Chiesa in giù
Murci
Usi
Semproniano
Rocchette
Montorgiali
Castello di Montepo
Podere San Lorenzo
Santa Maria di Rispéscia
Pàncole
Catábbio
Poggioferro
la Croce
Trappola
Valle Maggiore
Monte Bottigli 319
Fonte al Cárpine
Scansano
Piàn di Palma (Necrópoli)
Capanne
Spergoláia
Saturnia
Póggio Murella
Terme di Satúrnia
Alberese
Póggio Spináia 346
la Pieve
Marina di Alberese
Salaioli
Montiano
Cascata del Mulino
Parco Regionale della Maremma
Monti dell'Uccellina
Póggio Lecci 415
Torre di Collelungo
San Rabano
M. Cornuto 246
Bellavista
Pereta
Impostino
Pomonte
Montemerano
Cala di Forno
Colléchio
Casa Malpasso
Magliano in Toscana
Fattoria Colle Lupo
Casa Pergolacce
San Giorgio
Póggio Raso 280
Manciano
Casa Pereta
Necrópoli di Póggio Buco
San Brúzio
la Sgrilla
San Leonardo
Fonteblanda
Casalnovo
Casa Mariannáccia
Fornace
Talamone
Bengodi
Tre Gerri
Poggio della Perazzetta (Necrópoli)
Sgrillozzo
Terme dell'Osa
San Donato
Doganella
Marsiliana
Golfo di Talamone
San Donato Vécchio
Fiume Albegna
Banditella (Necrópoli)
la Campigliola
Via Aurelia Etrusca
la Barca del Grazi
Polverosa
M. Cavallo 234
Casa Piancalcáio
Monte Bellino 616
Albínia
Casa Lascone
la Parrina
Argentario
Lago Acquato
M. Maggiore 379
Quattrostrade
Póggio d. Léccio 353
Monteti 425
Lagaccioli
Bastia, Corse (F)
Laguna di Orbetello
Capálbio
Punta Lividónia
Porto Santo Stéfano
Orbetello Scalo
la Mándria
TOSCANA
LAZIO
Fortezza Spagnola
Porto Vecchio
Tómbolo della Giannella
Duomo
Pescia Fiorentina
Carige
Punta Cala Grande
Santa Liberata
ORBETELLO
Giardino dei Tarocchi
Garavícchio
Nunziatella
Isola del Giglio
Terrarossa
Monte Argentário
Convento dei Padri Passionisti
Tómbolo di Feníglia
Cosa (Città romana)
Tagliata etrusca
Via Aurelia
Ísola Argentarola
Cala Piccola
Ansedónia
Lago di Burano
Péscia Romana
il Telégrafo 635
Cala Galera
Museo Archeologico Nazionale di Cosa
Riserva Naturale Lago di Burano
Capo d'Uomo
Porto Vecchio
Porta della Rocca
Porto Ércole
Chiarone Scalo
Capalbio
Palazzo dei Governanti
Ísola Rossa
Póggio Bocca d'Inferno
Ísola Isolotto
Punta di Trorre Ciana 222
Punta Avoltore
Marina di Péscia Romana
Montalto di Castro
Mar Tirreno
California International Camping Village
Riva dei Tarquini
N
0
5 km
3 miles
E 78
E 80

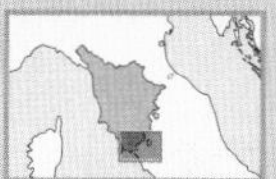

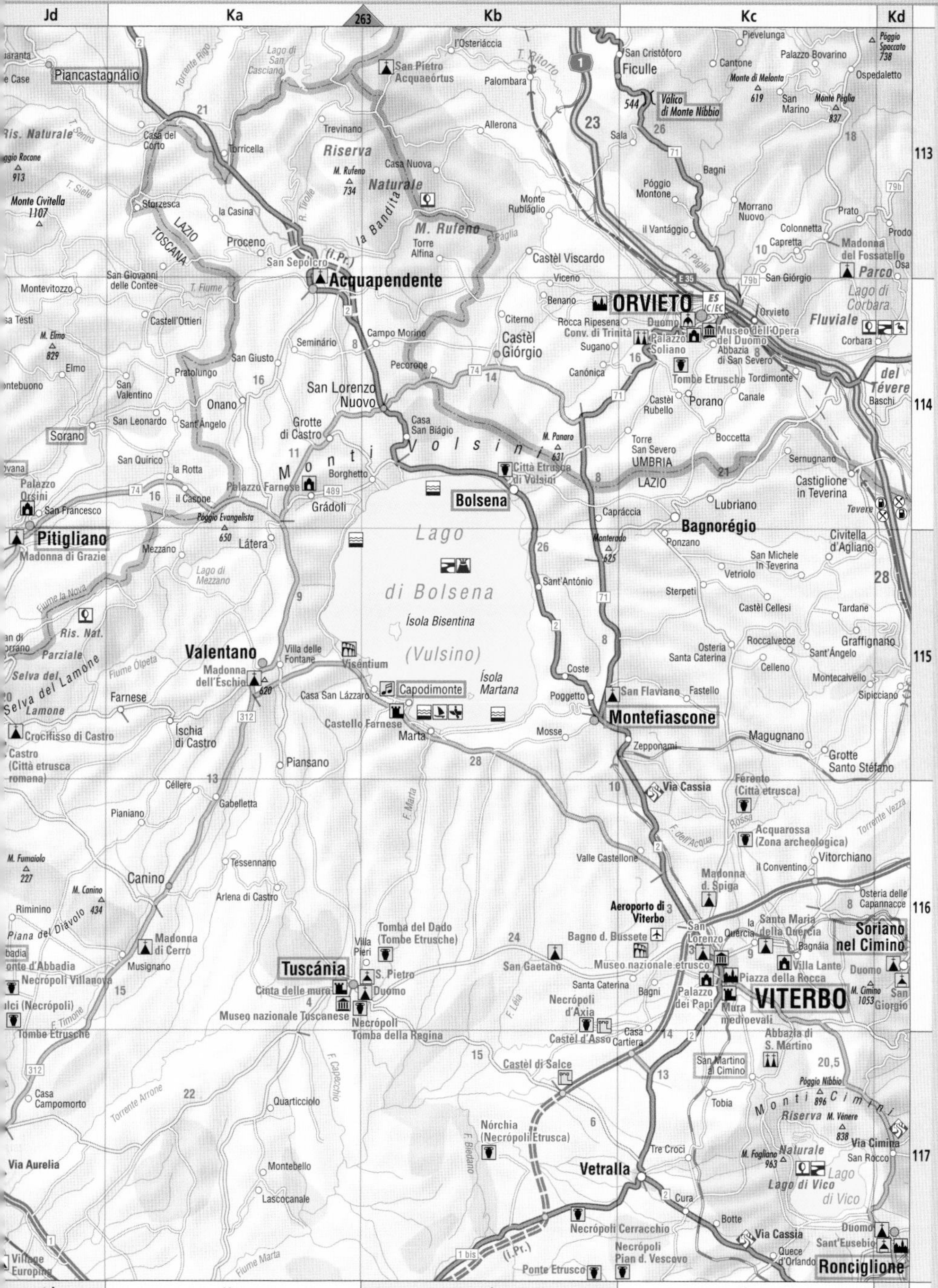

Jd | Ka | 263 | Kb | Kc | Kd

Piancastagnáio, Lago di San Casciano, Torrente Rigo, San Pietro Acquaeórtus, l'Osteriáccia, T. Ritorto, Palombara, San Cristóforo, Ficulle, Pievelunga, Cantone, Palazzo Bovarino, Póggio Spaccato 738, Ospedaletto, Monte di Melonta 619, San Marino, Monte Peglia 837, Vàlico di Monte Nibbio 544

Ris. Naturale, T. Senna, Póggio Rocone 913, Casa del Corto, Torricella, Trevinano, Riserva, Allerona, Sala, Casa Nuova, M. Rufeno 734, Naturale, Bagni, 113

T. Siele, Monte Civitella 1107, Storzesca, la Casina, R. Tirolle, la Bandita, Monte Rubláglio, Póggio Montone, Morrano Nuovo, Prato, Prodo

LAZIO, TOSCANA, Proceno, M. Rufeno, Torre Alfina, F. Páglia, il Vantággio, Colonnetta, Capretta, Madonna del Fossatello, Osa

San Sepolcro, (I.Pr.), San Giovanni delle Contee, T. Fiume, Acquapendente, Castèl Viscardo, Viceno, San Giórgio, Parco, Lago di Corbara, Montevitozzo

Benano, ORVIETO, ES IC/EC, Orvieto, Castell'Ottieri, Citerno, Rocca Ripesena, Conv. di Trinità, Duomo, Palazzo Soliano, Museo dell'Opera del Duomo, Fluviale, Corbara, Casa Testi, M. Elmo 829, Elmo, Seminário, Campo Morino, Castèl Giórgio, Sugano, Abbazia di San Severo

San Giusto, Pratolungo, Pecorone, Canónica, Tombe Etrusche, Tordimonte, del Tévere, Montebuono, San Valentino, San Lorenzo Nuovo, Castèl Rubello, Porano, Canale, Baschi, 114

Onano, San Leonardo, Sant'Ángelo, Grotte di Castro, Casa San Biágio, Monti Volsini, M. Panaro 631, Torre San Severo, Boccetta, Sorano, San Quírico, la Rotta, Borghetto, Città Etrusca di Volsini, UMBRIA, LAZIO, Sernugnano, Castiglione in Teverina

Palazzo Orsini, San Francesco, il Casone, Palazzo Farnese, Grádoli, Bolsena, Lubriano, Tevere, Pitigliano, Póggio Evangelista 650, Látera, Capráccia, Bagnorégio, Madonna di Grazie, Mezzano, Lago, Monterado 625, Ponzano, Civitella d'Agliano

Lago di Mezzano, di Bolsena, Sant'António, San Michele in Teverina, Vetriolo, Sterpeti, Fiume la Nova, Ísola Bisentina, Castèl Cellesi, Tardane, Ris. Nat. Parziale, Valentano, Villa delle Fontane, Visentium, (Vulsino), Osteria Santa Caterina, Roccalvecce, Sant'Ángelo, Graffignano, Celleno, 115

Selva del Lamone, Fiume Olpeta, Madonna dell'Eschio 620, Ísola Martana, Coste, Montecalvello, Farnese, Casa San Lázzaro, Capodimonte, Poggetto, San Flaviano, Fastello, Sipicciano, Crocifisso di Castro, Ischia di Castro, Castello Farnese, Marta, Mosse, Montefiascone, Magugnano, Castro (Città etrusca romana), Piansano, Zepponami, Grotte Santo Stéfano

Céllere, Gabelletta, Via Cassia, Ferento (Città etrusca), Pianiano, F. Marta, F. dell'Acqua, Acquarossa (Zona archeologica), Torrente Vezza, M. Fumaiolo 227, Tessennano, Valle Castellone, il Conventino, Vitorchiano, Canino, Madonna d. Spiga, M. Canino 434, Arlena di Castro, Aeroporto di Viterbo, Osteria delle Capannacce, Riminino, 116

Piana del Diávolo, Madonna di Cerro, Tomba del Dado (Tombe Etrusche), Villa Pieri, Bagno d. Bussete, San Lorenzo, Quercia, Santa Maria della Quercia, Bagnáia, Soriano nel Cimino, Badia, Ponte d'Abbadia, Musignano, Tuscánia, S. Pietro, San Gaetano, Museo nazionale etrusco, Villa Lante, Duomo, Necrópoli Villanova, Cinta delle mura, Duomo, Santa Caterina, Bagni, Piazza della Rocca, M. Cimino 1053, San Giorgio, Vulci (Necrópoli), Museo nazionale Tuscanese, Necrópoli d'Axia, Palazzo dei Papi, VITERBO, Mura medioevali

F. Timone, Tombe Etrusche, Necrópoli Tomba della Regina, F. Léia, Castèl d'Asso, Casa Cartiera, Abbazia di S. Martino, F. Capecchio, Castèl di Salce, San Martino al Cimino, Póggio Nibbio 896, Casa Campomorto, Torrente Arrone, Quarticciolo, Tobia, Monti Cimini, Riserva, M. Vénere 838, Nórchia (Necrópoli Etrusca), F. Biedano, Via Cimina, Via Aurelia, Montebello, Tre Croci, M. Fogliano 963, Naturale, San Rocco, 117

Vetralla, Lago di Vico, Lascocanale, Cura, Botte, Necrópoli Cerracchio, Via Cassia, Duomo, Village Europing, Fiume Marta, Necrópoli Pian d. Vescovo, Quece d'Orlando, Sant'Eusebio, Ponte Etrusco, Ronciglione

Jd | Ka | Kb | Kc | Kd

Pages 252–267

GENERAL INDEX

Pages 6–249

International dialing code for Italy from abroad:
+39

Emergency:
Tel 112 (Police, ambulance, fire; also from mobiles)
Also: 113 Police/115 Fire/118 Ambulance

Roadside assistance:
ACI (Automobile Club Italiano) Breakdown Service (Soccorso Stradale):
Tel 80 31 16,
from mobiles:
Tel 800 11 68 00 (24-hr, multilingual)

Information on driving in Italy:
http://www.initaly.com/travel/info/driving.htm
http://www.autostrade.it/en/index.html

Tuscany on the internet:
www.turismo.toscana.it
http://www.discovertuscany.com/
www.italiantourism.com

ENIT – Ente Nationale Italiana per il Turismo (Italian State Tourist Office)

Australia
Italian Government Tourist Office (ENIT)
PO Box Q802 – QVB NSW 1230
Level 4
46 Market Street
Sydney
NSW 2000
Tel 02 92621666
Fax 02 92621677
E-Mail: italia@italiantourism.com.au

Canada
Italian Government Tourist Office (ENIT)
Office National Italien du Tourisme
175 Bloor Street E. – Suite 907 South Tower
Toronto
M4W 3R8
Tel 416 9254882
Fax 416 9254799
E-Mail: toronto@enit.it

United Kingdom
Italian Government Tourist Office (ENIT)
1 Princes Street
London
W1B 2AY
Tel 020 74081254
Fax 020 73993567
E-Mail: italy@italiantouristboard.co.uk

United States
Italian Government Tourist Office (ENIT)
630, Fifth Avenue – suite 1565
New York
NY 10111
Tel 212 2455618
Fax 212 5869249
E-Mail: newyork@enit.it

Embassies and Consulates

Australian Embassy in Rome
Via Antonio Bosio, 5
Rome 00161
Tel 06 852 721
Fax 06 8527 2300
Email: info-rome@dfat.gov.au
http://www.italy.embassy.gov.au/

British Embassy in Rome
Via XX Settembre, 80a
I-00187 Rome RM
Tel 06 4220 0001
Fax 06 4220 2347
http://ukinitaly.fco.gov.uk/en/

Embassy of Canada in Rome
Via Zara 30
Rome
00198
Tel 06 85 444 2911/06 85 444 1
Fax 39 (06) 85 444 2912
Email: rome.citizenservices@international.gc.ca
http://www.Italy.gc.ca

Embassy of Ireland in Rome
Piazza di Campitelli 3
00186 Rome
Tel 06 697 9121
Tel 06 679 2354
http://www.embassyofireland.it/

South African Embassy
Via Tanaro 14
00198 Rome
Tel 06 85 2541
Fax 06 8535 7992
http://www.dfa.gov.za/foreign/bilateral/italy.html

Embassy of United States in Rome
Palazzo Margherita
Via Vittorio Veneto, 119/a
00187 Roma
Tel 06 4674 1
Fax 06 4674 2244
http://rome.usembassy.gov